STAYING ALIVE
IN AVALANCHE TERRAIN

second edition

STAYING ALIVE
IN AVALANCHE TERRAIN

Bruce Tremper

M THE MOUNTAINEERS BOOKS

To Bill and Barbara Tremper

~

The Mountaineers Books
is the nonprofit publishing arm of The Mountaineers Club,
an organization founded in 1906 and dedicated to the exploration,
preservation, and enjoyment of outdoor and wilderness areas.

1001 SW Klickitat Way, Suite 201, Seattle, WA 98134

First edition, 2001. Second edition, 2008.

Published simultaneously in Great Britain by Bâton Wicks, London
Distributed by Cordee, 3a DeMontfort Street, Leicester LE1 7HD

Manufactured in the United States of America

Copy Editor: Erin Moore
Illustrations: Gray Mouse Graphics
Cover, book design, and layout: Peggy Egerdahl
All photos by the author unless otherwise noted

Cover photograph: *Andrea Binning releases a slab avalanche on her second turn from the ridge*
top of the Coast Mountain Range near Mount Waddington, BC. © Mark Gallup.com
Frontispiece: *Snowbird avalanche expert Dean Cardinale with his avalanche search dog,*
Midas, on a search for two backcountry snowshoers who were killed in an avalanche they
triggered. Neither snowshoer wore a beacon; the only way to locate them was with ava-
lanche dogs and probes. (Wasatch Range, Utah)
Back cover photo: *Author doing field work*

Library in Congress Cataloging-in-Publication Data
Tremper, Bruce, 1953-
    Staying alive in avalanche terrain : how the pros keep themselves and
others alive / by Bruce Tremper.—2nd ed.
        p. cm.
        Includes bibliographical references and index.
    1. Mountaineering—Safety measures. 2. Avalanches—Safety measures.
I. Title.
    GV200.18.T74 2008
    796.9028'9—dc22
                        2008027104

CONTENTS

ACKNOWLEDGMENTS

If you like this book, please don't thank me; I'm just the messenger. Most of the ideas in this book came from the pioneers of avalanche research and education, which started in the United States with Ed LaChapelle, Monty Atwater, and Ron Perla, who ran the Alta Study Center from just after World War II to1972. Together, they came up with the bulk of what we now teach in modern avalanche schools, as well as most of the techniques now used in avalanche forecasting, control, and rescue.

As you will notice, the names of my mentors, Doug Fesler and Jill Fredston, come up repeatedly in this book, and for good reason. Doug Fesler has lived among the big Alaska avalanches for 40 years. He started the Alaska Avalanche School in the early 1970s; he was joined by Jill Fredston, now his wife, in the early 1980s. Together they now run the Alaska Mountain Safety Center. As near as I can tell, they know more about avalanches and more about teaching avalanches than anyone else in the world. Most of the organization and presentation of avalanche concepts in this book were pioneered and refined by Doug and Jill through hundreds of multiday avalanche courses.

Special thanks for the hard work of the manuscript review committee:

Dale Atkins	Colorado Avalanche Information Center
Roger Atkins	Canadian Mountain Holidays helicopter ski guide
Karl Birkeland	Forest Service National Avalanche Center
Doug Coombs	pioneer of the Valdez, Alaska, extreme skiing phenomenon
Doug Fesler	Alaska Mountain Safety Center
Liam Fitzgerald	Utah Department of Transportation avalanche forecaster
Bruce Jamieson	avalanche researcher, University of Calgary, Canada
Ron Johnson	Gallatin National Forest Avalanche Center
Tom Kimbrough	Forest Service Utah Avalanche Center
Ed LaChapelle	America's most venerable avalanche expert
Evelyn Lees	Forest Service Utah Avalanche Center
Ian McCammon	engineering consultant and National Outdoor Leadership School avalanche instructor
Mark Moore	Northwest Weather and Avalanche Center
Mark Newcomb	helicopter ski guide and world-class mountaineer
Peter Schaerer	Canada's most venerable avalanche expert
Juerg Schweizer	Swiss Federal Institute of Snow and Avalanche Research
Knox Williams	Colorado Avalanche Information Center

Thanks also go out to the many people who have made significant contributions to this book but, for various reasons, were not able to review the manuscript. Those include (in alphabetical order): Ed Adams, Duain Bowles, Bob Brown, Howard Conway, Rand Decker, Kelly Elder, Jill Fredston, Andy Gleason, Hans Gubler, Clair Isrealson, Janet Kellam, Nick Logan, Dave McClung, Art Mears, John Montagne, Halstead Morris, Ron Perla, Doug Richmond, Don Sharaff, Grant Statham, and Chris Stethem.

The second edition was reviewed by Karl Birkeland, Ian McCammon, and Ron Johnson, and thanks to Erin Moore for her wonderful editing.

INTRODUCTION

It's so wonderful finding out you were wrong, that you were ignorant,
that you know nothing, not squat. You get to start over.

—Rick Bass

WHAT HAPPENS WHEN YOU GET CAUGHT IN AN AVALANCHE?

It was November 1978. I was a cocky, ex-national-circuit ski racer, 24 years old, fresh out of college, and because I needed the money I was building chairlifts at Bridger Bowl Ski Area in Montana. In the ignorance and vigor of youth, I naturally enough considered myself to be an avalanche expert. I had grown up in the mountains of western Montana where my father had taught me about avalanches when I was 10 years old, and I had skied in the backcountry the past several years and had so far avoided any serious mishaps. In other words, I was a typical avalanche victim.

I was skiing alone (first mistake) and not wearing a beacon (second mistake). After all, I wasn't "skiing," I was "working," tightening the bolts at the base of each chairlift tower with a torque wrench. Even in my stubborn ignorance, I could see that it was clearly very dangerous. Over a foot of light snow had fallen the night before on top of fragile depth hoar and the wind was blowing hard, loading up the steep slopes beneath the upper section of the chairlift with thick slabs of wind-drifted snow.

Starting from the top, I skied down, stopping at each tower to torque the bolts. When I was finished with the tower at the top of the avalanche paths, I took off my skis and started walking back up the slope so I could gain the ridge and circle around to the tower beneath the avalanche paths. But I quickly discovered my third mistake. Since I didn't bring my backcountry skis or climbing skins, the easy ski down was now an exhausting pig wallow back up through chest-deep snow, and the nearby snow-free cliffs were too scary to climb in my slippery plastic boots. I couldn't help but notice that only a 15-foot-wide couloir at the base of the cliffs separated me from the safe slopes on the other side. Naturally enough, I thought a good skier like me should be able to get up speed and zip across it before anything too bad happened. (Ski cutting alone and without a beacon or partner—fourth mistake.)

I did my ski cut according to the book. I built up speed and crossed the slope at about a 45-degree angle so that, in theory, my momentum would carry me off the moving slab, in case it did break on me. Since I had never been caught in an avalanche before, I had no idea how quickly the slab—after it shatters like a pane of glass—can pick up speed. I heard a deep, muffled thunk as it fractured. Then it was like someone pulled the rug out from under me and I instantly flopped down onto the snow, losing all the precious speed I had built up. Like a startled cow, I sat there on my butt and watched soft slab shatter into little blocks and the blanket of snow rocketed down the slope as if sucked downward by extra-heavy gravity.

I jumped to my feet and tried to build up my speed again so I could jet off to the side, but it was far too late. The blocks of shattered slab were moving all around me, like a herd of tumbling cardboard boxes blowing in the wind. Nothing seemed to work. Even though only 2 or 3 seconds had elapsed, the avalanche, with me as its unintended passenger, was already moving a good 20 miles per hour (mph). Looking downhill, I saw a line of small trees coming toward me at a frightening speed. They looked like periscopes slicing through the water in an old World War II movie. I tried to maneuver to grab one of them. But the avalanche, as I discovered, pretty much has its way with you. Choice is an option you think you might have *before* you're caught in an avalanche, but never afterward. Luckily it took me directly into the smallest tree and I slammed it hard and held on with all my strength. The snow pounded me like I was standing under a huge waterfall, and it felt like my neck would snap as each block of wind slab smashed into my head. The tree snapped off, and I rocketed down the slope again.

Then the tumbling started, over and over like being stuck in a giant washing machine filled with snow. Hat and mittens, instantly gone. Snow went everywhere, down my neck, up my sleeves, down my underwear—even under my eyelids, something I would have never imagined. With every breath, I sucked in a mixture of snow and air that instantly formed a

Skiers triggering an avalanche (Columbia Mountains, British Columbia) © Brad White/Alpenstock

plug in my mouth and down into my throat. I coughed it out but the next breath rammed my throat full of snow again. Just when I needed to breathe the most, I couldn't—I was drowning, high in the mountains, in the middle of winter and miles from the nearest water.

After a long while, when I was about to pass out from lack of air, the avalanche began to slow down and the tumbling finally stopped. I was on the surface and I could breathe again. But as I bobbed along on the soft, moving blanket of snow, which had slowed from about 60 mph to around 40 mph, I discovered that my body tended to sink if I didn't swim hard.

So I swam. But something was pulling one of my legs down. These were the days before ski brakes and I had safety straps attaching my skis to my boots. I could swim but my skis couldn't. One safety strap had torn the heel piece out of my ski but the other one remained attached, and it felt like a boat anchor tied to my leg. The ski was beneath me in the slower moving debris and as the surface debris moved faster, it tipped me forward, shoving my face in the snow again and again. I struggled hard to pull that ski up through the debris with my furious swimming. Eventually, the swimming worked, and when the avalanche finally came to a stop I found myself upright and buried only chest deep, breathing hard, very wet, very cold, and very lucky.

I remembered from avalanche books that debris sets up like concrete the instant it comes to a stop, but it's one of those facts you don't entirely believe. Sure enough, I was in a body cast from the chest down. Barehanded, I chipped away at the rock-hard snow for a good 10 minutes with my shovel before I could finally work my legs free. On one foot, the heelpiece of the binding hung from the safety strap with a 6-inch section of the top-skin of the ski still attached to the screws. It had pulled completely off the ski. On my other foot, the ski was still intact but both the tip and the tail were broken. How I could have broken both skis, yet none of my bones, has always been a mystery to me.

I decided that day that, no, I wasn't an avalanche expert, not even close, and that was the real beginning of my avalanche education. Within a month I luckily landed a job on the ski patrol doing avalanche control where the old pros quickly took me under their wing. I have always been grateful to those guys, especially my childhood friend and ski racing buddy Doug Richmond, who patiently tutored me through those first couple of years. He could see that I was an accident waiting to happen, as full of myself as I was, and living with the delusion that I knew much more about avalanches than I did. His friendship, instruction, and love have saved my life many times over since then and helped set me on the path of a new career. I promised myself I would do the same for others, which I have, and this book is part of that promise.

I don't think it's possible to watch a huge natural event, especially a cataclysmic one, without having the experience change your life. Volcano watchers, tornado chasers, eclipse junkies—they all saw their first one and then nothing was the same anymore. The unspeakable power, the beauty, the horror, the insignificance of humanity in the face of it all. They spend the rest of their lives trying to find it again. In an avalanche, the mountainside shatters like a pane of glass and roars to the bottom at 60 mph, ripping out trees. I rode one down and somehow survived and have been haunted by them and hunted them ever since. Avalanches will probably never let me go.

WHAT HAPPENS WHEN YOU GET BURIED IN AN AVALANCHE?

Over 25 percent of avalanche victims in the U.S. die from trauma from hitting trees and rocks on the way down (about 6 percent of avalanche victims in Europe and as many as 50 percent in

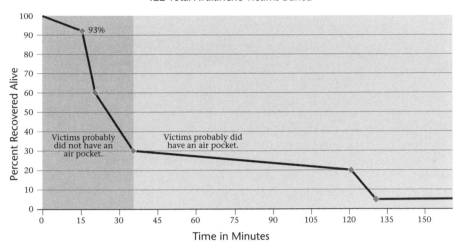

Avalanche Survival vs. Burial Time
422 Total Avalanche Victims Buried

Figure I-1. *A generalized graph of European avalanche victims who were completely buried and in total contact with the snow (no people in vehicles or houses). After 15 minutes the percent recovered alive drops precipitously. Half of victims are dead within 25 minutes. This graph does not include victims killed by trauma, which account for about a quarter of avalanche deaths in the U.S. and about half of avalanche deaths in Canada.*

Canada). Of those who survive the ride, the lucky ones end up with their head above the surface or close enough to the surface to breathe and they or their partners can often dig them out. Completely buried victims begin a desperate race against time, in which only half will live.

Even dense avalanche debris contains about 60 to 70 percent air, plus snow is very permeable, so avalanche victims would be able to breathe almost indefinitely if it were not for one little problem: Avalanche victims die from rebreathing their own carbon dioxide (asphyxia) rather than the lack of oxygen (suffocation). Moreover, the condensation of the victim's breath forms an "ice mask" around their mouth, further exacerbating the buildup of carbon dioxide.

How much time do you have? Not long. Avalanche books from 20 years ago said half the people are dead in the first half-hour. As avalanche rescue times become shorter and shorter, we're finding that people are not living as long under the snow as we thought. The latest research from Europe now indicates that 93 percent of completely buried victims can be revived if they are recovered in the first 15 minutes, but the number drops catastrophically after that, leaving only 27 percent alive after 35 minutes. It is thought that victims who survive after 35 minutes must have some sort of air pocket, which allows the final 27 percent of victims to survive to 100 to 120 minutes, after which the numbers sink to near zero. Most contemporary data suggest that half the victims are dead within the first 25 minutes (Figure I-1). This is a sobering number, especially considering that brain damage starts well before death—perhaps at 10 minutes for an average victim. I have known a number of people who were dug out within 5 minutes, and they were already unconscious and blue-faced.

U.S. Avalanche Fatalities 1986–2008

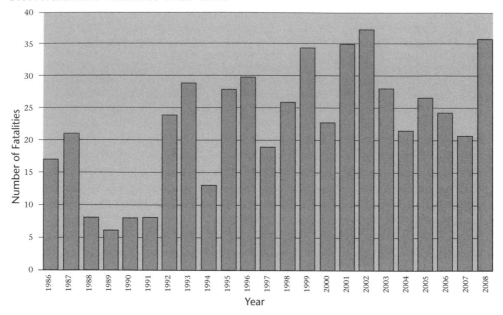

European and North American Fatalities 1986–2007

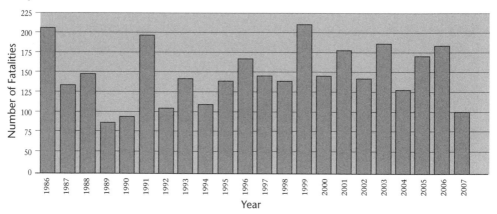

Figure I-2. Avalanche fatalities in the United States continue to rise at an alarming rate. In most western states, avalanches kill more people than any other natural hazard. Compare U.S. statistics with international statistics, which have remained more or less flat. As this book was published, European statisics for 2008 had not been released.

In other words, avalanche victims are like drowning victims. They have to be dug out of the snow *fast*. If the victim is wearing an avalanche rescue beacon (see Chapter 9, Rescue) *and* their partners escape or survive the slide *and* they have been regularly practicing with their beacons, then chances are good that they can dig the victim out in time—but this doesn't happen very often. In practice, for approximately every 10 people who die in an avalanche, only one is rescued from a complete burial by their partners. The numbers usually don't add up to many happy endings.

WHY THIS BOOK?

People are getting slaughtered by avalanches. I don't think slaughter is too strong a word considering that between 1990 and 2007, 423 people have died in avalanches in the United States, averaging 25 per year and 15 per season in Canada, and the trend is on a steep upward slope that shows no signs of abating (Figure I-2).

And no wonder. Pick your sport: skiing, snowmobiling, snowboarding, climbing, or snowshoeing. It's hard to pick up a magazine or watch one of the extreme videos without succumbing to the siren call—images of elite athletes in remote mountains, stunning scenery, on the edge of their sport, and almost always in dangerous avalanche terrain, yet almost never shown wearing shovels, turning on their beacons, or digging snowpits.

In addition, the equipment manufacturers make it easy to get into avalanche terrain. Snowmobilers can now go nearly any place skiers can go and can cover one hundred times the terrain skiers can and in nearly any kind of snow condition. Likewise, skis, snowboards, snowshoes, and climbing equipment have made quantum leaps in performance, weight, and variety. This translates into more people in the mountains, going more places, going more of the time, and getting killed in record numbers.

Fifteen years ago snowmobilers could only rarely access avalanche terrain right after storms, but modern snowmobiles can go nearly any place a skier or climber can go, and in a day they can cover nearly 100 times the amount of terrain as human-powered recreationists can cover. Consequently, snowmobiler avalanche fatalities have skyrocketed in recent years. (Wasatch Range, Utah) © Dan Gardiner

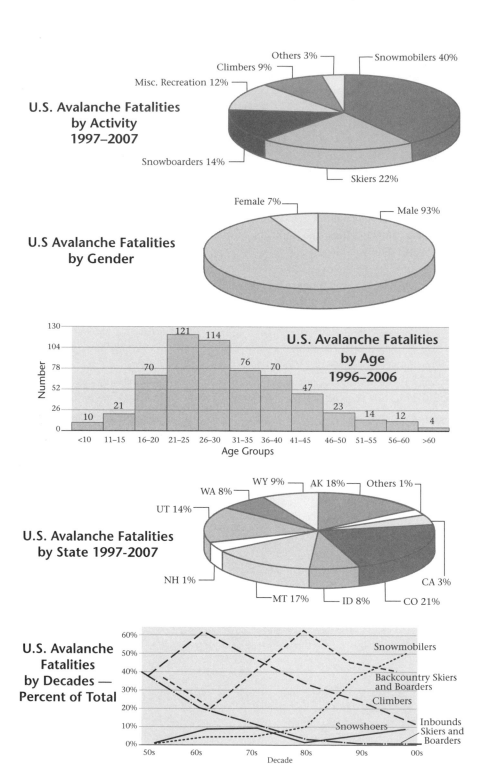

Figure I-3. U.S. avalanche fatalities by activity, gender, age, and state over time

Also, the profile of recreationists has changed dramatically in recent years. The high mountains used to be the exclusive playground of climbers and skiers, but they have since become the minority compared with rapidly increasing numbers of snowmobilers, snowboarders, snowshoers, hunters, hikers, and Boy Scout troops. Although most victims are very skilled at their sport, their avalanche skills invariably lag far behind their sport skills. Possibly because of this, nearly all avalanche victims overestimate their avalanche skills—usually vastly overestimate them. Combine these facts with a dearth of funding for public avalanche information services and the fact that avalanche training videos and books are scarce and poorly funded, and it's easy to see why an increasing number of encounters with avalanches end badly.

Almost all avalanche fatalities involve recreationists, most notably snowmobilers, backcountry skiers, snowboarders, and climbers, in that order. Almost all are very skilled in their sport, male, fit, educated, intelligent, middle class, and between the ages of 18 and 40 (Figure I-3). Does this sound anything like you?

There is hope. In 93 percent of avalanche accidents, the avalanche is triggered by the victim or someone in the victim's party. Which is good, because as the Pogo cartoon says, "We have met the enemy and he is us."

The good news is that we have two important things going for us: first, we have a choice, and second, we already know the enemy. The bad news is that the enemy is us, and that is the hardest enemy of all to conquer.

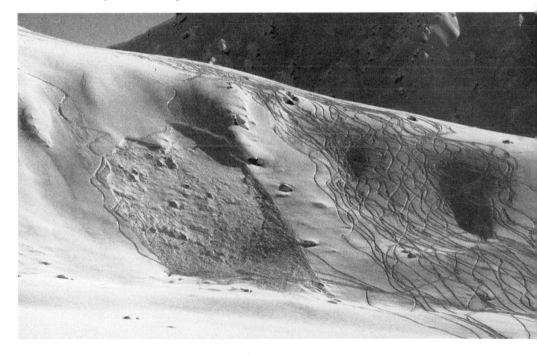

A skier-triggered soft slab avalanche in which the victim was uninjured. The victim or someone in the victim's party triggers 93 percent of avalanche accidents, making avalanches the only natural hazard usually triggered by the victim. This is good news because it means we can prevent most avalanche fatalities by mastering avalanche and decision-making skills. (Talkeetna Mountains, Alaska)

POPULAR MYTHS ABOUT AVALANCHES
(AND WHAT REALLY CAUSES AVALANCHE FATALITIES)

Myth

"Noise triggers avalanches."

Truth

Only in the movies. In 30 years as an avalanche professional I have never once seen an avalanche triggered by, say, a shout or even a sonic boom. I have heard of very rare incidents where low-flying helicopters triggered avalanches in extremely unstable conditions—most likely because of rotor wash, however, not noise. Most noise just does not exert enough force. Even with an explosive it's not the noise but the shock wave that is the trigger. In 93 percent of U.S. avalanche fatalities, the avalanche is triggered by the weight of the victim or someone in the victim's party.

Myth

"An avalanche is a bunch of loose snow sliding down the mountain."

Truth

Technically, yes, but avalanche professionals call these "sluffs," or loose snow avalanches, which account for only a small percentage of deaths and property damage. When we talk about avalanches, we generally mean "slab" avalanches—cohesive plates of snow sliding as a unit. Picture a magazine sliding off an inclined table, with the victim standing on the middle of the magazine.

Myth

"Avalanches strike without warning."

Truth

I often hear the word "strike" used in the popular media. Earthquakes, meteor impacts, and love may strike without warning, but avalanches usually have obvious signs. In addition, avalanches don't "strike." They happen at particular times and in particular places for particular reasons. I'll say it again because it's so important: *In 93 percent of all avalanche accidents, the avalanche is triggered by the victim or someone in the victim's party.*

Natural avalanches occur because new or windblown snow overloads weak layers or because of rapid warming or rain, but there are usually obvious signs of instability by the time avalanches come down on their own.

Myth

"If you see an avalanche coming, get out of the way."

Truth

Good luck. An average-size dry avalanche travels 60 to 120 km/hr (60 to 80 mph), so you'll need to be mighty cagey and mighty quick to get out of the way. People have been known to scoot off to the side in time, especially on a snowmobile, but as far as outrunning an avalanche, you will need to be either a world-class athlete or a very good driver of a very fast snowmobile with no obstacles in the way. Also, naturally triggered avalanches that descend from above kill few people. Do I sound like a broken record here? The vast majority of avalanche incidents are triggered by the victim or someone in the victim's party.

Myth

"When buried in an avalanche, spit to tell which way is up and dig in that direction."

Truth

It doesn't matter which way is up. You can't dig yourself out. If you could dig yourself out, few people would die in avalanches. Avalanche debris instantly entombs you in place, as if you were frozen in concrete, and most of the time you can't even move your fingers. Sometimes, if it's a small avalanche with soft debris and they have a hand near the surface, people have been able to dig themselves out, but the vast majority of the time there are only two ways to get out of the snow—to be dug out or to melt out.

Myth

"All the avalanche experts are dead."

Truth

Realizing that it may be bad luck to even say this, I'm happy to report that just the opposite is true. In the U.S. skilled avalanche professionals enjoy a very low avalanche fatality rate compared to other groups, especially when you consider the amount of time an avalanche professional spends in dangerous avalanche terrain. Only 1.5 percent of all avalanche fatalities involve avalanche professionals.

LEARNING ABOUT AVALANCHES THE HARD WAY

Nearly every one of us has to learn about avalanches the hard way, and I'm certainly no exception. I must have made every mistake possible, short of getting killed. I've taken a couple of very frightening rides in avalanches and I've worn a brace on my knee for a month because of one of them. I've had to ski off moving slabs on several occasions and I've cried over the deaths of students, friends, and even a coworker because I blamed myself for not teaching them enough.

I'm not sure what it is about avalanches, but people invariably overestimate their skills. This doesn't happen with, say, accounting or physics or gardening, so what is it with avalanches? Maybe we can chalk it up to a man-thing. Maybe it's like grizzly bears or hunting or starting a fire in the woods. We puff up our chests, tell our lies, and would literally rather die than admit our ineptitude. This would explain why 93 percent of avalanche fatalities are men and only 7 percent women. It's perhaps not a coincidence that these are the same percentages as males to females in the U.S. prison population.

I think one of the major contributing factors is known as "positive reinforcement." You go out into avalanche terrain, nothing happens. You go out again, nothing happens. You go out again and again and again; still no avalanches. Yes, there's nothing like success! But here's the critical fact: from my experience, any particular avalanche slope is stable 95 percent of the time. So if you know absolutely nothing about avalanches, you automatically get a nineteen-out-of-twenty-times success rate. It's like playing a slot machine where the quarters jingle into your cup on every pull but the twentieth, when that one-arm bandit not only takes all your quarters back, it charges your credit card $10,000 and three big goons throw a blanket over you, pummel you with baseball bats, and throw you in the street. After you recover, you think it *must* have been a fluke. I mean you were winning on every pull. So you get back in the game and the quarters jingle away, but eventually, here it comes again, the credit card, the blanket, and the baseball bats. It takes a lot of pulls to learn the downside of the game. Thus, nearly everyone mistakes luck for skill. (See Table I-1 later in this chapter.)

The frightening truth is that in most close calls, the average person has no idea they even had a close call—kind of like playing soccer on a minefield. You didn't weigh *quite* enough to set the thing off. In an ideal world, everyone would take a multiday avalanche class; then buy a beacon, probe, and shovel and practice with them; and finally, when they felt ready, they would venture into avalanche terrain, working their way into increasingly hazardous terrain as they gain confidence in their skills.

What happens in the real world? Just the opposite. While we're still in the ignorance-is-bliss stage, we jump into one steep slope after another and 95 percent of the time we come home with smiles on our faces, because after all, snow is stable about 95 percent of the time. But if a slope can produce an avalanche, it eventually will. When the inevitable happens, we get an expensive lesson, whereupon we realize that maybe we should buy one of those "beepers." After a couple more close calls, we realize we should practice with them, too. After a friend dies, we realize that maybe we should take an avalanche-awareness class. After a couple more close calls, we realize we should take a multiday class and read some books.

That's the way almost everyone learns about avalanches. I certainly did. So don't be like me. There's standing room only in the Dumb Mistakes Club. Read this book first, and then go out and practice everything you learned. Start slow in low-risk terrain and work your way into progressively more dangerous terrain as you gain more confidence. Building your avalanche skills to the point where you can safely travel in avalanche terrain 99.9 percent of the time—the minimum safety margin for a reasonably long career—usually takes several years.

Maybe you bought this book because you've had some close calls or lost a friend. Don't go back out until you finish the book and practice with what you've learned. Take the time. It will save on gray hairs, lost equipment, lost pride, hospital bills, tears shed at the funerals of friends, or devastating the lives of your loved ones.

WHERE DO PEOPLE GET KILLED IN AVALANCHES?

Ski areas and highway forecasters do an extremely thorough job of forecasting avalanches and controlling them with explosives before people arrive each morning. Because of this, less than 1 percent of avalanche fatalities since 1980 have occurred within ski area boundaries on open runs or on open highways. At least in Utah, you stand a hundred times better chance of being killed by lightning than by an inbounds avalanche. The vast majority of avalanche incidents occur in the backcountry, which we define as areas outside of ski area boundaries where no avalanche control is done. (Although highway departments often do avalanche control with explosives to protect the highway, we still consider those slopes as backcountry. Likewise for terrain occasionally explosive-controlled by helicopter skiing companies.)

WHO GETS KILLED IN AVALANCHES?

When I first started my avalanche career 30 years ago, avalanche fatalities were relatively rare and they occurred mostly to backcountry skiers wearing wool knickers and skinny wooden skis and to a few hardy mountaineers on big mountains. Since then, avalanche demographics have been completely turned upside down. Today, skiers and climbers represent the minority compared to the new kids on the block—snowboarders, snowshoers, and the group that currently leads the avalanche pack by a wide margin, snowmobilers.

The infamous Temptation avalanche path just out-of-bounds from Telluride Ski Area, Colorado. This was one of several fatal avalanche accidents through the years resulting from people crossing the rope line into uncontrolled avalanche terrain for untracked powder. Nearly all avalanche fatalities occur in the backcountry and nearly all fatalities involve recreationists who are quite skilled at their sport. However, there is almost always a large gap between sport skills and avalanche skills. (Telluride, Colorado) © Nick DiGiacomo

Fifteen years ago, existing technology did not allow snowmobilers to access the back-country right after a storm. But led by hill-climbing pioneers who tinkered in their garages, manufacturers began to build high-performance mountain sleds, which can now go virtually any place a skier can go and cover 10 to 100 times more terrain than a skier in a day. Nearly overnight, it seems, remote mountain ranges once open only to super-fit skiers on multiday trips are now completely tracked by snowmobilers after a sunny powder weekend. Today, a large new population of people with little experience with snow, or knowledge or understanding of avalanches, have easy access to thousands of square miles of pristine avalanche terrain. Not surprisingly, snowmobilers have begun to be killed in droves.

Similar but less dramatic accident spikes have occurred among a new generation of mountain aficionados, snowboarders, snowshoers, and skiers on super-wide, lightweight telemark and alpine touring equipment (Figure I-3). Avalanche centers such as ours in Utah have had to scramble to keep up with the rapidly changing demographics. We've all learned to snowboard and ride the new generation of snowmobiles. We've also had to adapt our avalanche classes and avalanche bulletins to a whole new culture and language, to new equipment and travel styles. It's helped to keep old farts like me young, or at least pretending I'm young.

DOING THE NUMBERS

To give you an example, let's make the following assumptions:

- You travel in avalanche terrain 100 days per year.
- You cross 10 avalanche slopes per day.
- The snow is stable enough to cross on 95 percent of the slopes.
- For every avalanche you accidentally trigger, you get caught every third time and killed every tenth time.

Table I-1 is a fictional actuarial table that uses these *conceptual* numbers to give you an idea of your odds in avalanche terrain.

TABLE I-1. FICTIONAL AVALANCHE ACTUARIAL TABLE			
Percent Correct Decisions	*Avalanches Triggered per Year*	*Number of Times Killed per Year*	*Expected Lifetime*
99.99	.1	.01	100 years
99.9	1	.1	10 years
99.8	2	.2	9 years
99.7	3	.3	8 years
99.6	4	.4	7 years
99.5	5	.5	6 years
99.4	6	.6	5 years
99.3	7	.7	4 years
99.2	8	.8	3 years
99.1	9	.9	2 years
99.0	10	1	1 year
95 *	50	5	2 months
* People with no avalanche skills and assuming snow is stable on 95 percent of the slopes			

If we believe these conceptual numbers, completely ignorant people who go out 100 days per year will probably get killed sometime that first year or perhaps the next year. If they avoid going out during storms, as many people do, they might go a few years without getting caught. On the other end of the spectrum, if skilled helicopter skiing guides expect to have a reasonably long career, they have to make the correct avalanche decision better than 99.9 percent of the time. How many people do you know who make the right decisions 99.9 percent of the time?

Because humans regularly make mistakes, we can't rely on our individual knowledge or prowess to keep us alive. Instead, avalanche professionals operate in a SYSTEM, which I capitalize here because it's so important. The pros travel a well-trodden path of proper training, mentorship, procedures, checklists, rituals, and step-by-step decision-making. And to further push the arrow toward the top of the actuarial chart, they know that, inevitably, they will make mistakes: so they always follow safe travel ritual and regularly practice rescue techniques. In contrast, most recreationists operate without any overall system, in a nerve-wracking chaos in which they repeatedly throw themselves into avalanche path after avalanche path, betting with their lives, depending on little more than luck, which eventually runs out. (See Figure I-4 for avalanche incidents

Avalanche Incidents By Severity—Utah Data 1997–2007

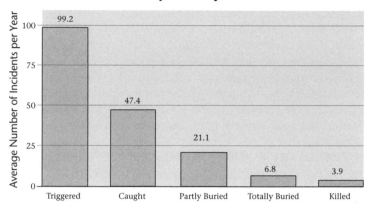

Percent Killed vs. Incident Severity—Utah Data 1997–2007

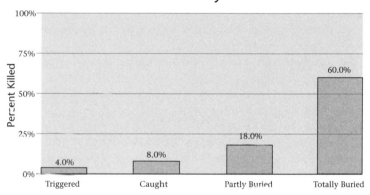

Figure I-4. Lucky for us, avalanches give us several cheap lessons before we get an expensive one. But sometimes, as Dave McClung says, "The final exam comes before the lesson."

U.S Beacon Use Among Fatalities—2000–2007

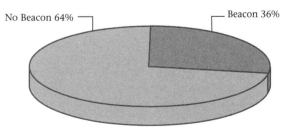

Figure I-5. Two thirds of avalanche victims were not carrying basic rescue gear—similar to the percentage of drowning victims who did not wear personal flotation devices.

in Utah, percent of people killed and incident severity.) Thus, in the U.S., the vast majority of avalanche fatalities occur to general recreationists while less than 2 percent occur to professionals. Similarly in Switzerland, a recent study by Beni Zweifel of the Swiss Federal Institute of Snow and Avalanche Research found that in the past two decades, avalanche fatalities among guided parties have significantly decreased while fatalities among non-guided parties has increased. In Utah and nationally, we estimate that three out of four avalanche victims did not consult the avalanche advisory before heading out and two out of three were not wearing beacons (Figure I-5). The bottom line is that for each day spent in avalanche terrain, more is better when it comes to avalanche knowledge and experience.

Avalanche professionals and skilled amateur recreationists gain this advantage in several ways:

- They make it their business to know everything they can about snow and avalanches and the terrain in which they work.
- They communicate closely with one another so that everyone stays abreast of rapidly changing avalanche conditions, and they use the wisdom of the group instead of relying on the fallible decisions of individuals.
- They base their decisions on systematically derived evidence, not emotion—very important!
- They use a largely unwritten set of safe travel rituals that help to minimize the damage in case something does go wrong.
- They regularly practice rescue techniques in realistic situations for the inevitable times when something goes wrong.
- Most important, they have seen bad things happen and know the consequences. They have seen unexpected things happen and know the limitations of their knowledge and technology. In other words, the pros survive by learning to master their arrogance and nurture their humbleness.

THE IMPORTANCE OF USING A SYSTEM

I used to think that just by teaching people about avalanches, they would automatically make the right decisions; but it has become painfully obvious through the years that education alone just doesn't work nearly as well as we had hoped. Nor has it worked in dozens of other fields ranging from anti-drug campaigns to industry to the military. In a 2000 study, Dale Atkins of the Colorado Avalanche Information Center found that among people with at least some avalanche education nearly 90 percent of accidents were caused not by avalanche factors such as snowpack, weather, or terrain but by "human factors"—thus Chapter 10 is entirely dedicated to human factors. In other words, smart people regularly do dumb things.

Fortunately, there's a way around this. The best defense against the human factor is to train people to systematically evaluate avalanche danger. Time-tested procedures, checklists, and rules are widely used not only by stock traders and business professionals, but by those working in commercial aviation, the military, and industry, and within many other environments where mistakes could be fatal. Hence an overarching theme of this book: Staying alive in avalanche terrain means learning and using a system for evaluating the snowpack and the risks associated with it.

USING THIS BOOK

When I first started learning about avalanches I continually became frustrated because very few hard-and-fast rules seemed to work. Avalanches are filled with double-edged swords, good news—bad news situations. For example, rain is bad, right? Well, it depends. In the short term rain makes the snow less stable, but in the long term rain makes it more stable. Anchors are good, right? Well, it depends. Sometimes trees and rocks anchor the snow, sometimes they are sources of snowpack weaknesses like depth hoar. You get the idea. That's just how avalanches are. You'll notice a number of good news—bad news sections in this book. Learn them and use them to your advantage. Here's the first one.

Good News—Bad News

The good news is that it's possible to spend a lifetime recreating safely in avalanche terrain.

The bad news is that it requires work. It is widely accepted that mastering most complex human endeavors requires 10 years' experience.

This book will *not* guarantee that you won't die in an avalanche. This is only the first baby-step in a lifetime of avalanche education. You didn't become an accomplished snowmobiler, climber, skier, or snowboarder by reading a book or taking one lesson, and avalanches are no different.

The more you know about avalanches and the more you follow standard procedures practiced by avalanche professionals, the farther you will be able to push the arrow toward the top of the avalanche actuarial chart. You can never push the safety arrow to 100 percent—never—but you can get very close. The more tricks you know, the more knowledge about snow stability, the better your travel skills and rescue skills, and most important, the more mastery you have over your own human foibles, the better the odds for living a long, stress-free life in avalanche terrain.

The other bad news is that research clearly shows that people with education and experience do not always make better decisions than novices. Both experts and novices tend to have similar success when 1) they encounter unusual conditions, 2) they do not get regular feedback, and 3) when human factors cloud their judgment. Thus, avalanche education and experience can only take us half-way to our goal. The rest depends on operating within a systematic decision-making framework which serves as check and balance against our inevitable human foibles.

In this book I attempt to pass along the current state of avalanche knowledge and practice among professionals and advanced recreationists—what we know and what we don't know—and the system of techniques, procedures, checklists, and protocols pros use to keep themselves and others alive in dangerous avalanche terrain. This book is a compilation of decades of avalanche knowledge learned by many smart people through science and from trial and error—sometimes tragic error. Along the way, I emphasize the human factors that cause the vast majority of accidents—even among people with some knowledge and training in avalanches—and how to avoid entirely all-too-human mistakes.

Staying Alive in Avalanche Terrain takes you step-by-step through the time-tested system practiced by avalanche professionals. This system allows them to enjoy long careers in dangerous avalanche terrain.

Rap on Measurement Units

In this book I primarily use metric units, but I also give American units in parentheses. I call them American units instead of English units because even England doesn't use them anymore. The United States is the only industrialized country in the world not on the metric system. It certainly makes the avalanche business difficult. Because scientists (and the rest of the civilized world) use the metric system, we always describe everything beneath the snow surface in metric units, but because the National Weather Service still communicates to the public in American units, we usually describe everything above the snow surface in American units. Crazy, I agree, but hey, we're Americans.

So to make this book understandable to people outside the United States, and to stick with international standards, I use metric units.

A NOTE ABOUT SAFETY

Safety is an important concern in all outdoor activities. No book can alert you to every hazard or anticipate the limitations of every reader. The descriptions of techniques and procedures in this book are intended to provide general information. This is not a complete text on avalanche safety. Nothing substitutes for formal instruction, routine practice, and plenty of experience. When you follow any of the procedures described here, you assume responsibility for your own safety. Use *Staying Alive in Avalanche Terrain* as a general guide to further information. Under normal conditions, excursions into the backcountry require attention to traffic, road and trail conditions, weather, terrain, the capabilities of your party, and other factors. Keeping informed on current conditions and exercising common sense are the keys to a safe, enjoyable outing.

The Mountaineers Books

chapter one

AVALANCHE BASICS

Life is short, the art long, opportunities fleeting, experience treacherous, judgment difficult.

—Hippocrates

DRY SLAB AVALANCHES

If you're looking for the killer, then this is your man. This is the White Death, the Snowy Torrent, the Big Guy in the White Suit. Dry slab avalanches account for nearly all the avalanche deaths in North America and, not surprisingly, 90 percent of this book focuses on how to avoid getting caught in them.

A "slab" is a cohesive plate of snow that slides as a unit on the snow underneath. Picture a magazine sliding off an inclined table. Then imagine you're standing in the middle of the magazine as the crack forms up above you. It feels like someone pulls the rug out from underneath you and suddenly there's no escape. The slab rockets downhill with you as its unintended passenger—off for the most terrifying and dangerous ride of your life.

A dry slab avalanche being triggered by an explosive (Adamant Mountains, Canada) © Roger Atkins

If you look at avalanche accidents in the U.S., a typical slab is 60 centimeters deep and 60 meters wide, in other words about 2 feet deep and about two-thirds the size of a football field wide. It usually reaches speeds of 30 km/hr (20 mph) within the first 3 seconds and quickly accelerates to around 130 km/hr (80 mph) after the first, say, 6 seconds. The bonds holding a slab in place fracture at about 350 km/hr (220 mph) and the slab appears to shatter like glass. As it continues down it breaks up further, forming furious and fast-moving piles of cascading snow.

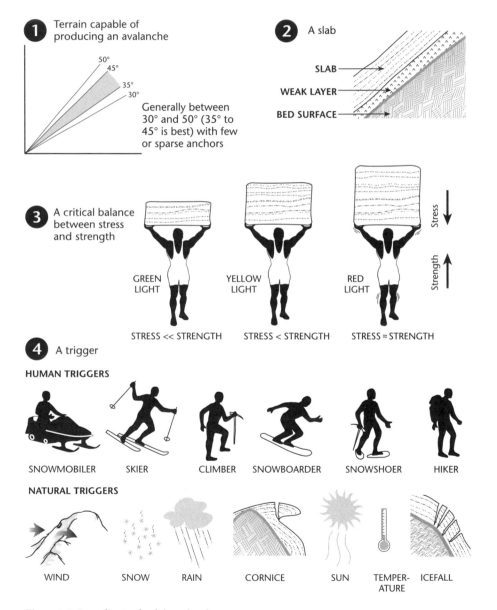

Figure 1-1. Ingredients of a slab avalanche

Dry slab avalanches can lie teetering on the verge of catastrophe, sometimes for several days. The weak layers beneath slabs are extremely sensitive to the rate at which they are stressed. Thus a rapid change to the snowpack, such as the quick addition of wind-blown or new snow, can make an otherwise benign snowpack very cranky. Then, the mere weight of a person can easily push it over the edge (Figure 1-1). Like a giant booby trap, avalanches can lie in waiting for just the right person to come along. The crack often forms well above the victim, leaving little room for escape. Does any of this sound dangerous to you?

PARTS OF A SLAB AVALANCHE (Figures 1-2 and 1-3)
- **Slab:** Relatively harder, or more cohesive snow that slides.
- **Weak layer or weak interface:** Relatively weaker or less cohesive snow that fractures, causing the slab to slide.
- **Bed surface:** Harder layer of snow the slab slides upon. The ground can also be a bed surface. A preexisting bed surface is not required but it helps. Often the avalanche creates its own bed surface.

What Makes a Slab?
Weather deposits snow in layers. Each different kind of weather affects the snow in a different way: Sunshine makes a sun crust. Wind erodes snow from the upwind side of a ridge and deposits that same snow on the downwind side in a dense wind slab. Clear skies at night create a layer of frost on the surface of the snow. And so on. As each storm buries the layers, the snowpack becomes a complex stack of layers, some relatively stronger and some relatively weaker. When stronger snow overlies weaker snow, we call it a slab. Or as Karl Birkeland of the Forest Service National Avalanche Center puts it, "A slab is when you have something sitting on top of nothing."

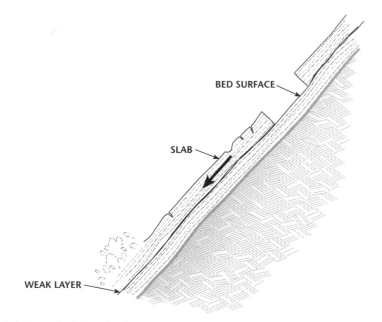

Figure 1-2. Parts of a slab avalanche

Average-size hard slab avalanche. Dry slab avalanches range from very hard to very soft. Soft slabs are composed of mostly new snow, while hard slabs are composed of either old, harder layers of snow or wind slabs. (Gallatin Range, Montana) © Karl Birkeland

Remember that a slab doesn't have to be so hard that you can hardly kick your boot into it. It just has to be *relatively* stronger than the snow underneath. Light, dry powder snow can behave as a slab as long as it has an even weaker layer underneath.

What Makes a Weak Layer?

Nearly any kind of snow can be a weak layer or a weak interface, but they tend to be (listed roughly in order of importance):

- Faceted snow, which is very weak, angular, larger-grained snow that forms within or on top of the snowpack because of large temperature gradients
- Surface hoar (a fancy name for frost)
- Low-density or poorly bonded layers within new snow, such as stellar crystals or plates (like a snowflake design on a sweater) or graupel (pellet snow like tiny Styrofoam balls, which can behave like little ball bearings)
- A weak interface, such as new snow sliding on a slippery ice crust

See Chapter 5, Snowpack, for more details on weak layers.

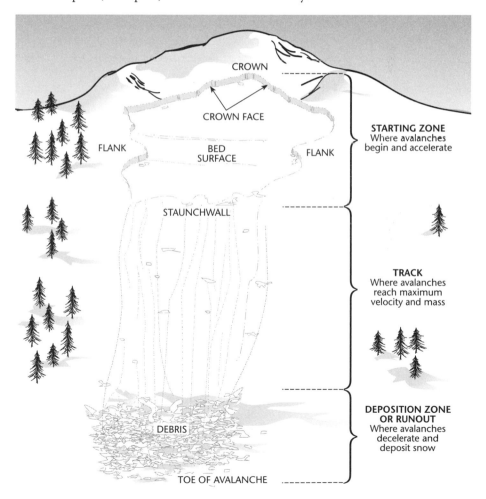

Figure 1-3. Parts of an avalanche slide path

What Makes a Bed Surface?

A bed surface is a layer of relatively harder snow (or ground) on which the slab slides. You don't need a pre-existing bed surface to make an avalanche. For instance, sometimes avalanches fracture within a thick layer of weak snow and the avalanche creates its own bed surface as the avalanche descends. But in most cases, avalanches descend on a harder, slicker snow surface like the surface of an inclined table as the magazine (the slab) slides off. Common bed surfaces include:

- Rain crusts
- Sun crusts
- Hard, old snow surface
- Wind-hardened snow
- Melt-freeze crusts

Good News—Bad News

The good news is that simple and easy observations and tests can detect potential avalanche hazard most of the time.

The bad news is that hundreds of combinations of slabs, weak layers, and bed surfaces commonly exist in the snowpack, and each combination behaves a bit differently.

A skier triggering a small loose snow avalanche, also called a "sluff" (Chugach Range, Alaska)
© Scott Markewitz

LOOSE SNOW AVALANCHES

Loose snow sliding down a mountainside is called a loose snow avalanche. Small loose snow avalanches are called "sluffs."

Loose snow avalanches usually start from a point and fan outward as they descend, and because of this they are also called "point releases." Few people are killed by loose snow avalanches because they tend to be smaller and they tend to fracture beneath you as you cross a slope instead of above you as slab avalanches often do. The avalanche culture tends to minimize the danger of loose snow avalanches, or sluffs, sometimes calling them "harmless sluffs." Of course, this is not always the case. Houses have been destroyed by "harmless sluffs," and if caught in one, the victim can be taken over a cliff, into a crevasse, or buried deeply in a terrain trap, such as a gully. Most of the people killed in loose snow avalanches are climbers who are caught in naturally triggered sluffs that descend from above—especially in wet or springtime conditions—or extreme skiers and boarders in very steep terrain.

Sluffs can actually be a sign of stability within the deeper snow when new snow releases as a sluff without triggering deeper slabs. Sluffs are also relatively easy to deal with, but slabs are definitely not. See Chapter 8, Routefinding and Safe Travel Rituals, for a discussion on sluff management techniques.

ICE AVALANCHES

When glaciers flow over a cliff they form the slow-motion, ice equivalent of a waterfall—an icefall. Falling blocks of ice create an avalanche of ice, which often entrains snow below it or triggers slabs. Especially in big mountains, ice avalanches can be large and travel long distances. Despite this, ice avalanches kill few people compared to dry slabs that people trigger themselves. Unlike slab snow avalanches, they are not triggered by people but most often naturally. Consequently, most of the deaths from ice avalanches occur to climbers in big mountains who happen to be in the wrong place at the wrong time.

Ice avalanches occur more or less randomly in time. In warmer climates, more ice tends to calve off in the heat of the day than at night. On a longer time scale, glacier velocity tends to vary over time. For instance, sometimes an icefall seems very dormant for several months, then suddenly the glacier surges, which produces more activity for several days to a month.

The best way to deal with ice avalanches, of course, is to avoid traveling on or beneath icefalls. When you choose to travel beneath them, do so quickly. At the risk of being too obvious—never camp under icefalls. Sometimes bad weather prevents climbers from seeing icefall hazard when they set up camp, or bad weather forces them to camp in the wrong spot. Many accidents with ice avalanches happen this way. The use of a map and a Global Positioning System (GPS) can eliminate many of these accidents.

CORNICE FALL AVALANCHES

Cornices are the fatal attraction of the mountains, their beauty matched only by their danger. Cornices are elegant, cantilevered snow structures formed when wind drifts snow onto the lee (downwind) side of an obstacle, such as a ridgeline. Similar to icefall avalanches, the weight of a falling cornice often triggers an avalanche on the slope below, or the cornice breaks into hundreds of pieces and forms its own avalanche—or both (Figure 1-4). Similar

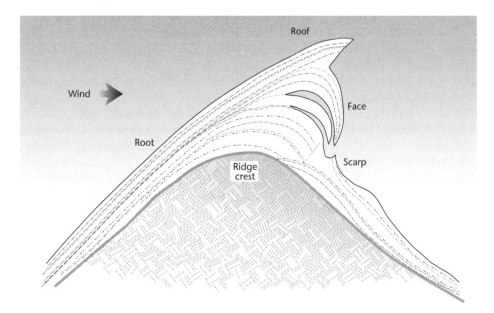

Figure 1-4. The structure of a cornice

Icefall avalanches in big mountains can be very large and catastrophic, representing a significant hazard to climbers and trekkers. (Pakistan) © Evelyn Lees and Rick Wyatt

to ice avalanches, cornice-triggered avalanches don't kill very many people. As with slab avalanches, the ones who get into trouble almost always trigger the avalanche; in this case, by traveling too close to the edge of the cornice.

Cornice fall fatalities, however, are a significant problem in big mountains, especially for climbers. Cornices have a nasty habit of breaking farther back than you expect. I have personally had three very close calls with cornices and I can attest that you need to treat them with an extra-large dose of respect. When reaching a ridge or a summit we are invariably drawn to the edge to see the view. In avalanche terrain, we have to resist the siren call of the edge, because most of the time the edge is a cornice. Although it feels like we are standing on solid ground, there's often nothing but air just a foot or more below our boots. Rule: *never, never* walk up to the edge of a drop-off without wearing a rope or first checking out the drop-off from a safe place. Many people needlessly die this way every year.

WET AVALANCHES

Most avalanche professionals make a hard separation between wet snow avalanches and dry snow avalanches. We forecast wet and dry avalanches very differently: much of their mechanics are different, they move differently, and it's only natural for us to think of them as two altogether separate beasts. But really, there's a continuum between wet and dry avalanches. For instance, there are damp avalanches, and often, large, dry avalanches start out dry and end up wet by the time they get to the bottom because they travel into a region of warmer snow.

Like dry snow avalanches, wet avalanches can occur as both sluffs and slabs. Wet avalanches usually occur when warm air temperatures, sun, or rain cause water to percolate through the snowpack and decrease the strength of the snow, or in some cases, change the mechanical properties of the snow. (See Chapters 2, 5, 6, and 7 for more details.) Once initiated, wet snow tends to travel more slowly than dry snow—like a thousand concrete trucks dumping their load at once instead of the hovercraft-like movement of a dry avalanche. A typical wet avalanche travels around 15 to 30 km/hr (10 or 20 mph, or less than half the speed of a dry avalanche), but on steeper terrain they can go nearly as fast as a dry avalanche. Probably because not as many recreationists are out on wet-snow days, wet avalanches don't account for nearly as many avalanche fatalities as dry snow avalanches. However, they still account for a sizeable percentage of avalanche fatalities in maritime climates, especially to climbers. Wet slides can also damage property or forests and often cause significant hazards on highways.

Glide Avalanches

A type of wet avalanche, the glide avalanche, occurs when the entire snowpack slowly slides as a unit on the ground, similar to a glacier (Figure 1-5). Glide is a slow process that usually takes place over several days or weeks. Glide occurs because melt-water lubricates the ground and allows the overlying snowpack to slowly "glide" downhill. The presence of glide cracks in the snow does not necessarily mean danger. Occasionally they can release catastrophically as a glide avalanche. It's often difficult for a person to trigger a glide avalanche, but at the same time it's not smart to be mucking around on top and especially not smart to camp under them.

Glide cracks and glide avalanches tend to occur more in wet climates on smooth slopes, but when they occur in dry climates, they do so in spring or sometimes during midwinter thaws when water has percolated through the snow.

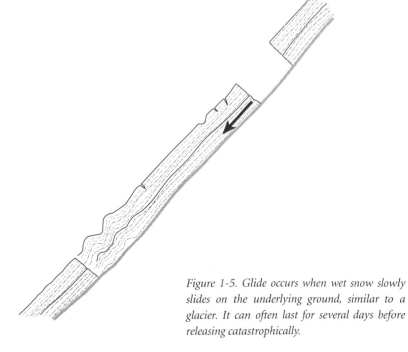

Figure 1-5. Glide occurs when wet snow slowly slides on the underlying ground, similar to a glacier. It can often last for several days before releasing catastrophically.

Glide avalanches are a type of wet avalanche that occurs when water lubricates the interface between the snow and the ground. The snowpack moves slowly for hours or days before it releases. (Wasatch Range, Utah)

Slush Avalanches

Slush avalanches are the snow equivalent of a flash flood. Although slush avalanches are rare in temperate climates, they are quite common in very northern latitudes, such as the Brooks Range of Alaska, northern Norway, Greenland, and northern Russia. They're unusual because they occur on very gentle slopes compared with other avalanches, typically 5 to 20 degrees, and they rarely occur on slopes steeper than 25 degrees. Similar to a flash flood, they can travel 40 to 60 km/hr (20 to 40 mph), overrunning a camp in low-lying areas well away from what most people would recognize as avalanche terrain. A typical slush avalanche occurs on impermeable permafrost soil, which allows water to pool up. In very northern latitudes, spring is brief: winter often turns into summer in just a week or two. When a cold, dry snowpack suddenly becomes saturated with water, it catastrophically loses its strength and the resulting slush often runs long distances on gentle terrain. Once again, very few people are killed by slush avalanches, possibly because so few people live or recreate in high-latitude permafrost mountains. But they can certainly be dangerous to people camped in gullies or alluvial fans or to structures built in the wrong locations.

Figure 1-6. A generalized map of the three avalanche climates: maritime, intermountain, and continental.

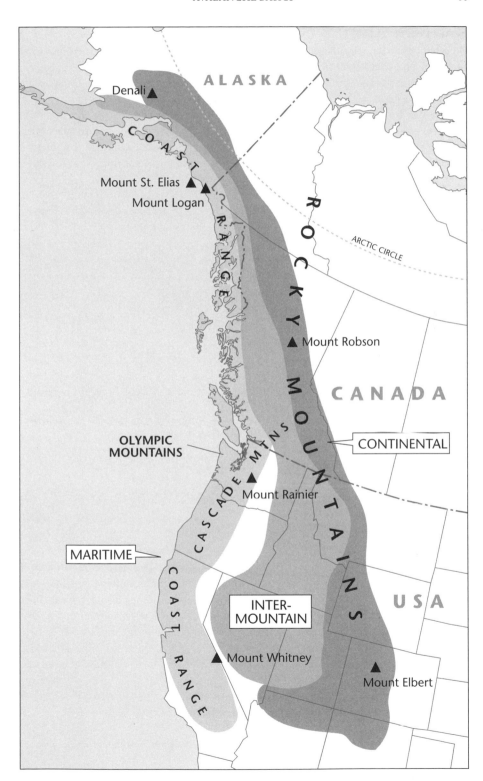

AVALANCHE CLIMATES

We often refer to three different avalanche climates in North America: maritime, inter-mountain, and continental (Figure 1-6). Maritime snowpacks tend to be thick, warm, and strong; continental snowpacks tend to be thin, cold, and weak; intermountain climates tend to be in between.

Although the climate is named for the region where we usually find it, remember that this is only a naming convention; each climate can occur anywhere and considerable overlap exists. For instance, often coastal mountains have a thin snowpack with cold temperatures in the early part of the season and therefore have a "continental" snowpack—at least for a

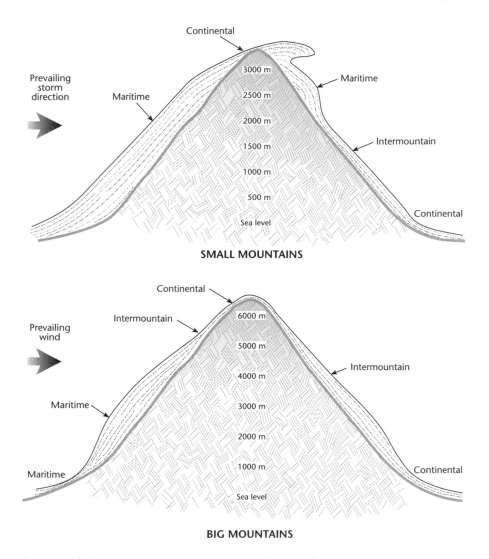

Figure 1-7. The three avalanche climates can occur locally, depending on the conditions.

few weeks. Likewise, an unusually warm and wet winter on the east slopes of the Rockies can create a "maritime" snowpack. On an even smaller scale, a windblown ridgeline may resemble a continental snowpack while a few feet away a thick wind drift might resemble a maritime snowpack (Figure 1-7).

Maritime—Mountains Bordering Oceans

Characteristics:

- Deep snowpack (over 3 meters; over 100 inches).
- Warm temperatures (near freezing; -5 to +5 degrees Celsius, 20 to 40 degrees Fahrenheit).
- High-density new snow (commonly 100 to 200 kg/m³ or 10 to 20 percent ice by volume).
- Frequent storms with high precipitation rates.
- Most avalanches occur as "direct action" avalanches, i.e., avalanches directly caused by precipitation or wind.
- Weak layers tend not to persist through time and avalanches tend to occur during or immediately following storms. Because of this fewer avalanche fatalities occur in maritime climates.
- Common weak layers include low-cohesion layers within new snow, graupel, weak interfaces such as ice crusts, and weak layers produced by rain or rapid warming. Faceted snow is more rare but does occur, especially in the early season. Surface hoar is common.
- Stability evaluation tends to utilize weather parameters and observed avalanche activity with less reliance on snowpit tests.
- Midwinter rain commonly falls and wet avalanches can occur throughout the winter.

Intermountain—Mountains with an Intermediate Influence of Oceans

Characteristics:

- Intermediate snowpack depths (1.5 to 3 meters; 50 to 100 inches).
- Intermediate temperatures (-15 to -3 degrees Celsius; 10 to 30 degrees Fahrenheit).
- Weak layers include both weak layers within new snow and persistent weak layers, such as facets and surface hoar.
- Instabilities often persist for several days after a storm and can linger for long periods, especially with persistent weak layers and cold temperatures.
- Stability evaluation tends to involve all factors: weather, avalanche activity, snowpit tests, and surface clues.
- Midwinter rain occurs, but only rarely.

Continental—Mountains Far from the Influence of Oceans

Characteristics:

- Thin snowpack (less than 1.5 meters; 70 inches).
- Cold temperatures (-30 to -10 degrees Celsius; -20 to 20 degrees Fahrenheit).
- Storms occur less often and deposit relatively smaller amounts of low-density snow.
- Common weak layers include faceted snow, depth hoar, and surface hoar—weak layers that are very persistent through time.

- Stability evaluation is difficult. Traditional tests do not work as well. The most common strategy is to simply avoid avalanche terrain for several days after wind or snowstorms.
- Avalanches can occur many days after storms and changes in stability from nonstorm-related events. Because of these notoriously persistent instabilities, we often see high fatality rates in areas with large mountain populations, such as Colorado.
- Midwinter rain is extremely rare.

chapter two

HOW AVALANCHES WORK

Avalanches cannot readily be subdivided, reconstructed, or reduced to laboratory scale.... They are best observed in their native habitat, and this is an occupation something like trailing a wounded African buffalo.
—Monty Atwater, grandfather of American avalanche study

This chapter describes the mechanical way that avalanches fail, fracture, and flow. As the old avalanche adage goes, *"The best rule of thumb in the avalanche business is that there are no rules of thumb."* Despite this, a number of simple, rule-based, decision-making methods have been created over the years, which, if used properly, can eliminate many avalanche

This large avalanche was triggered by a party of three, including the skier in this photo, who located his completely buried partner with a beacon and saved his life. Here, he returned the following day with me to investigate the close call. The avalanche was a meter deep and a half kilometer wide. Often, unstable snow can hang in the balance for hours or days, just waiting for a trigger. (Wasatch Range, Utah)

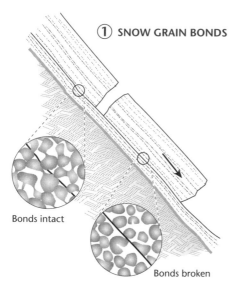

① **SNOW GRAIN BONDS**

Bonds intact

Bonds broken

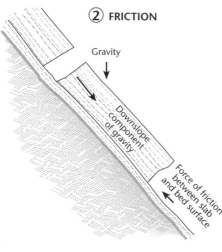

② **FRICTION**

Gravity

Downslope component of gravity

Force of friction between slab and bed surface

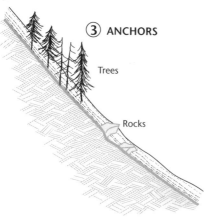

③ **ANCHORS**

Trees

Rocks

deaths. These methods have proven very useful for beginning avalanche students and in Chapter 7, Hazard Evaluation, I present a number of them. In this chapter, I want to take the opposite approach to give you an idea of how avalanches work. How do you, "think like an avalanche"? To do this you need to develop a three-dimensional, stress-and-strain feel for how avalanches work. When a mechanic wants to learn how an engine works, he takes it apart and then puts it back together again and we're going to do the same thing in this chapter with avalanches. As you progress on your own personal journey of avalanche mastery, you will eventually develop the skills, knowledge, and experience to make good decisions intuitively.

FORCES INVOLVED IN SLAB AVALANCHES

In order for a slab to become an avalanche the forces that pull the slab downhill must overcome the following forces that hold it in place:

- Snow grain bonds at the slab boundaries
- Friction between the slab and the bed surface
- Pinning effect of anchors

Let's look at these forces one at a time (Figure 2-1).

Snow Grain Bonds at the Slab Boundaries

Which slab boundary is the most important? Good question. For most typical avalanches the bond between the slab and the bed surface is the important one, and this has been confirmed experimentally, namely, that failure and fracture start within the weak layer first—not the slab. That's why we spend most of our time thinking about, testing, and worrying about the all-important weak layer (Figure 2-2).

Figure 2-1. Forces that hold a slab in place

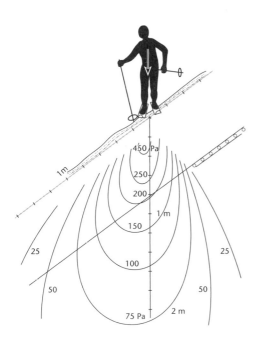

In the past, avalanche prediction tended to concentrate only on the stability of the snowpack (strength vs. strength, see Chapter 6, Stability) but recent work by Ian McCammon and others suggests that we need to also consider the propagation potential of the snowpack. In other words, just hitting someone won't start a barroom brawl. You also have to have enough pent-up tension in the room for the fight to spread to others. Fracture initiation depends on the stability of the snowpack, but fracture propagation depends on both the energy stored in the snowpack and the structure of the snowpack (Figure 2-3). In other words,

Figure 2-2. Additional stress the snow feels when you cross it. The units are pascals. Notice that the deeper a weak layer is buried, the less additional stress a person will exert on it. (From the Swiss Institute of Snow and Avalanche Research)

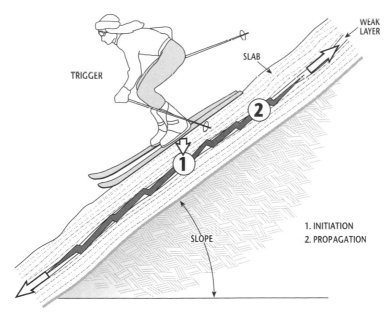

Figure 2-3. When a person triggers an avalanche, the initial fracture occurs within the weak layer under or near the person because their weight exerted too much additional stress on the buried weak layer. The fracture then spreads outward through the weak layer. Finally, after the slab has detached on the bottom, gravity pulls the slab downhill creating visible fracture lines in the snow on the surface, which although they are the most visible to us, are actually the last fractures to occur. (From Ian McCammon)

for snow to avalanche we need all three legs of the stool: 1) snow unstable enough to initiate a fracture, 2) sufficient stored, elastic energy to propagate that fracture, and 3) the proper snowpack structure to propagate a fracture. (See Chapter 6, Stability, for a more detailed discussion.)

Let's look at some numbers. Take the case of three different avalanches. First, let's look at a very small and very stout avalanche. Let's say it's 10 meters square and 1 meter deep (Figure 2-4). In this case the area of the bed surface is 2.5 times the combined surface area of the slab perimeter (crown face, flanks, and staunchwall). Since slabs are commonly ten times stronger than the weak layer under them, in this case the strength of the slab

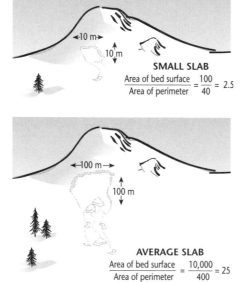

SMALL SLAB

$$\frac{\text{Area of bed surface}}{\text{Area of perimeter}} = \frac{100}{40} = 2.5$$

AVERAGE SLAB

$$\frac{\text{Area of bed surface}}{\text{Area of perimeter}} = \frac{10,000}{400} = 25$$

becomes a significant factor. But let's take a look at a larger avalanche, for example, one 100 meters square and 1 meter deep. In this case, the area of the bed surface or weak layer is 25 times that of the perimeter. An average-size avalanche might be 100 meters square and only 50 centimeters deep, making the bed surface 50 times the area of the perimeter. Finally, let's look at a very large avalanche, 1000 meters square and 1 meter deep. In this case the bed surface layer is 250 times the size of the slab perimeter. In other words, the strength of the slab compared to the weak layer varies with the size and proportion of the avalanche. The take-home point here is that for most avalanches the strength of the slab is insignificant compared with the strength of the weak layer.

Having said this, it certainly doesn't mean that we completely ignore the strength of the slab. For instance, Figure 2-4 illustrates that with stout slabs on small avalanche paths, the strength of the slab can become an important factor. Also, the "bridging" effect of slabs is very important (more on this later). To understand all of this, let's head to the kitchen and do an experiment.

Find three different "slabs" of about the same size but different strength: a paper towel, a piece of cardboard, and a wooden cutting board. Even though they have about the same bed surface area, it's easiest to tear the paper towel, harder to tear the cardboard, and impossible to tear the wooden board. Thick, stout slabs are more difficult to fracture and they form much better bonds to the crown, flanks, and staunchwall than thin, flimsy slabs.

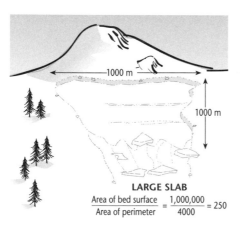

LARGE SLAB

$$\frac{\text{Area of bed surface}}{\text{Area of perimeter}} = \frac{1,000,000}{4000} = 250$$

Figure 2-4. Three sizes of avalanches with a 1-meter-thick slab. The bonds around the slab perimeter fracture (crown, flanks, and staunchwall) are more important in smaller slabs than in larger slabs.

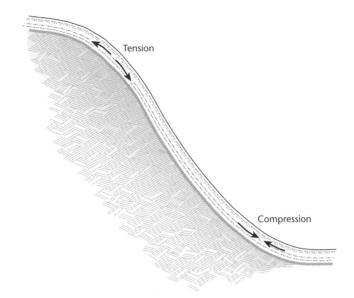

Figure 2-5. A stout slab on a small avalanche path is difficult to trigger because of the compression support at the bottom and tensile strength at the top.

Because of this, it's difficult to trigger stout slabs on a very small avalanche path. These slabs have a relatively large amount of compressive support at the bottom, shear strength at the flanks, and tensile strength at the crown face. Even with little or no bonding on the bottom, the strength of the slab itself can usually hold it in place (Figure 2-5).

On the other end of the spectrum, soft slabs with little internal strength (paper towels) can slide on nearly any slope, even small slopes and slopes with lots of anchors (trees, etc). Because they're so soft, the strength of these slabs plays a relatively insignificant role in keeping the slab in place.

Although the bed surface is by far the most important boundary, like a jazz trio the mechanics of an avalanche release depend on the interactions of all three members of the avalanche band: the slab, the weak layer, and the bed surface. Even though one has the solo while the other two follow along, it still takes all three to make music (more on this later).

Friction Between the Slab and the Bed Surface

To make a magazine slide off the table, you need to tip up the table to the point where gravity overcomes friction. For avalanches, this usually happens somewhere between 35 and 45 degrees. Not coincidentally, a pile of sand begins to slide at 38 degrees. With a very weak and slippery weak layer and bed surface, avalanches can occur on gentler slopes. Remember that without friction, only snow grain bonds and anchors hold snow on steeper slopes.

An example of a very slippery surface would be a stout and smooth rain crust with a layer of surface hoar on top of it. When we quickly put a heavy slab on top of it, avalanches can occur on unusually low slope angles. The shallowest avalanche I have ever seen is 25 degrees at the trigger point, but they have been known to slide on slopes as shallow as 18 degrees in extremely unusual circumstances.

Pinning Effect of Anchors

Anchors such as trees and rocks help to hold the slab in place. The effectiveness of anchors depends on the following factors:

- **Stiffness of the slab.** Returning to our paper-and-cardboard experiment: take a paper towel and attach it to a bulletin board with a thumbtack. Do the same with the piece of cardboard. Now pull down on both of them with an equal amount of force. The paper towel will tear away first.
- **Number of anchors.** The more thumbtacks you use, the harder it will be to rip either the cardboard or the paper off the bulletin board.
- **Effectiveness of the anchors.** If we use nails instead of thumbtacks, it will be harder still. For instance, trees with few branches, such as aspens, anchor the snow-pack much less effectively than spruce trees, with their lower branches frozen into the slab.
- **Size (or weight) of the slab.** It's easier for a thumbtack to secure a piece of cardboard the size of this book than one the size of your living room. (See Chapter 3, Terrain Management, for more details on anchors.)

HOW SLABS FRACTURE

The Bridging Effect of Slabs

If you hang around avalanche pros you will hear them talk about the slab "bridging." To understand bridging, you need to go sit on the edge of your bed. Notice that your weight makes the mattress springs sink down right under your bouncing butt, yet the springs just a foot away hardly compress at all. Now go get your biggest cutting board from the kitchen—the big one that slides out from under the countertop—put it on the bed, and sit on the cutting board. Notice that the springs under your butt don't sink down as far. Your weight is "bridged" outward (Figure 2-6). Now imagine that you are in a spy movie and that someone has planted a pressure-sensitive bomb under your mattress. As soon as the switch feels your full weight, KAPOW! So what are you going to do? Are you going to sit on the cutting

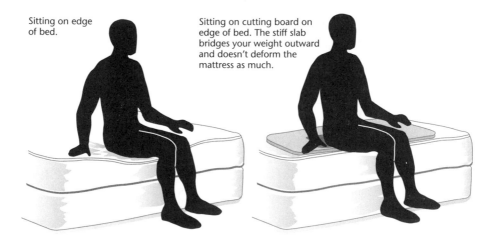

Sitting on edge of bed.

Sitting on cutting board on edge of bed. The stiff slab bridges your weight outward and doesn't deform the mattress as much.

Figure 2-6. Bridging. A strong slab can bridge the weight of a person outwards, which puts less stress on buried weak layers. The good news is that bridging makes avalanches harder to trigger, but the bad news is that if you do trigger one, it is a larger and more dangerous avalanche.

Although it appears solid, snow can shatter like glass. Utah Avalanche Center forecaster Evelyn Lees investigates an avalanche that caught a skier the previous day. (Wasatch Range, Utah)

board or not? Maybe you'll go get a bigger, stiffer cutting board—how about a big piece of plywood? This is why it's much easier for a person to trigger soft slabs than hard slabs.

There are two reasons for this:

1. Stiff slabs tend to spread a person's weight over a larger area.
2. Even with very poor weak-layer bonding directly beneath the person, a stiff slab can bridge outward to places where the slab might be better bonded to the bed surface, like a drunkard stumbling along supported on the shoulders of two sober friends.

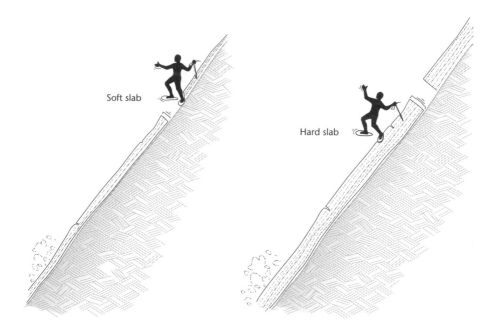

Figure 2-7. Soft, shallow slabs tend to break at your feet. Hard or thick slabs tend to break above you.

Good News—Bad News

The good news is that hard slabs are more difficult to trigger, but the bad news is that they tend to propagate farther and make a much larger and more deadly avalanche. Also, the stiffer the slab, the farther above you the fracture line will usually form, and the harder it will be to escape (Figure 2-7). Finally, remember that the stiffness and/or thickness of slabs can vary a lot from place to place, so just because you may not be able to trigger a slab in a thick spot, as soon as you cross to a thinner area—for instance, where it may thin near a ridgeline—you may be able to trigger the whole shebang. Which brings us to the next point.

Trigger Points

The strength of the bond between the slab and its bed surface varies, as well as the stiffness of the slab, sometimes dramatically from one place to the other. For instance, imagine a pane of glass sprinkled with a thin layer of flour. We then blow the flour off only one part of the glass. Finally, we spread glue on the bottom of a piece of plywood and lay it down on top of the floured glass. The glue will stick to the bare glass, but it won't stick to the floured glass. The slab is well bonded in one place but not as well bonded in another. A similar scenario happens in the mountains when, for instance, surface hoar (frost) forms on the surface of the snow, a little wind comes up which destroys the surface hoar in localized areas, and then finally new snow falls, creating a slab—a slab that is only sporadically bonded to the underlying snow (Figure 2-8). Other areas of poor bonding include around bushes and rocks or areas of shallow snowpack. (See Chapter 5, Snowpack, for more details.)

These areas of poor bonding have been called "deficit areas" or "superweak zones" by some researchers. Ski patrollers call them "sweet spots" because they can trigger avalanches with explosives when they hit just the right spot. I like to call them "trigger points."

The trouble, of course, is that they're invisible. We know about them only because patrollers bang away at the slope with explosives until they finally find the trigger point or snowmobilers track up a slope all afternoon until one person finally brings the entire slope down. By the time we finally find out where they are, it's too late to avoid them. This phenomenon alone accounts for most of the so-called mysterious and unpredictable nature of avalanches (Figure 2-9).

And no wonder. Danger is one thing, but invisible danger is quite another. But just because it's invisible doesn't mean that it's mysterious. It just means that we don't yet know how or where to look. So how do we deal with invisible danger? One way is to gather more information—perhaps dig more snowpits to see the aerial extent of the deficit areas, or throw more explosives. If you don't have the time or resources to get more information, your only hope is to take a giant step backward from the "stupid line"—the line between reasonable and unreasonable risk. Then a lot of the old pros take another giant step back. In other words, we need to always remember that a snowpit test or an explosives test or even trundling a cornice down a slope tells us what is going on in only one place. Since the strength of the buried weak layer often varies from place to place, we have no choice but to either do additional tests or different tests to eliminate the uncertainty—or simply take a more conservative approach. Always be suspicious when you have a lot of variability in your test results. The trend is your friend and surprises are not.

As you gain more experience and mountain-smarts, you will learn what kinds of weak layers tend to be more continuous, which ones tend to be localized, which ones you can trust, and which ones you can't. (See Chapter 5, Snowpack, for more details.)

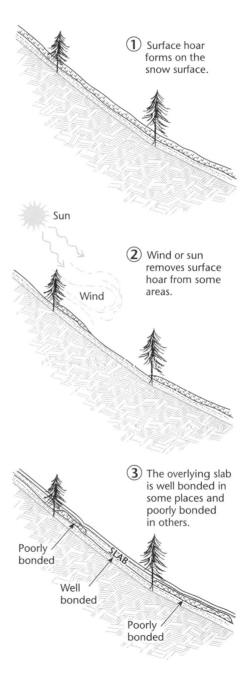

① Surface hoar forms on the snow surface.

Sun

② Wind or sun removes surface hoar from some areas.

Wind

③ The overlying slab is well bonded in some places and poorly bonded in others.

Poorly bonded

SLAB

Well bonded

Poorly bonded

Figure 2-8. The creation of a slab that is only sporadically bonded to the underlying snow

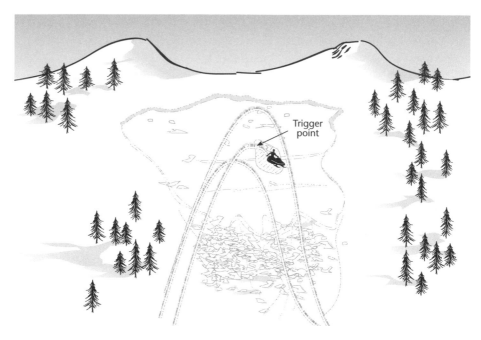

Figure 2-9. A snowmobiler finds the trigger point of the avalanche, where the slab is thinner or the weak layer is more fragile.

A snowmobiler found the trigger point of this avalanche after his party tracked up the entire slope. Luckily, he was not caught. This is typical of a faceted weak layer because it grows best in shallow areas near rocks. Shallow snowpack areas are common trigger points for avalanches in intermountain and continental climates. (Wasatch Range, Utah)

A common pattern with soft slab avalanches. Here we see many smaller avalanches occurring during or immediately after a storm. As the slab gains strength, avalanches become harder to trigger but fractures propagate farther and create larger, more dangerous avalanches. (Switzerland) © Juerg Schweizer

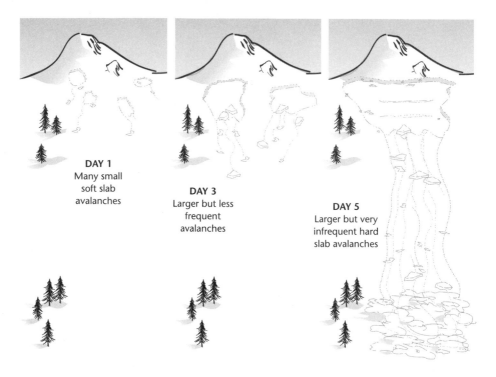

Figure 2-10. The number and type of avalanche occurring in a particular area often depend on how much time has passed since the last storm.

Slab Strength and Propagation Distance

In general, the stiffer the slab, the farther the fracture can propagate. In other words, the stiffer the slab, the bigger and scarier the avalanche, and it tends to fracture above you instead of at your feet.

Here is an example that we notice in many areas of North America: During and right after a storm, we see widespread natural avalanche activity on all kinds of slopes, even small slopes with a lot of compressive support and relatively thick trees, but the fractures typically don't propagate very far. Since the slab is soft, we can also trigger avalanches easily, and they usually fracture at our feet instead of above us.

But as time passes, the slab settles and gains strength—and the slab typically gains strength much more quickly than the weak layer beneath it. When this happens, we usually see fewer avalanches because they are less sensitive to triggers, but the ones we do see will occur on large, open slopes without anchors, the fractures will occur above us instead of at our feet, and, because of the stiffer slab, the fractures will propagate much longer distances. With "persistent" weak layers (see Chapter 5, Snowpack), such as surface hoar and faceted snow, it's not unusual for fractures to propagate around corners and over ridges, or to trigger the slopes "sympathetically," meaning from a distance away. This is because the stiffer slab transmits energy farther and can store more elastic energy (Figure 2-10). (See also the Silly Putty example below.)

Although most avalanches occur during or immediately following storms, especially with persistent weak layers, avalanche danger to people is sometimes worse after a storm than during a storm—after the slab has had a chance to stiffen up. Most avalanche professionals I know would rather deal with the slab while it's still soft because it's easier to manage the hazard.

Snow Is Like Silly Putty

Go to nearly any lecture on avalanches and chances are good that you will see the instructor pull out their trusty Silly Putty. (I've also seen people use a mixture of cornstarch and water.) This is the only way I know to demonstrate the visco-elastic nature of snow. Silly Putty, like snow, exhibits both a viscous and an elastic nature. If you roll it in a ball, you can bounce it (elastic energy). But snow (and Silly Putty) also flow viscously; like the proverbial molasses in January.

The most interesting part of the snow–Silly Putty metaphor is that when deformed slowly, it flows like taffy, but when deformed rapidly, it fractures like glass. The take-home point is: *Snow is very sensitive to the rate at which it is deformed.* This is probably the most important property to remember about snow, and it's the cause of most avalanche fatalities. In other words, snow, just like people, does not like rapid change. (If you raise taxes slowly enough, no one will notice. If you raise taxes 30 percent overnight, there will be riots in the streets.)

For example, let's add 60 centimeters (2 feet) of slab on top of a weak layer, but let's add it over the course of two weeks—a few centimeters here, a few there. Will we have any avalanches? Probably not. The snow has time to adjust to its load. (See the "Settlement and Sintering" section below.) Let's add 60 centimeters (2 feet) of snow in, say, two days. Any avalanches? Probably. Now let's add 60 centimeters (2 feet) of snow in 2 hours. Any avalanches? You bet.

Wait, 60 centimeters (2 feet) of snow in 2 hours? Have any of you ever seen that happen? Yes, you have—from wind. Wind can deposit snow ten times more rapidly than snow falling out of the sky, making it usually the most important weather factor to consider.

Finally, let's deform the snow at an *extremely* rapid rate. A 90 kilogram (200 pound) rider gets a 200 kilogram (500 pound) snowmobile stuck on a steep slope, and now you can begin to understand why

Snow behaves viscously when it moves slowly as demonstrated by this roof glide. When strained to its breaking point, it behaves elastically and fractures. (Switzerland) © Juerg Schweizer

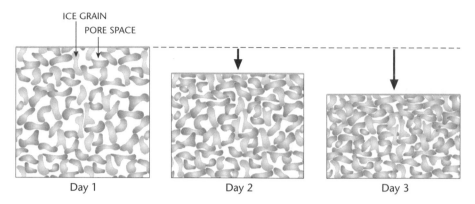

Figure 2-11. Settlement occurs when snow slowly deforms and becomes more dense over time due to rounding metamorphism and gravity. This is why powder doesn't last long.

people make such great avalanche triggers. The stress is being added over the course of seconds or milliseconds instead of over hours or days.

Snow can adjust to a certain amount of stress in a certain amount of time. If you reach that limit, you get an avalanche. This is why we pay such close attention to what we call "loading rate" (discussed in more detail in Chapter 4, Weather). By loading rate I mean the rate at which new snow, wind-drifted snow, rain, or people add weight to the snowpack. Rapidly added weight rapidly deforms snow and that means avalanches (Figure 2-11).

Settlement and Sintering

A newborn snowflake that falls out of the sky doesn't stay that way for long. As soon as it lands on the snow surface it begins a rapid process of change. Just like people, as a snowflake ages, its beautiful, angular shape becomes progressively more rounded through time and it forms bonds with its neighbors. In people, it's called growing up; in the snowpack it's called "sintering"—forming bonds with neighboring crystals to create the fabric of the snowpack.

As sintering progresses, the snow becomes denser and stronger, which we call "settlement." Sometimes you will hear people incorrectly use the term "settlement" to describe the catastrophic collapse of a snowpack that often makes a giant WHOOMPH sound, as in, "Hey, did you hear that settlement? Maybe we should get out of here." Instead, we call these collapses, or "whoomphing," which has been adopted as the technical term for a collapsing snowpack because it is such a great descriptive term. Settlement is the *slow* deformation of the snow as it becomes denser and sags under the influence of gravity.

At warmer temperatures, new, fluffy snow settles relatively quickly, within minutes to hours, and at very cold temperatures it settles very slowly (more details on this later) (Figure 2-12). When new snow settles, it forms "settlement cones" around trees and bushes where the snow bonds to the bush which props up the snow like a circus tent.

Caveat: When we see signs of settlement, such as settlement cones, many people feel that it means that the snowpack is stable, right? Whoa, not so fast.

As I have said, slabs usually gain strength much faster than the weak layers beneath them. As we will see in Chapter 5, Snowpack, the old snow may contain persistent weak layers, such as surface hoar and facets, which gain strength much more slowly than new

When new snow slowly settles (becomes more dense and forms internal bonds) it remains propped up by bushes like the center pole in a circus tent. We call these settlement cones. (Wasatch Range, Utah)

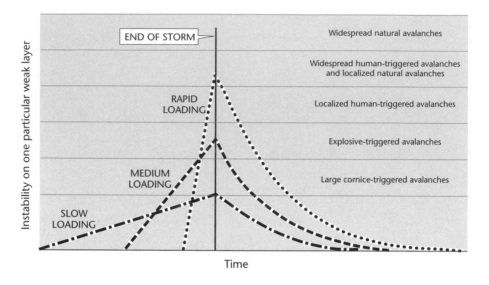

Figure 2-12. If we add the same exact load but vary the loading rate, fast loading rates produce more instability because the snow has not had time to adjust to its load.

snow. These persistent weak layers have just been loaded by the new snow—weight rapidly added onto its shoulders—and it may still be staggering under the strain. So it's important to make the distinction; are we talking about stability within the new snow or within the old snow? Yes, settlement cones may indicate stability within the new snow, but they tell us nothing about the preexisting snow underneath. In fact, this is precisely the setup that creates many deadly avalanches. The old snow is brittle and overloaded with a fresh layer of "sucker snow" on top—sucker snow with settlement cones, which indicate stability, right? Wrong. They indicate settlement only within the new snow.

Creep

"Creep" is simply settlement on an inclined slope, which causes the snow to actually flow downhill (Figure 2-13). Most people are surprised to learn that snow on a slope is in constant motion, slowly flowing down the slope—not the entire snowpack sliding on the ground like a glacier (we call this glide) but a slow deformation within the snowpack. This downhill movement of snow occurs more in the upper, low-density layers than in the older, denser snow below. For instance, when I studied avalanches in college, we would drill a completely vertical hole in the snow and fill it with sawdust. When we come back in a week or two and dig it out, the sawdust column will be bent downhill like a willow tree blowing in the wind.

Very interesting, you say, but what does this have to do with avalanches? Creep is very important in the snowpack because the surface layers travel downhill faster than deeper layers, which causes "shear stress." Shear stress tends to concentrate along any discontinuity in the snowpack, such as a weak layer or a weak interface, which can cause avalanches.

Temperature

Beginning avalanche students tend to focus too much attention on temperature, possibly because it's such an easy number to measure. Temperature plays a critical role in

near-freezing or wet snow (more on this later), but in dry snow, temperature is a complicated, often contradictory, factor in the avalanche game. Most of the time, temperature is
a minor player, especially when compared to loading. We can point to loading as the cause
of avalanches far more often than temperature changes—perhaps ten or a hundred times
more often, depending on the conditions. Usually loading requires *rapid* warming, not slow
warming, combined with a tender buried weak layer. Rapid loading plus rapid temperature
change plus a tender weak layer is an especially powerful combination. Once again, we have
to return to our mantra: *snow does not like rapid change*. Dry snow is highly sensitive to
rapid change—mostly mechanical change—and to a lesser extent, thermal changes. Having
said this, it's still important to know how temperature affects the mechanical properties of
the snowpack.

Ray Smutek, an avalanche educator from the Pacific Northwest, uses an analogy he calls
the "Betty Crocker principle" to explain the role of temperature in the snowpack. Say you
want to bake a cake. The directions on the Betty Crocker box say "bake the cake at 350 degrees for 20 minutes." Well, you're in a hurry so what do you do? That's right, you turn up
the heat to maybe 450 degrees.

Everything happens faster at warmer temperatures than colder temperatures. The battery
in our car works better, trees grow faster, paint dries faster. All chemical reactions—including metamorphosis of the snow—work faster at warmer temperatures than cold ones.

Warm snow deforms faster and easier than cold snow. This also includes creep, and an
increase in the creep rate of snow will also increase the rate of shear deformation along

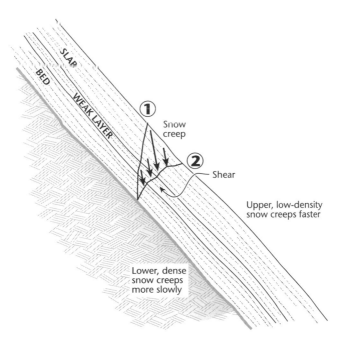

*Figure 2-13. Creep is the slow, downhill movement of snow, which can cause shear deformation to
concentrate in weak layers or weak interfaces. It should not be confused with glide, which occurs when
the entire snowpack slides on the ground like a glacier.*

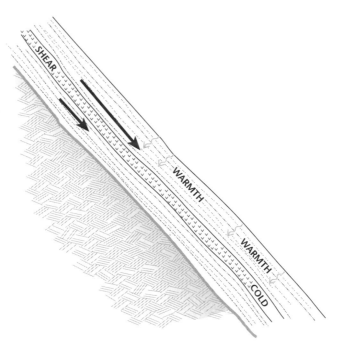

Figure 2-14. A rapidly warmed slab can accelerate settlement and creep in the slab, causing shear failure on cold, brittle, weak layers.

buried weak layers within the creeping snow and this means avalanches. Let me give you an example.

I remember once in Alaska, where I used to work as an avalanche forecaster, we had several weeks of cold, clear weather that turned the entire snowpack into depth hoar. Then slowly we got a couple of light snowstorms on top of the depth hoar with no avalanches and temperatures remained cold. Finally, a warm, wet air mass from the Pacific pushed into the interior, warming up the surface of the snow for the first time in several weeks, and localized avalanches started even before any precipitation fell.

When I measured the temperature profile in the snowpack, I found that the warmer temperatures had penetrated much of the slab, but the warmth had not yet reached the weak layer. In other words, the warmer temperatures caused avalanches by affecting the properties of the slab, not the weak layer. A commonly accepted explanation is that as a slab warms up, it increases the settlement and creep rate of the slab, which can accelerate shear within the still cold and brittle weak layer (Figure 2-14).

Ed LaChapelle and Swiss avalanche scientist Hans Gubler explain the process using the term "viscosity." Viscosity simply means how much a fluid resists flow. For instance, molasses in January resists flow much more than molasses in July. When the viscosity of the slab is about the same as the viscosity of the weak layer, the snow tends to be stable. But things get sketchy when the slab flows more easily (through settlement and creep) than the weak layer, or when the weak layer flows more easily than the slab. Back to the mantra: *snow does not like rapid change*, whether it is the rapid addition of weight or a rapid increase in temperature.

Most important in terms of human-triggered avalanches: cold slabs mean stiff slabs, and stiff slabs not only bridge better (bridging the weight of a person over a wider area) but the deformation of the snowpack from the weight of a person doesn't penetrate as deeply in a cold slab as a warm one. This would explain why we have noticed that people tend to trigger avalanches more easily after a slab has been warmed by sun or rain—especially after rapid warming (Figure 2-15). This, however, is a complicated and poorly understood process and, as we will learn later, with dry avalanches you should never base your entire stability evaluation on temperature when several other factors are usually more important.

Perhaps Ed LaChapelle, one of the grandfathers of American avalanche research, said it best: "Any rapid change in the mechanical or thermal energy state of the snowpack is a precursor to avalanching. And I emphasize rapid."

Deformation

Avalanches don't "strike without warning" as we so often read in the press. They are only the most spectacularly visible event in a long series of precursors leading up to the grand finale.

The process begins many hours—or even days—before, usually when new snow or windblown snow begins to pile weight on top of a buried weak layer. Added weight causes

Cold slabs bridge better and spread weight over a larger area.

Warm slabs allow weight to be transferred more directly to buried weak layers.

Figure 2-15. People tend to trigger avalanches more easily after a cold slab has been warmed by the sun, warmer air, or rain because warm slabs are softer than cold slabs and do not bridge someone's weight as effectively, and also because of the accelerated creep rate of the warming slab.

the underlying snow to deform; rapidly added weight causes snow to deform rapidly. On an inclined slope, the deformation tends to concentrate within buried weak layers in the form of shear.

Inside a weak layer under stress, bonds are being both broken (from deformation) and reformed (from sintering) at the same time. Let's look at three different rates of deformation: slow, medium, and fast.

Slow Deformation Rate

If the weak layer shears slowly, it simply deforms the bonds between the snow grains. As the deformation speeds, some bonds break; yet more bonds are formed than break. This means that the weak layer adjusts to its load and gains strength.

Medium Deformation Rate

With an increasing rate of deformation, the snow reaches a point where nearly as many snow grain bonds break as form and the strength of the weak layer remains about the same.

Rapid Deformation Rate

If shear occurs rapidly—past a certain critical threshold—then more bonds break than form. The weak layer inexorably loses strength and begins the slippery slide toward disaster. With sensitive microphones we can actually hear the rupture of individual bonds between the snow grains, like the sound of slowly ripping Velcro. We call this "failure"—when the snow begins to progressively lose strength. We also call this "strain softening." To understand failure and strain softening, do this experiment: Take a paper clip and bend it in the same place repeatedly. After about 10 bends you'll notice that it is getting weaker (failure) and after about 15 bends, it snaps right off (fracture).

Stretching the Rubber Band

Rapid changes create what we call "stored elastic energy" in the snowpack. To understand the concept of stored elastic energy, try another experiment: Take a rubber band and a sharp knife. Hook one end of the rubber band around a doorknob and stretch the rubber band but just a little. Now touch the rubber band with the knife and you'll see that it is very hard to cut the rubber band. Next, stretch the rubber band about halfway and touch it with the knife again, and most of the time it still won't cut the rubber band. Finally, stretch the rubber band all the way and touch it with the knife again. Now the knife easily cuts the rubber band. Climbers experience this with climbing ropes when falling rocks or sharp rock edges cut a taut climbing rope much more easily than a rope that isn't under tension or is coiled at their feet.

A stable snowpack is like a limp rubber band. Even large disturbances usually don't trigger avalanches, but after rapid changes occur in the snowpack (stretching the rubber band) even small disturbances can trigger avalanches. Remember that this stored elastic energy exists throughout the entire snowpack, including both the slab and the weak layer, and tickling either of them can have the same effect.

Caveat: Having said this, scientists still don't know all the details of how avalanches fail and fracture because snow is such a devilishly difficult substance to study. First, large variations commonly exist over both distance and time. Second, as you can imagine, catching a natural avalanche in the act is stupendously difficult and dangerous. So 10 or 20 years from

A very large, natural avalanche crashes into the valley bottom beneath a 4,000-vertical-foot avalanche path. Three snowboarders were killed in this same area the previous year when 14 people were recreating at the bottom during a very large snowstorm. The dust cloud of this avalanche billows up into a stunningly beautiful facade, concealing the destructive horror within it, which mowed down nearly an acre of trees. (Mt. Timpanogos, Wasatch Range, Utah)

now, these paragraphs—like so many of the "facts" we believe about avalanches—may seem like yet more quaint, geezer ramblings.

Good News—Bad News

The bad news: all of this is invisible. It happens underneath the perfect façade, and it becomes visible only through other evidence or from someone getting out the old shovel and doing some honest work.

The good news is that whenever the slope is close to fracture, it will usually give obvious signs—such as other avalanches, collapsing, and cracking. Plus, if you dig a snowpit in a representative spot, the instability is usually very obvious. Your columns will often fall off before you can even saw them out and most of your other tests will be just as apparent (see Chapter 6, Stability). So don't get too freaked out quite yet. Read on.

AVALANCHE FLOW
Dry Avalanches

Few sights on Earth are as stunningly beautiful as a big avalanche storming down the mountain in the golden light of dawn. Ski patrollers live a life of renunciation just to be able to witness it at close quarters on a daily or weekly basis—renouncing high pay, steady work, peaceful morning slumber, and a youthful face unblemished by wind

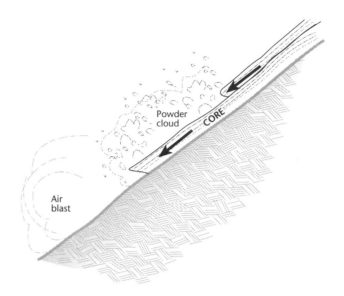

Figure 2-16. Parts of an avalanche in motion

and sun. But the beauty of the billowing powder cloud belies the violence that goes on underneath.

Inside the misty envelope of the powder cloud is a rushing mass of snow called the "core" of the avalanche that is a fluidized mixture of air and snow—about 70 percent air and 30 percent ice particles. Thirty percent doesn't seem like very much, but it's about the same density as seven adults standing within a 1-meter-square box drawn on the floor, in other words, about like a very crowded dance floor. Now, picture a basketball court tightly packed with people at a rock concert tipped up to a 40-degree angle and imagine the force of all the people slamming against the wall. This would exert about the same amount of force as a 2-meter-thick avalanche sliding 100 meters—not very far in the avalanche world. Now imagine that same basketball court of people traveling down a large avalanche path at 100 km/hr (60 mph) and slamming into a brick wall at the bottom and it's easy to imagine how avalanches can rip out trees and turn houses into toothpicks. This is also why more than a quarter of avalanche victims die from trauma, by hitting trees and rocks on the way down.

As the snow rushes through the air, it kicks up an envelope of powder, appropriately enough called a "powder cloud," which is composed of only about 1 percent snow and 99 percent air—the part of the avalanche that gives it beauty. In front of the powder cloud is the invisible "air blast," which is, as you might imagine, a burst of air that is pushed out in front of the moving snow. The air blast typically carries only about 10 percent of the wallop of the core of moving snow (Figure 2-16).

The avalanche is slowed down mainly by the friction with the surface it runs upon—rocks, vegetation, and the snow surface. To a lesser extent, the friction with the air slows the avalanche down. The snow nearest the bed travels more slowly than the snow above. Often, if you look close enough, you can see avalanches come down in waves. One wave shoots out in front, is slowed by friction with the ground and air, and then the next wave—traveling on the back of the first wave—shoots out ahead of the first wave, and so on. It looks kind of like pulses of snow being spit out the front of the avalanche once every few seconds.

The extreme violence inside the flowing debris grinds up all the snow into finer and finer particles and even if the snow started out light and fluffy, it can become very dense by the time it finally comes to a stop. It's not uncommon for a large avalanche that starts out with a density of 5 to 10 "percent" (weight of ice divided by the volume of the sample) to end up as 30 to 40 percent at the bottom. This means that when everything comes to a stop, the dense snow packs very tightly. Also, small grains sinter much more quickly than large grains, and the tiny grains making up avalanche debris can sinter as much as ten thousand times faster than the larger grains of the initial slab. Finally, all of the kinetic energy liberated on the way down heats up the snow a little and can create small drops of liquid water on the surface of the ice grains. (I remember once walking around on the debris of a big avalanche right after it came down and my goggles steamed up from all the warm moisture rising off the debris.) Combining all these factors, it's easy to see why avalanche debris in anything but the smallest avalanches (where less energy is released) seizes up like concrete the instant it comes to a stop. Great beauty and great power also bring great horror and great destruction. Although avalanches look like flowing white water in a river they do not flow as a liquid. Instead avalanches exhibit "granular flow" composed of millions of bouncing particles. And lucky for us. Since avalanche debris is around 30 percent density and the human body is close to 100 percent, if avalanches flowed like water we would always end up on the bottom.

In granular flow, larger objects tend to rise to the surface, just as shaking a bag of tortilla chips brings the larger, unbroken pieces to the top. (Which also means, in a cruel twist of fate, that the snowmobile, which in a lake would sink like a rock, usually ends up on the surface while the snowmobile rider often lies buried.) This explains the phenomenal success of the avalanche airbag (see Chapter 9, Rescue) which, with one pull of the rip cord, makes a human into a much larger object. Granular flow makes the human body more or less neutrally buoyant, and an airbag causes a person to quickly rise to the surface.

Wet Avalanches

A wet avalanche resembles 10,000 concrete trucks dumping their loads all at once. Wet avalanches travel more slowly than dry avalanches, typically less than half the rate of dry slides, or 15 to 40 km/hr (10 to 30 mph) as opposed to 70 to 130 km/hr (40 to 80 mph) for dry slides. However, wet avalanches in steep terrain can travel nearly as fast as dry slides. Wet avalanches travel down the hill looking like a giant Slurpee, typically following the drainage and terrain features much more precisely than dry slides. Although wet avalanches don't usually travel as far as dry slides, they can sometimes run long distances on flat slopes, often moving very slowly like a lava flow. They often leave spectacular, vertical grooves in the bed surface and they dig out a defined channel with high banks on the sides.

Wet avalanches sometimes have impact pressures about twice that of dry avalanches and can be extremely destructive to forests and structures. They tend to leave a sharp line of demarcation when they travel through forests with a line of untouched trees just a foot away from cleanly snapped-off trees. Wet avalanches tend to break off trees with near surgical precision compared with the ragged strand lines left by dry avalanches.

Mechanical Properties of Wet Avalanches

Dry avalanches and wet avalanches are two different beasts, especially the mechanics of how they are triggered. To visualize this, imagine a tower of gymnasts standing on each other's shoulders. There are two ways to make them crumple: first, you can add too many gymnasts to the pile until one of the guys below gives way, or second, you can tickle one of the gymnasts until he starts to giggle and loses his strength (Figure 2-17). The take-home point here is that the difference between dry and wet avalanches is that dry avalanches are triggered because stress overloads the strength of the weak layer (adding too many gymnasts) while wet avalanches occur for the opposite reason: by decreasing the strength of the weak layer (tickling one of the gymnasts).

When I worked as a ski patroller doing avalanche control, this would drive me crazy. To trigger a dry snow avalanche, you use an explosive to overload the strength of the buried

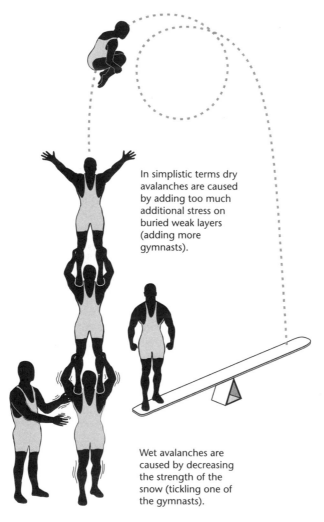

In simplistic terms dry avalanches are caused by adding too much additional stress on buried weak layers (adding more gymnasts).

Wet avalanches are caused by decreasing the strength of the snow (tickling one of the gymnasts).

Figure 2-17. Visualize the layers in the snowpack as a tower of gymnasts standing on each other's shoulders. Dry avalanches are caused by adding too much stress on buried weak layers while wet avalanches are caused by decreasing the strength of buried weak layers.

weak layer. But when I would try the same thing with wet avalanches, nothing happened. You pronounce it safe and a half-hour later, the wet slab pulls out on its own. What happened? Wet avalanches are like stubborn mules, they come down when they're good and ready, not before. Explosives don't work as well because explosives work by adding a large and rapid load—the wrong tool for the job. Also, wet snow tends to behave more viscously while dry snow tends to behave more elastically; wet snow does not transmit explosive shock waves nearly as well. It's not that you can't trigger wet slides with explosives or the weight of a person, it's just that triggers tend to work only when the avalanche is on the verge of coming down on its own anyway.

Some people think that wet avalanches are easier to forecast, but most of these people are from dry climates. Even after working for 30 years as a professional avalanche forecaster, wet avalanches often mystify me. (See more details on weather controls of wet avalanches in Chapter 4, metamorphism of wet snow in Chapter 5, and forecasting for wet slides in Chapter 7.)

Runout Distance

How far will an avalanche run? It depends on four factors (Figure 2-18):

1. **Size (mass) of the avalanche.** The greater the mass, the farther an avalanche runs. Small sluffs may run only about 10 percent of the maximum runout distance while "climax" avalanches that "break to the ground" (taking out the entire season's snowpack), or ones that involve a large amount of new snow, often run to the maximum runout.

2. **Slope configuration.** Planar slopes or slopes with gentle transitions produce longer running avalanches than slopes with abrupt transitions. Plus, larger vertical drops produce longer-running avalanches than short vertical drops.

3. **Slope roughness.** Slope roughness includes rocks, trees, or shrubs that stick up above the bed surface that can slow down an avalanche. Typically, avalanches don't run nearly as far in the early season when shrubs and rocks in the track slow the avalanche down. After the snowpack has accumulated enough to cover the shrubs and rocks, or after the roughness is smoothed over by avalanches—"greasing the track" as professionals call it—then avalanches can run much farther. Forecasters for highways, railroads, and work sites regularly take this into account.

4. **Type of snow in the avalanche.** An avalanche composed of blocky, hard, old snow doesn't run as far as an avalanche composed of new, powdery snow. Usually, the longest running and most destructive avalanches occur during very large storms that lay down unprecedented amounts of low-density (light) snow. This snow has little internal friction and once it gets going, it goes into "hovercraft mode" as Dave Medara, a Utah highway avalanche forecaster, puts it. These avalanches can do nearly unimaginable things, like running long distances across flats and even traveling uphill. Big, dry avalanches can jump off terrain features and fly through the air for long distances before they come back down, often leaving the trees beneath their flight untouched. They can easily "jump their track"—when the momentum of the avalanche takes them outside their normal drainage. They can wipe out large swaths of mature trees.

Researchers have estimated that as much as seven times the mass of some avalanches comes from snow entrained on the way down (picking up snow as they descend) with only a small amount from the initial slab. (See Chapter 3, Terrain Management, for details on a simple way to judge how far an avalanche will run.)

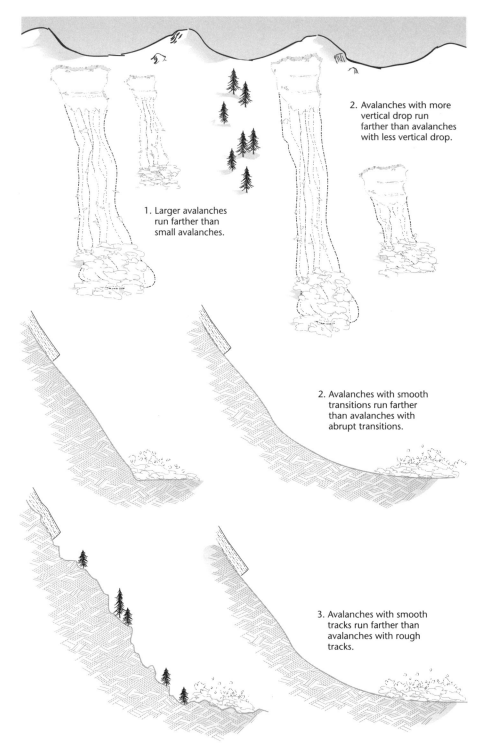

Figure 2-18. Three of the four factors that determine how far an avalanche will run: 1) the mass of the avalanche; 2) the slope configuration; and 3) the slope roughness.

This is only the lowest one-fifth of a large avalanche path. The portion visible in this photo was filled with 50-year-old trees before this avalanche wiped them out in January of 1996. (Wasatch Range, Utah)

AVALANCHE SIZE

Avalanche geeks commonly refer to avalanches by size using the following international standard five-point scale.

DESTRUCTIVE AVALANCHE SIZE SCALE	
Class 1	Relatively harmless to people
Class 2	Could bury, injure, or kill a person
Class 3	Could bury and destroy a car, damage a truck, destroy a wood frame house, or break a few trees
Class 4	Could destroy a railway car, large truck, several buildings, or a substantial amount of forest
Class 5	Could gouge the landscape. Largest snow avalanches known.

To make things really confusing, about 25 years ago American avalanche workers also started using a 1-5 relative size scale, describing the avalanche size relative to the size of the avalanche path. So you will often see avalanche size listed with a "D" or an "R" in front of the number to indicate whether it is on the Destructive or the Relative scale. For instance, R3, D2.

RELATIVE AVALANCHE SIZE SCALE	
R1	Very small relative to path
R2	Small relative to path
R3	Medium relative to path
R4	Large relative to path
R5	Major or maximum relative to path

chapter three

TERRAIN MANAGEMENT

Don't trivialize the importance or the subtlety of terrain. It takes a lifetime to get a handle on reading terrain—maybe two lifetimes.
—Chris Stethem, prominent Canadian avalanche consultant

The snowpack is a capricious and erratic acquaintance who you never get to know very well. The terrain is a steady and predictable friend that you can always depend on.
—Karl Klassen, Canadian avalanche specialist, providing a sanitized version of something his mentor, Ernst Buehler, used to say

Now we will start on the basic building blocks of avalanches. Everything we know about avalanches fits into one of three categories: terrain, weather, and snowpack. This is the data triangle made famous by Alaska avalanche specialists Doug Fesler and Jill Fredston (Figure 3-1).

I will start with terrain first because it is by far the most important. If you're going to learn nothing else about avalanches, at least learn how to manage terrain. You can be a complete klutz at stability analysis, yet you can live a long and happy life if you can learn the basics of terrain and how to manage it. Helicopter ski guides spend most of their time during their morning and evening meetings talking about which terrain is appropriate for the conditions. They consider the stability of the snowpack, the pattern of the instability, the kind of avalanche dragon they are dealing with, and the skill of their clients to come up with a run list—the kind of terrain they feel they can safely negotiate. Terrain management; it's the skill that separates the cagey from the inept, the ones that will live a long life from the accidents soon to happen.

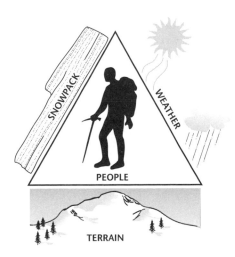

Figure 3-1. The data triangle (from Jill Fredston and Doug Fesler)

Once again, let's make like Aristotle and take terrain apart, piece by piece, and then we'll put it back together again in an organized way at the end of the chapter.

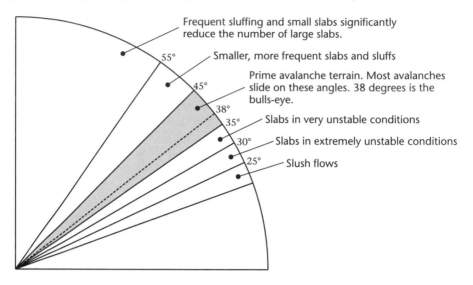

Figure 3-2. The vast majority of avalanches occur on slopes between 33 and 45 degrees.

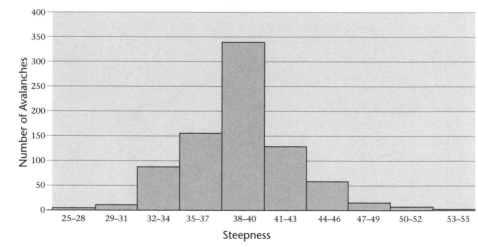

Figure 3-3. Slope steepness of 809 human-triggered avalanches in Canada and Switzerland. The steepness of human-triggered avalanches is probably slightly steeper than for natural avalanches. Also, don't be fooled by low numbers of avalanches on steep slopes. This is partially the result of fewer people traveling on steep slopes than on moderate slopes.

STEEPNESS

Gravity never sleeps. The steeper the slope, the more snow wants to slide off the mountainside, but avalanche *danger* doesn't necessarily work that way. Danger increases with increasing slope steepness and bull's-eyes around 38 to 40 degrees, on steeper slopes, avalanche danger counterintuitively starts to decrease. Especially as the slope climbs above 50 degrees, sluffs and smaller slabs run more frequently and significantly reduce the number of deeper, more dangerous slabs. This does not mean that large slab avalanches don't occur on 60-degree slopes, because they certainly do. It just means that they are less common than on 40-degree slopes.

Good News—Bad News

The good news is that the intermediate slope angles cause most of the problems. The bad news is that those are the exact ones where most of us like to recreate.

Slopes between 35 and 45 degrees cause the vast majority of avalanche fatalities (Figure 3-2). Recent statistics from Canada and Switzerland indicate that half of human-triggered avalanches occur between 37 and 42 degrees (Figure 3-3). The bull's-eye is around 38 degrees. Memorize this number — 38 degrees.

Table 3-1 illustrates the relationship between steepness and avalanche danger.

TABLE 3-1			
Steepness	*Slope Rating at a Ski Area*	*Avalanche Activity*	*Perception of Danger*
10–25	Beginner to intermediate slopes (green slopes).	Slush flows in arctic climates. Infrequent wet avalanche runouts. Dry slabs in extremely unusual situations	What is this, a golf course?
25–30	Intermediate slopes (blue slopes).	Infrequent slabs in unstable conditions. Those that do occur tend to be large.	OK, but not steep enough to have fun.
30–35	Advanced slopes (black diamond).	Slabs increasing rapidly in frequency as you approach 35 degrees. Usually requires fairly unstable conditions.	Starting to get steep enough to have fun.
35–45	Expert slopes (double black diamond).	This is prime avalanche terrain with the bull's-eye around 38 degrees. Frequent slab avalanches, some large.	Perfect! (But this is where most avalanches happen.)
45–55	Extreme terrain (couloirs in cliffs—usually roped off).	Frequent smaller slabs and sluffs reduce the number of larger slabs.	Whoa, this is seriously steep. I'm scared.
55–90	Alpine climbing terrain (cliffs and very steep couloirs).	Frequent sluffs and small slabs dramatically reduce the number of larger slabs.	Wow, it's a cliff. Give me a rope.

Caveat: In continental and intermountain climates, we rarely see avalanches on slopes steeper than about 50 degrees. Maritime climates are wetter, so the snow tends to get plastered onto steep slopes, like a giant spatula icing the side of a cake. I have seen several large slab avalanches on 60-degree slopes in maritime climates. I think the main reason they

Slope Steepness

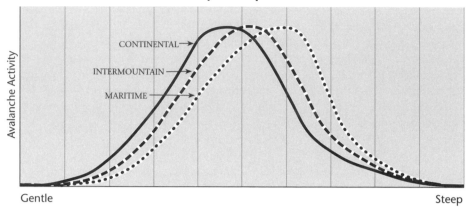

Avalanche Activity

CONTINENTAL →

INTERMOUNTAIN →

MARITIME →

Gentle   Steep

Figure 3-4. A conceptual diagram of how slope steepness of avalanches varies by climate

This slope is about 33 degrees – definitely steep enough to slide but not very often. (Wasatch Range, Utah)

This slope is about 50 degrees and is actually safer than slopes of 40 degrees as far as avalanches go—but then again, there's a whole new set of hazards. © Scott Markewitz

don't show up in the statistics and on the slope steepness graphs is that no one is willing to go up and measure them (Figure 3-4).

The most important point to remember with slope steepness is that within the range of 30 to 45 degrees, avalanches are extremely sensitive to slope steepness. Thirty degrees is barely steep enough to slide yet avalanche activity reaches a maximum at 38 degrees. This difference of only 8 degrees doesn't seem like much to humans but it's monumentally important to avalanches.

Therefore, skilled avalanche professionals quickly develop a keen distinction between subtle differences in slope angles, especially in the range between 30 and 40 degrees. This skill, more than any other, distinguishes those with what Doug Fesler and Jill Fredston call "avalanche eyeballs" from those without.

If you watch a skilled backcountry skiing guide break a climbing track uphill, they will work the terrain like a hound dog, back and forth, seeking the lowest angled terrain possible to get to the top of the slope. They will study a slope for a long time to see how to most efficiently connect all the lower angled sections. They will follow sub-ridges and sub-ridges of sub-ridges to get to main ridges. The closer the slope is to 38 degrees, the more they will avoid it. This skill takes years to develop, and it's an important testing criteria for certification of winter mountain guides. More than any other skill, it separates the master artists from the apprentices. It's a beautiful thing, to watch a true artist at work—reading the terrain, working the terrain, drawing their line on the mountain.

Avalanche instructors spend a lot of time in the field quizzing students on slope steepness, asking them to first guess the steepness of a slope, and then measuring the slope angle to settle the argument. The exercise proves very quickly that most people are generally lousy at judging slope steepness. Part of the problem is simple inexperience, but most of the problem is that perception plays a number of tricks on us.

Of course, perception is something that happens to humans and not avalanches. To an avalanche, the closer the slope is to 38 degrees, the more it wants to send a slab rumbling down the mountain. And the avalanche doesn't care about our peculiar perceptions. That's

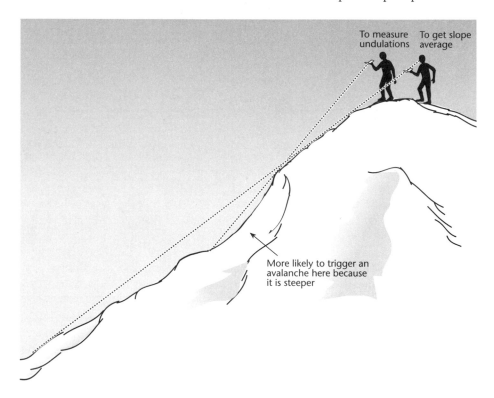

Figure 3-5. With an inclinometer, the most accurate measurement is to simply sight along the tangent of the slope either from the top or bottom. Local measurements of steepness (such as using a ski pole) are less accurate because you measure small variations in the snow surface instead of the average steepness.

Climber Kitty Calhoun measures slope steepness using a compass with an inclinometer built into it. Simply fold the mirror back so you can see the dial and sight along the top edge. (Wasatch Range, Utah)

why an inclinometer is one of the most important tools to carry in avalanche terrain.

Inclinometers

An inclinometer measures the steepness of a slope, and some avalanche educators say that if you're going to carry only one avalanche prediction tool, this should be it. Many relatively inexpensive compasses feature an inclinometer. Avalanche safety supply companies also distribute a small, inexpensive inclinometer card that uses a string as a plumb-bob. But I prefer the compass-inclinometers because they work better. You're going to need a compass anyway, so you might as well get one with an inclinometer.

Some avalanche books recommend laying a ski pole on the slope and setting the inclinometer on top of the ski pole to measure the slope angle, or using the ski pole plumb-bob system (see page 74). I have found these methods to be less inaccurate. The best way is to sight up or down the slope with the inclinometer because you can average out all the small undulations that would fool the ski pole method. You can also measure the medium-scale undulations from some distance away, thus not putting yourself at risk. Avalanches are often triggered when crossing the steepest part of a slope, which may be just a small undulation (Figure 3-5).

Note: From my experience teaching avalanche classes, it seems that most inexperienced people overestimate slope steepness by about 5 to 10 degrees; they'll tell you they just snowboarded a 50-degree slope that upon measurement is barely 40 degrees. You can get a general idea of slope steepness by practicing with an inclinometer on slopes at a ski area as illustrated in Table 3-1.

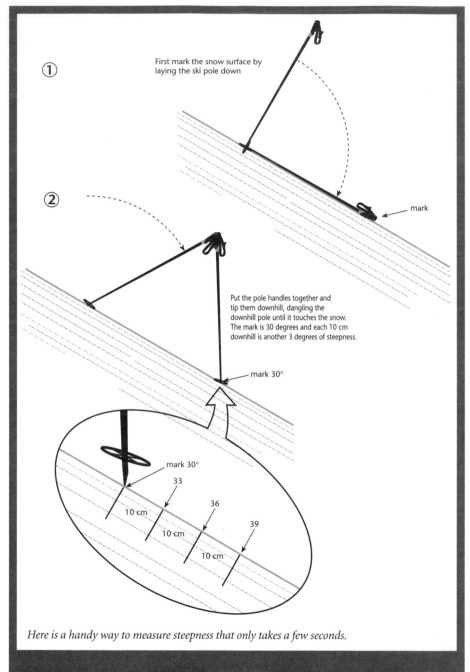

① First mark the snow surface by laying the ski pole down

mark

② Put the pole handles together and tip them downhill, dangling the downhill pole until it touches the snow. The mark is 30 degrees and each 10 cm downhill is another 3 degrees of steepness.

mark 30°

mark 30°
33
10 cm
36
10 cm
39
10 cm

Here is a handy way to measure steepness that only takes a few seconds.

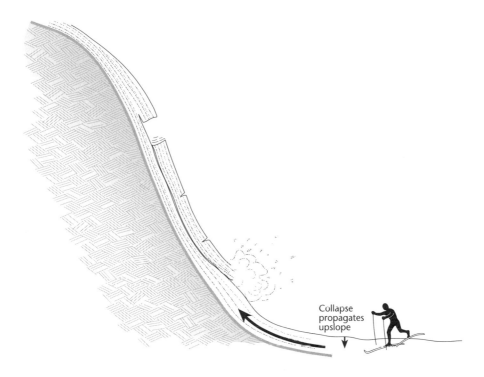

Figure 3-6. Especially in very unstable conditions, you can trigger an avalanche nearly as easily from the bottom as from the slope itself.

What Is the Slope Connected To?

You don't have to be on a steep slope to trigger it—very important. Especially in extremely unstable snowpacks, it's common to trigger steep slopes from an adjacent slope connected to it. We call these "remote" triggers when a person can trigger an avalanche from a distance. In extreme conditions, fractures can propagate long distances. Remote triggers are common in the following circumstances:

- You can trigger a steep slope above by crossing a gentle or flat slope below nearly as easily as crossing the steep slope itself. In Alaska I have collapsed flat slopes that triggered avalanches on steep slopes up to a quarter mile away. I have lost a couple of friends who died doing this very thing—people who should have known better (Figure 3-6).
- You can trigger avalanches below you from a flatter slope and especially from a ridge top. In extreme conditions, especially with thick, hard slabs, victims have been pulled off flat ridges this way—like when a child grabs onto the edge of a tablecloth and pulls all the dishes down onto the floor (Figure 3-7).
- You can trigger an adjacent slope. The slope you are standing on might not be steep enough to slide, but an avalanche on the adjacent steeper slope might pull your slope along for the ride.

Figure 3-7. Especially in very unstable conditions, you can trigger slopes from the top— or have the slab pulled out from under you, like a tablecloth being pulled off a set table.

ESTIMATING RUNOUT DISTANCE

Speaking of remote triggers, once I was skiing in the backcountry on an extremely unstable day with my friend Rip Griffith, a very experienced Utah Department of Transportation forecaster. Avalanches were coming down everywhere, so we traveled on "maximum security," that is, we stayed strictly on gentle slopes and ridges or in thick trees and kept our avalanche antennae fully extended.

We were following an old ski track, which made trail breaking easier even though it was now buried under a couple of feet of new snow. The old ski track went right underneath a 35-degree slope and as soon as we got close enough that the inclinometer in my head started giving me the alarm signal, I veered off the trail and started breaking a new trail through the thick trees off to the left, to skirt around the steep slope. Even though it was a royal pain to break a new trail through the thick trees, there was no way I was going under that steep slope on a day like that. I didn't have to say anything to Rip. He knew what I was doing. And if I hadn't broken a new trail, he certainly would have insisted on it.

On the way back a couple hours later we found ourselves on the flat ridge at the top of that same 35-degree slope. "Hey," he said, "I'll bet we can trigger the slope down there from up here on the flat ridge if we both jump at the same time."

"Okay," I said. "On three."

We jumped and the crown fracture opened up about 20 meters away from us, down over the edge where we couldn't see it but we could hear the slope below erupt into action. We saw the trees waving around and the dust cloud roll up into the air at the bottom. Then we did what most avalanche professionals do after they trigger a slide, we jumped into the avalanche path and did a snow profile. No better way to learn than that—direct, fresh data on a slope that is now very safe.

As we exited the bottom of the path, we noticed that the debris stopped about 10 feet away from where we decided to break another trail instead of following the existing one. The debris completely covered up the preexisting track. If we had followed the old track we would almost certainly have triggered the avalanche from the bottom and the newspaper headlines would have read: "Two Avalanche Experts Killed in Avalanche." The embarrassment alone would have killed us.

Like guys, we slapped each other on the back and said, "Hey, are we good or what?"

I tell this story not only to brag about myself, which I greatly enjoy, but also to illustrate the point that the road to destruction is sometimes paved by a well-broken trail. The person who broke the trail might not have known much about avalanches and even if they did, they broke it during different conditions. You must make your own decisions. The story also shows the importance of always measuring slope angles. Do it over and over until you can guess a slope angle within a couple of degrees. Many of the old-timer avalanche experts I know can guess a slope angle to within a half degree.

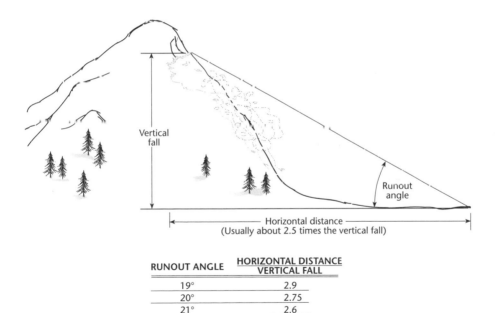

RUNOUT ANGLE	HORIZONTAL DISTANCE / VERTICAL FALL
19°	2.9
20°	2.75
21°	2.6
22°	2.4
23°	2.3

Figure 3-8. When choosing a campsite in avalanche terrain, avoid camping in avalanche runouts. In poor visibility or in areas without vegetation clues, you can tell if you are in an avalanche runout by using a topographic map. As a general rule of thumb, from the map, simply read the vertical fall of the avalanche path you're worried about and make sure you camp more than 2.5 times that distance horizontally away from the top of the starting zone.

Runout Angles

How far will an avalanche run? It's an important question when you set up camp, cross under a slope, or decide where to build your dream home. The runout angle, or "alpha angle," provides a quick, easy estimate of the maximum runout distance. To measure a runout angle, either stand at the toe of an avalanche and measure the angle to the crown fracture or stand at the top and measure the angle to the bottom (Figure 3-8).

Ballpark values for typical avalanches you may see on a yearly basis range from about 25 degrees for a damp snowstorm, unconfined avalanche paths without much snow in the track to be entrained in the avalanche, down to 19 degrees for storms with dry snow, confined avalanche paths, and lots of dry snow in the track to be entrained in the avalanche. In unusual conditions, runout angles can be much shallower.

Each local area seems to have a characteristic runout angle, so your friends will think you're an incorrigible nerd, but I suggest that you measure as many avalanche paths in your area as you can to get a feel for the common runout angles. I often wear an inclinometer around my neck when I'm out in the winter and sometimes I take one on summer hikes. Someday it may save your life.

Caveat: Remember that runout angles are only a general tool. If determining avalanche runout was that easy, then avalanche consultants wouldn't be able to charge premium prices

Anchors such as thick trees can effectively hold slabs in place. Here the lack of vegetation makes the big avalanche paths obvious. (Wasatch Range, Utah)

for doing avalanche zoning and figuring out if someone's trophy home is going to get hit.

Combine the runout angle with all your other information—other local runout angles, vegetation clues, path shape and path roughness, storm snow densities, entrainment, etc. (See Chapter 2, How Avalanches Work, for more details on avalanche flow.)

Vegetation Clues

You can often determine the maximum runout of an avalanche path from the vegetation—missing trees, knocked down trees, or "flagged" trees—trees with the branches stripped off the uphill side but still existing on the downhill side. Plus, by looking at the trees, you can usually tell how many years have passed since an avalanche last hit them. For instance, you might find a uniform blanket of 10-year-old trees in the lower section of the avalanche path, which suddenly terminates in 100-year-old flagged trees on the lower boundary of the path, indicating that 10 years ago an avalanche ran to its maximum runout—or at least the maximum runout in the past 100 years. Avalanches run to their *apparent* maximum runout about every 20 to 50 years, but their real maximum runout is usually much farther. About every 100 years an avalanche will run far enough to rip out fully mature trees and about every 500 years it will run bigger and farther than you could have ever imagined. Remember that these large slides could occur any time, not just every 100 years, and also no matter how big or how far you've seen an avalanche run in the past, given enough time, it will always run bigger and farther.

ANCHORS

Anchors such as trees, rocks, and bushes help to hold the slab in place. However:

- Anchors need to be densely spaced to be effective. Sparse anchors, especially combined with a soft slab, have very little effect (Figure 3-9).
- Anchors that don't stick up through the weak layer have no effect. They need to penetrate well into the slab (Figure 3-10).
- Spruce and fir trees with branches frozen into the slab are much more effective anchors than trees with few low branches, such as aspen or lodgepole pine. Also, snow falling off trees tends to stabilize the snowpack around trees and they tend to capture and reradiate more heat, which also affects the surrounding snow (Figure 3-11).

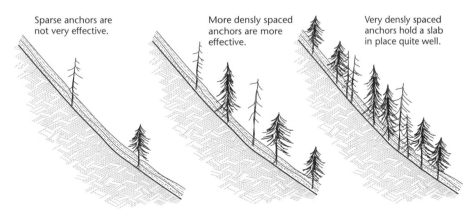

Sparse anchors are not very effective.

More densely spaced anchors are more effective.

Very densely spaced anchors hold a slab in place quite well.

Figure 3-9. More densely spaced anchors are much more effective than sparse anchors.

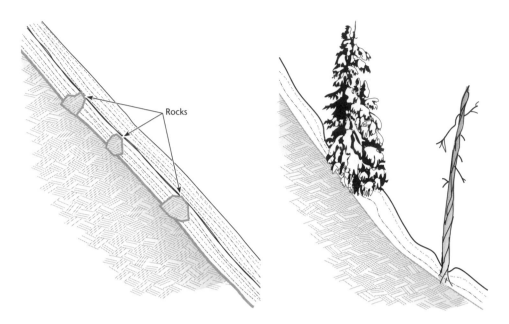

Figure 3-10. These anchors hold the lower slab in place but do nothing for the upper slab.

Figure 3-11. Evergreen trees with branches frozen in place such as spruce and fir, are more effective than bare-trunk trees like aspen or lodgepole pine.

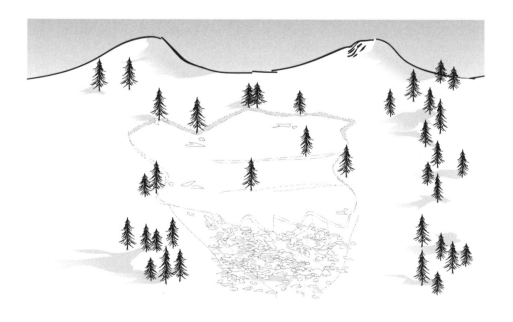

Figure 3-12. Anchors tend to be stress concentration points and fracture tends to break from anchor to anchor—another reason it is probably better to stand on the uphill side of trees.

- Anchors hold in place hard slabs much better than soft slabs.
- Avalanche fracture lines tend to run from anchor to anchor because they are stress concentration points, rather like the perforations between sheets on a roll of paper towels. In other words, you stand a better chance of staying on the good side of a fracture line by standing above a tree instead of below it (Figure 3-12). Also, anchors tend to break up the continuity of the slab so fractures tend not to propagate as far as they would without anchors.
- Flagged trees—trees with all the uphill branches stripped off—indicate trees that regularly get hit by avalanches.

Figure 3-13. Avalanche paths that terminate in trees are very dangerous. Remember that trees such as aspen are a disaster species, which recover quickly in places where avalanches or fire tend to destroy them.

Good News—Bad News

The good news is that anchors are our friends; they help to hold a slab in place.

The bad news is that if they fail to anchor the slab, your best friends suddenly turn into your worst enemies; trees and rocks turn into giant baseball bats that will break your bones and/or kill you (Figure 3-13). Remember that about a quarter of U.S. avalanche fatalities and as many as half of Canadian fatalities result from the trauma of hitting trees and rocks on the way down. (See the "Consequences" section in this chapter.)

Caveat: In continental climates, or in any depth hoar snowpack, faceted snow commonly forms around rocks because they conduct the ground heat to the surface very efficiently and because snow tends to thin around a rock (thin snow means weak snow). Because of this, it's common to trigger avalanches while crossing near rocks or other shallow snowpack areas. Therefore, in continental climates, don't think of rocks as islands of safety or anchors; they can be trigger points (Figure 3-14). (See Chapter 5, Snowpack, for more details on this.)

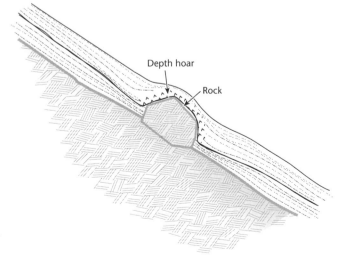

Figure 3-14. Depth hoar tends to grow around rocks.

SLOPE ASPECT WITH RESPECT TO THE SUN

The direction a slope faces with respect to the sun (aspect) has a profound influence on the snowpack. Developing an appreciation for the importance of aspect often takes several years of experience in avalanche terrain. You might not know your north, south, east, and west, but you had better learn, because someone who doesn't know the aspect of the slope they are standing on has missed one of the most important pieces of the avalanche puzzle. Buy a compass, use it often, and work on developing a constant awareness for slope aspect.

The influence of aspect with respect to the sun is most important at mid-latitudes, say, from about 30 degrees to around 55 degrees—from about the southern U.S. border to about the northern British Columbia border. At equatorial latitudes, the sun goes almost straight overhead, shining more equally on all slopes. At arctic latitudes, in the winter, the sun is too low on the horizon to provide much heat, but in fall and spring, aspects

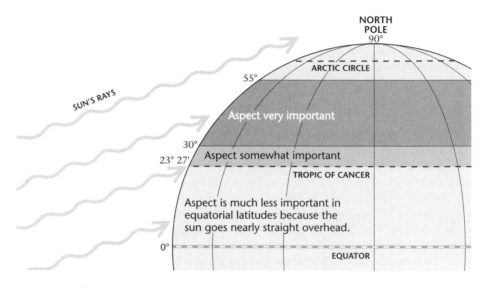

Figure 3-15. The importance of aspect varies with latitude. In the continental U.S., aspect is very important but is increasingly less important as you travel north or south.

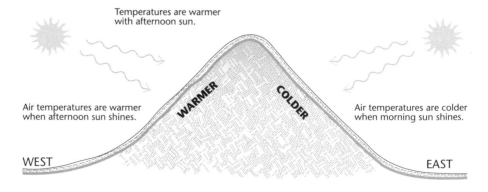

Figure 3-16. East-facing slopes are colder than west-facing slopes.

are nearly as important in arctic latitudes as temperate latitudes (Figure 3-15).

Consider the following points with regard to slope aspect with respect to the sun at mid-latitudes in the Northern Hemisphere:

- North-facing slopes receive very little heat from the sun in midwinter. Conversely, south-facing slopes receive much more heat. Therefore, a north-facing slope will usually develop a dramatically different snowpack than a south-facing slope.
- East-facing slopes catch sun only in the morning when temperatures are colder; west-facing slopes catch the sun in the warm afternoon. Consequently, east-facing slopes are colder than west-facing slopes (Figure 3-16).
- A cold snowpack tends to develop more persistent weak layers than a warm snowpack as long as it's not too cold (see below). A cold snowpack commonly develops notoriously fragile weak layers, such as facets and surface hoar. (See Chapter 5, Snowpack, for more details.) Largely because of this, the lion's share of avalanche accidents occur on north- and east-facing slopes, partly because that is where we find the best snow and consequently people tend to trigger more avalanches there, but mostly because those slopes exhibit more persistent weak layers (Figure 3-17).

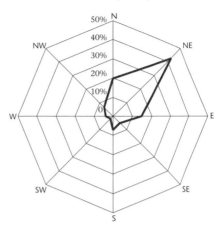

Figure 3-17. Avalanches plotted by aspect for Utah (40 N), Switzerland (46 N), and Canada (52 N). Each graph shows what percentage of the region's total avalanche count occurs in the different aspects. It's no surprise that northeast comes up repeatedly in avalanche accident reports. Aspect is more important in mid-latitudes and becomes less important as you travel north or south.

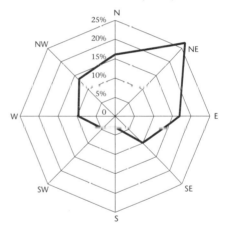

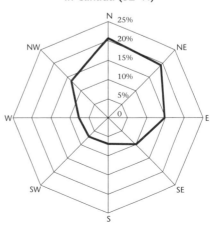

The direction a slope faces with respect to the sun makes a huge difference in snow stability. Here we can see a typical scenario in which avalanches occur on the shady north-facing slopes while the south-facing slopes are quite stable. (Wasatch Range, Utah)

- In wet snow conditions due to strong sun, it's just the opposite of a dry snowpack: south- and west-facing slopes usually produce more wet avalanches than the more shady slopes—at least at the beginning of a wet slide avalanche cycle in spring. The north-facing slopes are less dangerous (see Chapter 6, Stability, for more details).
- During prolonged cloudy or stormy conditions when the sun seldom shines on the snow, little difference exists between sunny and shady slopes.
- Here's a tricky one: When it's too cold, the situation is often reversed. During arctic outbreaks of very cold air, or in very cold climates, it's sometimes so cold on north-facing slopes that the avalanches are in a deep freeze and nothing much happens. On south-facing slopes, it's warm enough to produce persistent weak layers and thin sun crusts. Consequently, midwinter instabilities occur more on sunny aspects than on shady ones (Figure 3-18). (See Chapter 5, Snowpack, for more details.)

Remember that in the Southern Hemisphere the situation is just the opposite. South-facing slopes are colder than north-facing ones.

Seemingly subtle differences in slope aspect can have a huge effect on the stability of the snow. I can't count the number of accidents I have investigated in which people start skiing or snowmobiling in a bowl on a safe aspect, but as they use up the snow, they not only gain confidence but also tend to slowly work their way around the bowl onto the progressively more dangerous aspects, until someone finally triggers an avalanche.

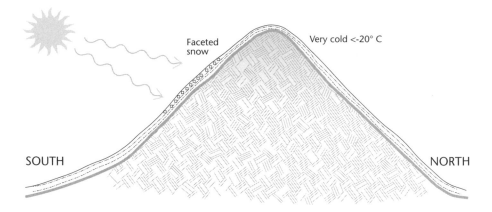

Figure 3-18. In very cold climates or during arctic outbreaks with temperatures less than about -20 degrees C, faceted snow grows better on sunny slopes because shady ones are just too cold.

Wind can deposit snow ten times more rapidly than snow falling out of the sky. Wind erodes from the windward side and deposits on the lee side of any obstacle such as a ridge, and can quickly overload buried weak layers. (Alta, Utah)

WIND

What direction the slope faces with respect to the wind is a *huge* factor. This takes many people by surprise, but ignore wind at your own peril. Human beings are big, heavy creatures and, most of the time, wind doesn't affect our lives very much. But imagine yourself as a bird, where wind is your entire world. Then imagine yourself as something even smaller and lighter—like a feather or, how about new fallen snow? Wind to a delicate snowflake is like the ocean current to plankton.

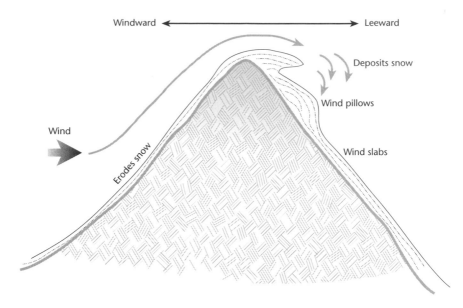

Figure 3-19. Typical wind-loading patterns

Figure 3-20. Cross-loading and top-loading

Why is wind important? As we have learned, loading (added weight) causes most avalanches and the fastest way to load a slope is with wind-drifted snow. Wind erodes from the upwind side of an obstacle, such as a ridge, and it deposits on the downwind side. Wind can deposit snow ten times more rapidly than snow falling from the sky (Figure 3-19).

Wind deposits snow most commonly on the leeward side of upper elevation prominent terrain features, such as ridges, peaks, and passes. We call this "top-loading." Wind can also blow across a slope, which we call "cross-loading," and wind can even cause loading when it blows down a slope (Figure 3-20). Remember that wind can blow from any direction and thus deposit snow on most any slope. (See Chapter 4, Weather, for weather factors that affect wind slab development.)

Wind slabs are dangerous because of the following reasons:

- As the wind bounces eroded snow across the snow surface, it grinds up the snow into small, dense particles. When they come to a rest on the lee of an obstacle— where the wind slows down—they pack into a heavy, dense layer that can not only overload any buried weak layer but can be stiff enough to propagate fractures.
- When strong wind starts to blow, within minutes, wind can turn nice fluffy powder into a dangerous wind slab. Safe conditions that quickly turn into dangerous conditions take people by surprise.
- Wind slabs can form in extremely localized areas. Often only a few inches separates safe snow from dangerous snow. We often hear people say, "I was just walking along and suddenly the snow changed. It started cracking under my feet, and then the whole slope let loose."

Bottom line: be suspicious of any steep slope with recent deposits of wind-drifted snow.

HOW TO RECOGNIZE WIND SLABS

Lucky for us, wind creates easy-to-read textures on the snow surface and characteristically shaped deposits. No one should go into avalanche terrain without first learning how to read these obvious signs. An old avalanche hunter's adage: if you have developed a good eye for slope steepness and the effects of wind, you can avoid about 90 percent of all avalanches.

It's extremely important to develop your avalanche eyeballs to see the difference between wind-eroded snow and wind-deposited snow. Here, wind has cross-loaded gullies in the early season and the wind slabs have overloaded fragile depth hoar. Eroded snow (usually safe) has a rough, sandblasted look while wind-deposited snow (usually dangerous) is smooth and rounded. Often just a few inches separate very safe snow from very dangerous snow. (Wasatch Range, Utah)

ERODED SNOW SUMMARY

Also called: "Sastrugi."
Looks like: Has a sandblasted, scoured, scalloped, roughed-up look.
Feels like: Often hard snow and difficult to negotiate on skis, snowboard, or snowmobile.
What it means: Weight (snow) has been removed from snowpack and it usually means that the snow has become more stable than before.

DEPOSITED SNOW (WIND SLABS) SUMMARY

Also called: Pillows, wind slabs, snow transport.
Looks like: Smooth and rounded, lens-shaped, pillow-shaped, chalky white color (Figure 3-21).
Feels like: "Slabby," i.e., harder snow on top of softer snow.
Sounds like: Often hollow like a drum—the more drumlike, the more dangerous.
Often notice:
- Cracks shooting away from you—the longer the crack, the more dangerous.
- Falling through a harder surface layer into softer snow below. You can easily feel this with a ski pole or by digging down with your hand, or as a snowmobile track punching through.
- Can be difficult trail-breaking. You keep falling through the slab.
- Hardness: Can range from very soft to so hard that you can hardly kick a boot into it.

What it means: Weight has been added to the snowpack. If the weight has been added recently, and it's on a steep slope without anchors, then it almost always means danger.

What you should do when you find a wind slab on a steep slope:
- Stop immediately! Don't go any farther!
- Back off to a safe spot and dig down to investigate how well the slab is bonded to the underlying snow (see Chapter 6, Stability).
- Jump on a few safe, test slopes to see how the snow responds.
- If the slab breaks away easily on your tests, don't cross larger slopes. Go back the way you came or find another route that avoids wind slabs or utilizes slopes of less than 30 degrees.
- If you absolutely have to cross the slope (and I can think of damned few reasons why you have to cross a dangerous slope without delving into B-movie plot devices), stay on the extreme upper edge of the wind slab, wear a belay rope tied to a solid anchor, and hope the crown fracture breaks at your feet instead of above you.

SLOPE SHAPE (CONFIGURATION)

Whether a slope is concave, convex, or planar makes some difference in avalanche danger, although usually not a significant difference. Avalanches happen on any steep slope without densely spaced anchors despite the shape of the slope. Slope shape makes more difference on smaller slopes than on larger ones.

Concave Slopes (Bowl-shaped)
- On small concave slopes, often there is enough compressive support from the bottom to prevent hard slabs from releasing, but on medium to large slopes, compressive support plays very little role (Figure 3-22).
- Concave slopes often accumulate wind-deposited snow.

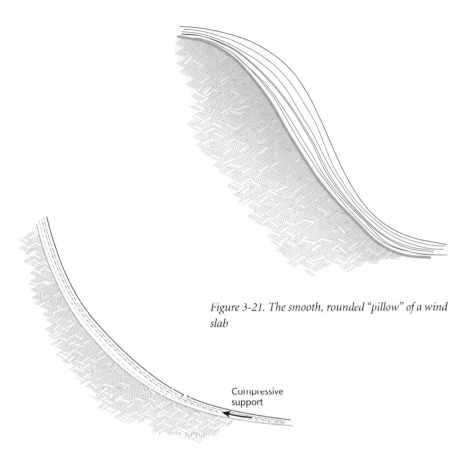

Figure 3-21. The smooth, rounded "pillow" of a wind slab

Compressive
support

Figure 3-22. Concave slope (remember "caved in")

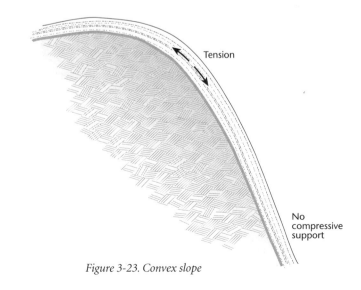

Tension

No
compressive
support

Figure 3-23. Convex slope

Convex Slopes (Basketball-shaped)
- Convex slopes statistically produce more avalanches and more avalanche accidents than other kinds of slopes, partly because they are inherently less stable and, I think, mostly because they present more routefinding problems than other slopes (Figure 3-23).
- Convex slopes have less compressive support at the bottom than other slopes, which makes a difference for small avalanche paths, makes some difference on medium-sized avalanche paths, but has little effect on large avalanche paths.
- Convex slopes are tricky to descend because each step or turn you take adds another degree of steepness until suddenly you find yourself on terrain that's too steep. You can also use this characteristic to your advantage. With a soft slab, if you descend slowly, especially jumping on the snow or slope-cutting while you descend, the avalanches tend to break at your feet instead of above you more so than on planar or concave slopes. (Remember that hard slabs tend to break above you.)
- Convex slopes are difficult to assess because the conditions you find on the upper flat part of the slope often are much different than on the steepest part of the slope where you will most likely trigger an avalanche. For instance, I have heard of many cases in which someone digs a snow profile or does a slope cut on the upper section, pronounces the slope safe, and then triggers an avalanche on the steeper part below.
- Snow conditions often change gradually on convex slopes. By the time you realize it has become too dicey, it's often too late.
- Convex slopes are difficult to exit while descending if you start to find dangerous conditions. You have to climb back up. All too often people would rather risk their life by descending than climb back up.
- Probably the most dangerous shapes are double convexities—convex vertically and horizontally—like dropping off the edge of a basketball. These slopes tend to wind-load both from the top and from the side, have no compressive support, and are difficult to descend, ascend, or cross safely. If you're lucky, the wind will erode one side of the slope and load the other side, allowing you to choose the safer, eroded side.

Good News—Bad News
The good news about convex slopes is that avalanches are much easier to survive, because they tend to drain off to the sides on double convexities and break at your feet on vertical convexities. The bad news is that people tend to trigger more avalanches on convex slopes.

CONSEQUENCES
What will happen if the slope slides? Consequences can range from very safe to absolutely unsurvivable.

Avalanche Paths with Very Dangerous or Unsurvivable Consequences
- Avalanche paths of nearly any size that terminate in trees, brush, a large cliff, or an icefall (Figure 3-24).
- Terrain traps, such as a gully or an avalanche path that suddenly flattens out at the bottom. Even a small slide off the side of one of these paths will bury someone

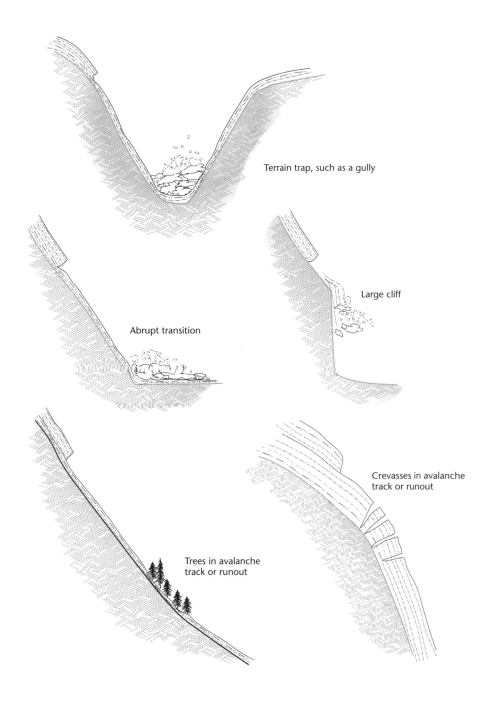

Figure 3-24. Different types of terrain with bad consequences. You should be obsessed with consequences—what will happen if it slides?

Terrain traps such as gullies are very dangerous because even small slides can bury a victim very deeply. Here two people approach this very dangerous, yet very popular, terrain trap near Alta Ski Area in Utah. It seems safe since it's right next to the road with houses above the gully, but it has been the site of many close calls.

very deeply, and deep burials have almost no chance of survival. Snowboarders—remember gullies are not half-pipes, they are terrain traps that can kill in the wrong conditions.

- Funnel-shaped avalanche paths that terminate in a gully because even small avalanches will bury a victim very deeply.
- Very large avalanche paths. It's difficult to survive a 1000-vertical-meter (3280-foot) ride in an avalanche path.

TERRAIN SUMMARY

Dangerous avalanche terrain:
- Is between 30 and 50 degrees—35 to 45 degrees is prime time
- Is leeward or cross-loaded
- Has few anchors
- Has bad consequences

Safer avalanche terrain:
- Is either gentle (0 to 25 degrees) or very steep (55 to 90 degrees)
- Has densely spaced anchors
- Has less dangerous consequences
- Is windward

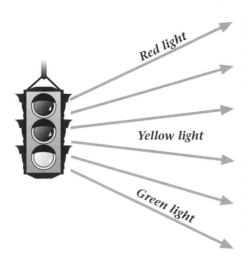

MORE DANGEROUS TERRAIN
- Steep 30° to 50°, especially 35° to 45°
- Leeward or cross-loaded
- Few anchors
- Bad consequences

Red light

Yellow light

Green light

SAFER TERRAIN
- Gentle 0° to 25° or very steep 55° to 90°
- Windward
- Densely spaced anchors
- No bad consequences

Figure 3-25. The trusty, Tremper "terrain-o-meter" illustrates the spectrum of terrain between very safe and very dangerous.

TRIP PLANNING TOOL—AVALANCHE TERRAIN ON A LARGER SCALE

Recently, Canadian avalanche forecaster and guide Grant Statham came up with a wonderful checklist to rate the danger of the terrain on a larger scale, and this basic terrain classification has proved very useful in planning the general area for an outing. The Canadians rate most of their popular tours using this system and they assign each tour with a three-step rating, which they call "Simple, Challenging, or Complex." This rating system has proved to be quite popular and you will likely see it used more and more in the U.S. It reflects not only the amount of avalanche terrain but how committing it is. For instance, on a day of high or extreme avalanche danger, the worst place to plan the day's outing is in "complex" terrain, which has large avalanche paths, overlapping runouts, many terrain traps, and few options to avoid danger (Figure 3-25).

TABLE 3-2 BASIC TERRAIN CLASSIFICATION	
Terrain Rating	*Summary of Characteristics*
Simple	Exposure to low angle or primarily forested terrain. Some forest openings may involve the runout zones of infrequent avalanches. Many options to reduce or eliminate exposure. No glacier travel.
Challenging	Exposure to well-defined avalanche paths, starting zones, or terrain traps; options exist to reduce or eliminate exposure with careful routefinding. Glacier travel is straightforward but crevasse hazards may exist.
Complex	Exposure to multiple, overlapping avalanche paths or large expanses of steep, open terrain; multiple avalanche starting zones and terrain traps below; minimal options to reduce exposure. Complicated glacier travel with extensive crevasse bands or icefalls.
If the tour you plan does not have a published rating from the local avalanche center, you can rate it yourself using Table 3-3.	

Simple Terrain—mostly low angle, forested terrain with many terrain choices—is a good place to recreate in red light avalanche conditions.

Challenging Terrain—well defined avalanche paths with options to reduce exposure. If you know what you are doing, you can recreate here in yellow or red light avalanche conditions (stay in densely spaced trees and lower angled terrain).

Complex Terrain—multiple, overlapping avalanche paths and large expanses of open terrain with minimal options to reduce exposure. You can go here only during green light avalanche conditions.

TABLE 3-3. AVALANCHE TERRAIN RATINGS		
	1 - Simple	*2 - Challenging*	*3 - Complex*
Slope angle	Angles generally < 30°	Mostly low angle, isolated slopes >35°	Variable with large percentage >35°
Slope shape	Uniform	Some convexities	Convoluted
Forest density	Primarily treed with some forest openings	Mixed trees and open terrain	Large expanses of open terrain. Isolated tree bands
Terrain traps	Minimal, some creek slopes or cutbanks	Some depressions, gullies, and/or overhead avalanche terrain	Many depressions, gullies, cliffs, hidden slopes above gullies, cornices
Avalanche frequency (events:years) and size	1:30 ≥ size 2	1:1 for < size 2	1:3 for ≥ size 2 1:1 < size 3 1:1 ≥ size 3
Start zone density	Limited open terrain	Some open terrain. Isolated avalanche paths leading to valley bottom	Large expanses of open terrain. Multiple avalanche paths leading to valley bottom
Runout zone characteristics		Abrupt transitions or depressions with deep deposits	Multiple converging runout zones, confined deposition area, steep tracks overhead
Interaction with avalanche paths	Runout zones only	Single path or paths with separation	Numerous and overlapping paths
Route options	Numerous, terrain allows multiple choices	A selection of choices of varying exposure, options to avoid avalanche paths	Limited chances to reduce exposure, avoidance not possible
Exposure time	None, or limited exposure crossing runouts only	Isolated exposure to start zones and tracks	Frequent exposure to start zones and tracks
Glaciation	None	Generally smooth with isolated bands of crevasses	Broken or steep sections of crevasses, icefalls or serac exposure

Note: Terrain ratings are provided courtesy of Parks Canada. Many published routes in Canada have been rated using these criteria and we will likely see these ratings used on an increasing number of routes in the U.S.

chapter four

WEATHER

You don't need a weatherman to know which way the wind blows.
—Bob Dylan

Obviously, weather plays a critical role in the avalanche business. Weather creates the snowpack, weather changes the snowpack, and weather can overload the snowpack. Weather is the mother of avalanches, and one of the first lessons we learn in life is that when Momma ain't happy, ain't nobody happy.

Weather is so important that professional avalanche forecasters keep a detailed, up-to-date graph of their local weather either pinned to the wall or just a mouse click away on their computer screens. They labor over weather record-keeping on a daily basis, and during storms they keep a close eye on up-to-the-minute graphs from their automated weather stations.

It was a dark and stormy morning. Weather is the mother of all avalanches and when Momma ain't happy, ain't nobody happy. (Wasatch Range, Utah)

Good avalanche forecasters can look at a seasonal history chart and then draw a detailed snow profile from it. They can also do the process in reverse. However, this kind of expertise comes from years of watching the weather and watching what effect the weather has on the snowpack, day in and day out. If you grew up in a snowy climate, you probably already have an intuitive feel for how the weather affects the snowpack, or at least the snow surface. How weather affects the deeper layers in the snow takes more study.

Weather is a big subject and this is not a book about weather. So I won't talk very much about how weather works or how to forecast weather. (See Bibliography for suggested weather books.) This chapter focuses instead on how weather works in the mountains and how weather affects the snowpack and snow stability.

TEMPERATURE AND ELEVATION

The higher you go, the colder the temperature is (with the exception of temperature inversions—see below). This is because the sun warms the ground, which in turn warms the air,

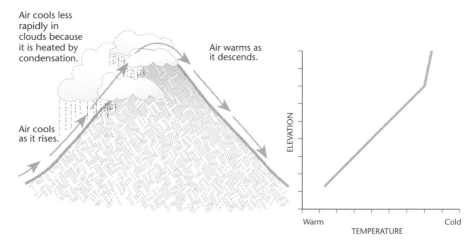

Figure 4-1. As air is pushed up a mountain by wind, it expands and cools, then precipitates.

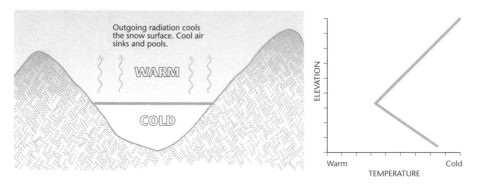

Figure 4-2. Temperature inversion. During calm conditions with a clear sky, often a temperature inversion develops with cold air trapped under a cap of warm air.

which means that air is warmed from the bottom, not from the top, like the way a pan of water is warmed.

Air also cools as it expands, which is called "adiabatic" cooling. In other words, when wind pushes the high-pressure air near the ground up the mountainside, it cools, and by the time the air reaches the mountaintop, it will be much cooler than when it started out. To understand adiabatic cooling, try this experiment: Let some air out of a bicycle tire. You can feel that the escaping air has cooled because it has suddenly lost pressure. You can use a sensitive thermometer to test this theory. To try the experiment in the other direction, pump up the bicycle tire and notice that the pump gets hot. The muscle power you put into pushing the pump handle compresses the air molecules together, gives them energy, and warms them up.

Very interesting, but what does this have to do with avalanches? Adiabatic cooling is the main cause of something dear to our hearts—precipitation. Rising air expands, and when it expands, it cools. When air cools, it causes the water vapor in the air to precipitate, thus the miracle of snow and rain. Without it, none of us would even be here.

How fast does air cool with elevation? As you go up in elevation, the air usually gets colder between 6 to 10 degrees Celsius per 1000 vertical meters (3 to 5 degrees Fahrenheit per 1000 vertical feet). How fast it gets colder as you go up depends on the layering of the atmosphere and relative humidity at the time (Figure 4-1).

TEMPERATURE INVERSIONS

Now that I've told you that air gets colder the higher you go, let me tell you about when it doesn't. "Temperature inversions" occur when, as the name implies, cold air lies underneath warm air. Cold air is denser than warm air, so it tends to sink and pool in valleys. This actually happens quite often in the mountains during calm, clear conditions. Snow is a very efficient radiator of heat, and on clear nights, it radiates most of its heat away into space and gets very cold. (See the "Radiation and Snow Temperature" section later in this chapter.) Thus, the cold air sinks into the valleys.

Temperature inversions often create surface hoar forms at lower elevations, "below the inversion" as it is called. Surface hoar is a particularly nasty weak layer when buried. (Wasatch Range, Utah)

Temperature inversions also occur during a warm front when warm air "overruns" cold air. In other words, when warm air pushes in at higher elevations, it rides up over the denser, colder air, thus trapping it in the valleys.

You can usually recognize inversions because in many populated mountain valleys the dreaded winter smog (or fog if you're lucky) sets in with every temperature inversion. When you scrape frost off your windshield in the morning, there's often a temperature inversion going on as well (Figure 4-2).

Temperature inversions are important to avalanche hunters for the following reasons:

- Temperature inversions tend to form surface hoar on the snow surface, which is a notoriously dangerous and persistent weak layer. (See Chapter 5, Snowpack.)
- Temperature inversions tend to create more faceted snow at lower elevations than upper elevations. This is a double whammy since the snowpack is usually shallower at lower elevations anyway. (Remember that shallow snow combined with cold temperatures means high temperature gradients, which means weak snow.)
- Temperature inversions cause freezing rain. When rain falls from the warmer air above into subfreezing air below, the rain instantly freezes on contact with the cold ground surface. This can dramatically warm the cold snow below the inversion layer, which sometimes initiates avalanches, not to mention that it can create a slippery bed surface for future avalanches.
- Temperature inversions that suddenly dissipate can cause the snow surface to warm rapidly. This can make dry snow less stable or increase melting or initiate melting of wet snow.
- Temperature inversions can fool you. For example, let's say it's spring with a clear sky overnight with no wind (with clear, calm conditions you should always assume there's a temperature inversion). You start out in the morning from the valley where

Cornices are a good sign of prevailing wind direction. **Caution:** *they always break farther back than expected. Never walk up to a drop-off in the mountains. (Wasatch Range, Utah)*

the snow is supportable and well refrozen. As you gain elevation and get above the inversion layer, you get into snow that did not refreeze overnight, and you're suddenly triggering wet avalanches. You think, "Wow! This snow sure warmed up quickly today." But no. The snow didn't suddenly warm up, you traveled into warmer snow—by going up—just the opposite of what you're used to.

WIND AND MOUNTAINS

Prevailing Winds

Almost every part of the world has a "prevailing" wind, meaning the direction the wind usually blows. For instance in the continental United States, Canada, Europe, and every other place at mid-latitudes, prevailing winds blow from the west, since global circulation at that latitude comes from the west. Between the latitude of about 15 degrees to about 30 degrees the prevailing winds blow from the east (trade winds).

You can usually tell the direction of prevailing winds by looking at the ridgelines. The prevailing winds tend to erode snow from the windward side of the ridge and cornices form on the lee side. After a season of prevailing winds, the snow can become very deep on the lee side of a ridge.

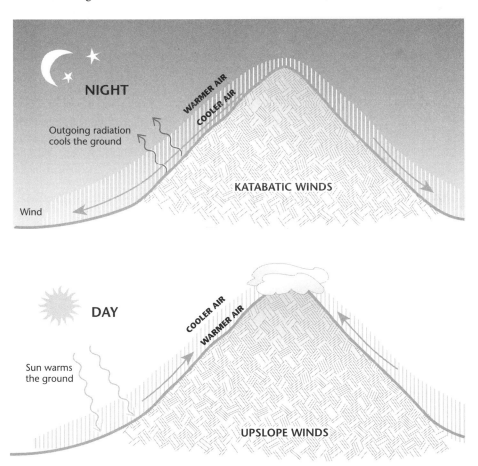

Figure 4-3. Katabatic drainage winds and upslope winds

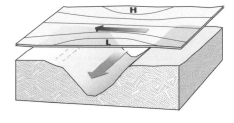

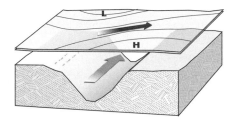

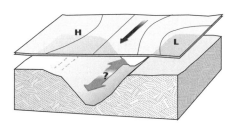

Figure 4-4. *Winds in mountain valleys seldom blow the same direction as winds along the peaks.*

Drainage Winds

Drainage winds, or "katabatic" winds, are winds that blow down a valley or mountainside. When clear skies cause the snow surface to cool, the air cools above it, making it denser than the warm air above, and it drains out of the mountain valleys like a river of air. This happens especially on clear, calm nights and the winds often blow stronger and stronger until they reach their maximum in the morning. Especially in large, glacial valleys, these drainage winds can cause significant snow transport (Figure 4-3).

Upslope Winds

Upslope winds are the opposite of drainage winds—they blow uphill or upcanyon. When the sun warms the mountains, it warms the air, which rises up the slopes making upslope winds. Air is also sucked up the drainages. Upslope winds are usually strongest in the afternoon on clear days.

Channeling of Winds

When wind encounters mountains, the wind is often channeled either up or down the local mountain valleys (Figure 4-4). Because of channeling, winds in mountain valleys seldom blow the same direction as the winds on the peaks.

HOT TIP!

You don't need a weatherman to know which way the wind blows.

The direction in which the wind blows in the mountain valleys is seldom the same as that on the ridge tops. How do you tell the ridge-top wind direction? Look at the clouds near the ridges. Remember that clouds at different elevations will move in different directions, so pick clouds near the ridge tops. With no clouds, you can sometimes see the plumes of snow blowing off the ridges. Avalanche geeks are constantly watching ridge-top clouds and snow plumes and taking a lot of teasing from their friends—until it's time to choose a route. Ha! Revenge of the nerds again.

LOADING PATTERNS FROM WIND

Storms rarely deposit snow uniformly over a mountain range. You need to know the common loading patterns that occur in the mountains, and you also need to recognize unusual loading patterns produced by unusual storms because, after all, unusual weather makes unusual avalanches. Here are some of the common patterns.

Loading and Elevation

More snow usually falls at high elevations than at low elevations. As air rises, it expands; as air expands, it cools; and when air cools, it precipitates. Thus, "orographic lifting"—air rising to get over a mountain—is the main mechanism responsible for more snow falling at high elevations than low elevations.

Caveat: See the "Loading Patterns in Big Mountains" section.

Loading and Wind Direction

Here's another tricky situation. How much snow falls on a mountain depends on scale. On a large scale, more snow falls on the windward (upwind) sides of mountain ranges than the lee (downwind) side. As air rises up the windward side of a mountain range, it cools and condenses its moisture into snow. When the air passes over the crest and begins its descent, it warms, thus ending snowfall. The windward side of a large mountain range typically has twice as much snow as the lee side, or more (Figure 4-5).

On a smaller scale, however, such as near the ridges of that same mountain range, it's a different story. Near the ridges, as we know, wind erodes snow from windward slopes and drifts that snow onto lee slopes, forming cornices along the ridgeline and wind pillows in the first hundred vertical meters of the summit. Also, especially with strong winds, orographic lifting occurs so rapidly that by the time the snowflakes form and fall out of the clouds, much of the snow ends up on the lee side of the mountain crest.

Wind usually increases with elevation. From the valley (top photo), it's obvious that it's a scary day in the mountains. Partway up (middle photo), it's still not too windy where we are. On top (bottom photo), we can barely stand up. A good day to avoid lee terrain where wind slabs are rapidly forming. (La Sal Mountains, Utah)

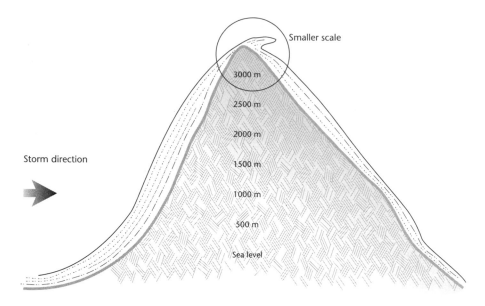

Figure 4-5. On a larger scale, more snow falls on the upwind side; on a smaller scale, near the ridge tops, more snow falls on the downwind side.

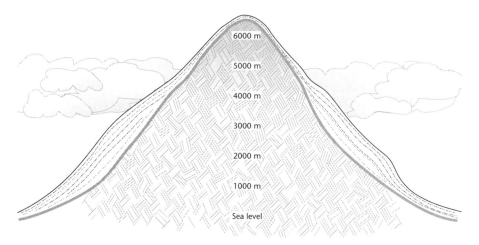

Figure 4-6. In big mountains, often more snow falls below 4,000 meters (14,000 feet) than above because most weather exists at lower elevations.

In other words, the heaviest loading during a storm with moderate winds occurs in the following areas:
- On the upwind side of the mountain range—more at high elevation than low elevation and within 1 km (0.5 mile) or so downwind of the ridge crest.
- On a smaller scale, near the ridge crest, wind erodes snow from the windward side and deposits deep drifts on the lee side.

Storms with Little Wind

Although orographic precipitation accounts for most of the difference between upper elevation and lower elevation snow, some storms come in with little wind, and as such, don't have enough oomph to push the moisture up the mountainsides. In storms like this, just as much—if not more—snow falls in the valleys as in the mountains. For instance, in Utah where I live, if 6 inches of snow falls in Salt Lake City, most people expect several feet of snow in the mountains because the air has to rise over 2000 vertical meters (7000 vertical feet) to get over the mountains—which is a lot of vertical relief. But several times each winter, a big storm will arrive with the center of the low directly overhead, so there's no wind to push the moisture up the mountains. Six inches in town. Yahoo! You head up to the mountains but there's only 3 inches. What happened?

Loading Patterns in Big Mountains

In big mountains, especially mountains over 4000 to 5000 meters (14,000 to 17,000 feet) or ones with more than about 3000 meters (10,000 vertical feet) of relief, the mountains are large enough to block low-level moisture and shallow cold fronts. Thus, more snow falls at lower elevations than at upper elevations. In winter, most of the weather exists below 4000 meters (14,000 feet) anyway, so big mountains stick up above the clouds and often receive much less precipitation. They get most of their precipitation in the summer when deeper, warmer layers of moisture can rise to higher elevations (Figure 4-6). However, more snow and ice accumulates at higher elevations, because the temperatures are cold enough that snow seldom melts.

WEATHER FACTORS AFFECTING WIND SLAB DEVELOPMENT
Wind Speed

Wind usually starts drifting snow at around 15 km/hr (10 mph) and most of the real action happens between about 25 to 80 km/hr (15 to 50 mph). Wind faster than about 80 km/hr actually blows less snow around because, at least in dry conditions, it tends to blow the snow into big plumes that jet off the ridge tops, and most of the snow evaporates before

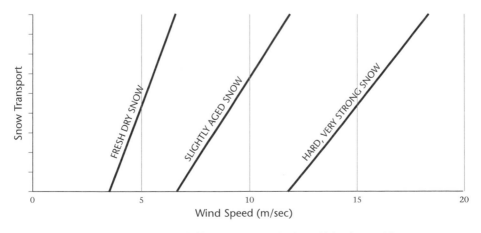

Figure 4-7. Wind can transport light, fluffy snow more easily than old, hard snow. The amount of potential wind-blown snow is called "snow available for transport."

it ever reaches the ground again. The snow that does make it back to the ground tends to be not only far, far away but also spread out more evenly instead of in discrete drifts. So just like slope steepness, it's the intermediate values that cause the problems (Figure 4-7).

Professional avalanche forecasting operations maintain at least one anemometer (a device for measuring wind speed) and wind vane in a representative location. They pay close attention to the average wind speed and especially the speed of the gusts, because once the easily transported snow has been moved, the gusts transport the rest of it.

Wind Duration

Ten minutes of wind is a whole different story than 10 hours of wind. More time equals more transport—but once again, only up to a point. Most of the damage usually comes in the first couple of hours of the windstorm. Once all the light fluffy snow gets blown around, then the wind has to work harder to blow the rest of it.

Snow Type

Obviously, wind can blow around light fluffy snow easier than dense, heavy snow. How easily the snow blows around is called "snow available for transport" by avalanche professionals. In other words, if a lot of snow is available for transport (light fluffy snow), then not much wind speed is required to blow it around. On the other hand, if no snow has fallen in several days and the snow is old and hard, then there's just not much to blow around. Even a storm with lots of huff and puff won't form many wind slabs.

Humidity

Humid air forms denser, stiffer wind slabs than dry air and they tend to be more dangerous because they weigh more and their stiffness tends to propagate fractures farther. Imagine a pile of dry, windblown leaves versus a pile of damp, windblown leaves. Most avalanche professionals pay close attention to humidity during windstorms. Also, humidity plays a critical role in how cold air becomes at night. (See the "Wet Snow Avalanches" section in Chapter 6, Stability, and the "Humidity and Mountains" section in this chapter.)

TEMPERATURE AND NEW SNOW

A common mistake among avalanche neophytes is to focus on the *amount* of snow instead of the *weight* of the snow. Snow that falls at near freezing temperatures can easily weigh several times as much as light fluffy snow falling at cold temperatures. Most avalanche professionals communicate with each other in units of water weight, for example, "This last few centimeters of snow brings us up to 14 centimeters of water for the storm."

I remember a storm in Montana that laid down slightly less than a meter (3 feet) of snow that contained only 2.5 centimeters (1 inch) of water—less than 3 percent water. In other words, if a barrel of new snow melted down, it would leave only a 2.5-centimeter (1-inch) puddle on the bottom. It was as insubstantial as a cloud of smoke and even though it was a meter deep, my skis clattered off the old icy surface underneath. Although some large sluffs occurred in the new snow that day, the new snow was so light that it had almost no effect on the preexisting snowpack. On the other side of the coin, we have all suffered through storms we would rather forget in which 7 centimeters (3 inches) of soggy snow contained the same 2.5 centimeters (1 inch) of water. Yet both of these examples weigh exactly the same and exert exactly the same stress on buried weak layers. The moral of the story is to pay attention to weight, not depth.

Right Side Up or Upside Down?

The perfect storm starts out as relatively heavy, wet snow, so it bonds well to the old snow, then progressively turns colder, thus depositing lighter and lighter snow. We call this "right-side-up snow." It bonds well to the old snow, the new snow doesn't have a slab, and if there are no instabilities in the old snow, everything is hunky-dory. Conveniently, most winter storms are associated with cold fronts, so they tend to produce right-side-up snow. Occasionally, however, warm fronts or occluded fronts or strong winds following a snowstorm will produce "upside-down snow"—heavy snow on top with light snow on the bottom. People often describe upside-down snow as being "slabby." You can feel the surface slab as you punch through it into softer snow underneath. It usually makes horrible skiing and boarding and snowmobiles get stuck easily.

Upside-down snow, especially accompanied by wind, commonly produces soft slab avalanches within the new snow, especially during the storm and in the first few hours after the storm. Often variations in temperature or wind during a storm cause a corresponding variation in the density and strength of the new snow. For instance, a storm may begin with dense, wet snow, then colder temperatures will lay down light, dry stellar flakes, then wind might blow, or warmer air suddenly arrives making a denser, stronger slab on top. We often describe avalanches in this kind of snow as "soft slabs running on a density inversion within the new snow."

HUMIDITY AND MOUNTAINS

Humidity, or relative humidity, simply means the amount of water vapor the air *does* hold compared to the amount of water vapor the air *can* hold. Knox Williams, retired director of the Colorado Avalanche Information Center, explains it best: "You can drink more beer on a warm day than a cold day." In other words, warm air can hold more water vapor than cold air.

When air rises to get over a mountain range, it cools, becomes more humid, and when it becomes saturated (no thanks, I just *couldn't* drink another beer), it forms clouds. If the clouds continue to rise and cool, precipitation occurs. Because of this, upper elevations tend to have more humid air than lower elevations.

Sometimes the situation is just the opposite, however, with clear, calm conditions that create temperature inversions. Then the colder, humid air tends to sink and pool in low areas, such as mountain valleys or basins. Also remember high humidity causes stiffer slabs to form on the snow surface than low humidity.

RADIATION AND SNOW TEMPERATURE

Radiation usually controls snow surface temperature much more than air temperature—something that takes most people by surprise. If you want to understand snow and avalanches, you need to get this concept firmly down, so let's take a moment to dive in under the hood and get our hands dirty.

As I type this, the morning sun is streaming in my window and the heat radiated by the sun has heated up the floor under my chair and it feels nice and toasty on my bare feet. Dark

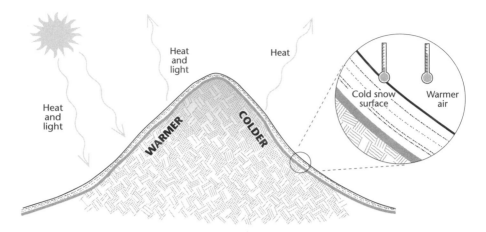

Figure 4-8. In the shade on a clear day, the snow surface is always much colder than the air temperature because the snow surface loses so much heat to outgoing radiation.

objects, like the legs of my chair, absorb heat more than light objects, like the white stacks of paper on the floor (edited chapters of this book, in this case). If I pull the shade, the heat from the floor then radiates outward in all directions and the floor slowly cools down again. Objects that *absorb* heat efficiently also tend to *radiate* heat just as efficiently.

Now here's the tricky part. The energy that reaches the Earth from the sun is composed of different wavelengths. First, there's visible light and ultraviolet radiation, which scientists call short-wave radiation, and second, there is heat, which we call long-wave radiation. Even though snow is white—meaning that it reflects most *visible* light—when it comes to the *heat* part of the spectrum (long-wave radiation), snow is a nearly perfect "black body radiator," as physicists describe it. This means that it absorbs almost all the radiant heat that reaches it and likewise, it very efficiently reradiates any heat it contains. In other words, if you shine a flashlight on the snow, it reflects most of the energy, yet if you shine a heat lamp on the snow, it absorbs the energy and warms up quickly. When you turn the lamp off, the snow cools down just as quickly by radiating its heat away. Since it is such an efficient heat radiator, the surface of the snow can easily be several degrees colder than the air above (Figure 4-8).

Try this experiment: Find a shady spot on a clear day where the snow surface is exposed to the clear sky. Lay your thermometer on top of the snow surface (in the shade, remember), wait a minute for it to adjust, and read the temperature. Then measure the air temperature in the shade (remember to give the thermometer a minute to adjust). I will buy you a case of your favorite beverage if the snow surface temperature isn't several degrees colder than the air temperature. At night often an even greater difference in temperature exists—even by as much as 10 degrees Celsius. As we will see in Chapter 5, Snowpack, it is important to understand this process because it accounts for many of the nastiest weak layers in the snowpack.

Cloud Cover and Radiation

It's obvious enough that clouds can prevent much of the radiation from the sun from reaching the snow surface, but much less obvious how clouds block and trap radiation from going in the other direction—from the snow surface to the sky. When the snow radiates its heat toward the sky, clouds can capture that same radiation and reradiate it back to the ground again, which we call a greenhouse effect (Figure 4-9). In other words, we can think of clouds like giant heat lamps in the sky. The snow surface can become much colder without clouds overhead than with clouds.

During the day, the greenhouse effect warms the snow surface most dramatically when the clouds are thin enough to allow some solar radiation to get through but thick enough to capture some of the outgoing radiation as well. This commonly happens with thin, wispy clouds, such as cirrus, or with a thin layer of fog or low clouds. For instance, you may be enjoying great, cold powder on a clear day and then when fog or thin high clouds appear, suddenly the powder turns to something resembling mashed potatoes. Usually the air temperature didn't change very much, just the radiation balance.

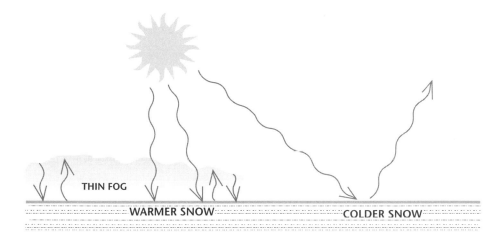

Figure 4-9. Thin fog can create a greenhouse effect by trapping outgoing radiation.

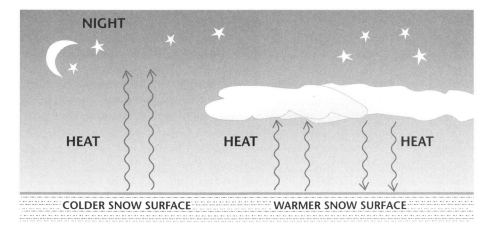

Figure 4-10. Clouds trap and reradiate outgoing radiation, acting like giant heat lamps in the sky.

At night, any kind of cloud cover can capture and reradiate the outgoing radiation. Thus, the snow surface usually stays much warmer on cloudy nights than on clear nights (Figure 4-10).

HOW TO GRAPH WEATHER

Professional avalanche forecasting operations keep either hand-drawn or computer-generated weather charts on the wall so that workers can keep up-to-date on weather trends. Most avalanche professionals feel out of touch with the snowpack and weather after only a couple of days off, especially if they were away from the mountains. A glance at the weather chart can catch them up (Figure 4-11).

Weather charts usually contain the following parameters:

- New snow amount
- New snow water equivalent
- Total snow
- Temperature (maximum and minimum)
- Wind speed
- Wind direction
- Avalanche activity
- Cloud cover

I know many professional forecasters who diligently maintain their own notebook with a seasonal history chart, snow profiles (see Chapter 5, Snowpack), and copies of field notes.

The average weekend warrior probably doesn't need to keep a chart at home, especially since you can go on the internet on Friday and look at a time profile of several local automated stations that gives you the specific information you need. (Consult www.avalanche .org or www.weather.gov for links.) However, if you recreate in a remote area without an avalanche forecast center or even any automated mountain weather stations, then keeping a little weather station in your backyard and charting your own weather is a good idea. By diligently following the weather every day, and then comparing it with changes in the snowpack and snow stability, even after one season, you can get a very good feel for how weather affects the snowpack.

HOW TO FORECAST WEATHER

For the past 25 years, part of my job has been forecasting mountain weather. I can personally attest that forecasting weather is a difficult proposition and forecasting mountain weather is doubly so. Even when I have all the latest computer models and satellite and radar images in front of me, I'm generally right about four out of five times and specifically right only about half the time. When I don't have all the technology in front of me—when I'm out in the mountains without even my trusty National Oceanic and Atmospheric Association (NOAA) weather radio—and I'm in an unfamiliar area, I feel like I'm doing pretty well if I'm right half the time—only about the same as flipping a coin. In other words, without technology, I suck. The moral of the story is: Use technology.

First, if you don't own a NOAA weather radio, run, don't walk, to the local electronics store and buy one. The National Weather Service maintains a network of low-power radio transmitters throughout the United States that broadcast a continuous loop of weather information. Just turn on the radio and 5 minutes later you have a pretty complete picture of the general weather setup. The bad news is that, especially in the Rocky Mountain states

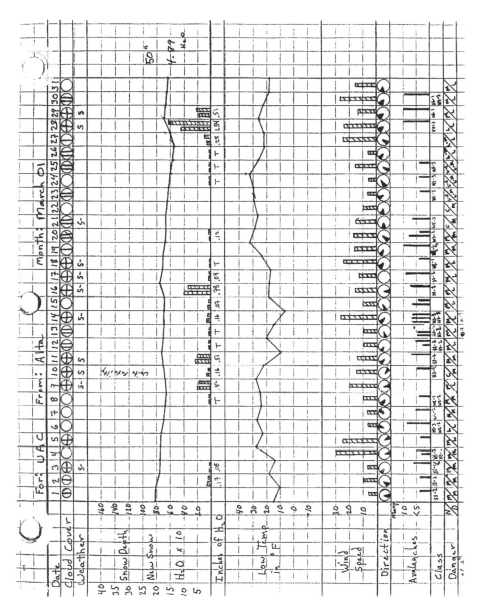

Figure 4-11. An example of a hand-drawn seasonal weather chart. This one was drawn by Tom Kimbrough of the Utah Avalanche Center who prefers to draw charts by hand instead of relying on computers because it gives him a better intuitive feel for weather history. Now that Kimbrough has retired, his lovingly hand-drawn charts hanging on the wall have been replaced by computerized charts on the screen. They're just not the same.

where, at least in my opinion, weather seems to have a more profound influence on people's lives, the transmitters are frustratingly few and far between. Sometimes you have to be on a mountaintop to pick up anything, and in the bottom of a mountain valley or a canyon you can pretty much forget about it.

The weather radio is rapidly being replaced by more useful and detailed products available on the internet. When all else fails, tune in your little AM/FM radio and listen to the local stations. The big disadvantage, of course, is that you have to listen to the top 40 and furniture store ads for an hour before you get a woefully brief forecast, but it's better than nothing. Remember that forecasts are always for the valleys unless stated otherwise and mountains almost always have worse weather than valleys. A 30 percent chance of rain in the valleys often means a 100 percent chance of snow in the mountains. Also remember that at night, AM radio waves can bounce off the ionosphere and travel long distances. You may find that your weather forecast is from east Texas. FM frequencies don't travel as far, but in remote areas you may not be able to get FM stations and will have to take your chances with AM.

Luckily, most people now have easy access to technology, where an astounding variety of high-quality weather information is at your fingertips. Many avalanche professionals are also Weather Channel junkies and they have bookmarked all their favorite weather sites on their browsers and smart phones. The information on the internet changes so rapidly that it's not worth discussing here, but you can visit www.avalanche.org or www.weather.gov or your local avalanche forecast center for links to the best sites and directions on how to use them.

chapter five

SNOWPACK

*Dragons live under the hills. Address them properly and they'll tell you
all they know. Ask them the wrong questions and they'll burn you up.*
—Fredric Lehrman

RAP ON METAMORPHISM

In this chapter, we learn, as Doug Fesler
likes to say, what kind of "avalanche dragon"
we're dealing with, how it forms, how it behaves, and how to deal with it. Why do we
need to know? Well, I'll sheepishly admit
here that we really don't *need* to know about
all the subtleties of crystal identification
and metamorphism. I've known a number
of very cagey avalanche pros who would
be hard-pressed to tell a facet from a fau-
cet, but they have nevertheless managed to
develop a nearly infallible feel for the snowpack. The truth is many avalanche pros and
advanced amateurs never take out their
shovels and dig in the snow and yet they all
seem to operate very safely for years on end
without getting caught. They have learned
to manage terrain, keenly observe weather,
and follow good routefinding and safe travel
rituals, and have a good mastery over their
own human foibles.

So having said this, why even take the
hard trip into the nerdy realm of snow science? For the same reason that Attila the
Hun said "Know your enemy." As we will
see, each different avalanche condition has
its own characteristic patterns, routefinding considerations, and forecasting considerations. Knowledge of the snowpack is an
extremely powerful tool in the battle against
the White Death, and I personally would

*First things first. Before we introduce you to the
cast of characters, go out and get acquainted.
(Wasatch Range, Utah)*

feel very naked without knowing what kind of avalanche dragon I'm dealing with.

In this chapter we will delve into the esoteric and sometimes scary world of snow crystal morphology and metamorphism. The words alone are enough to hurl you back. But "crystal morphology" is just a fancy word for what a snow crystal looks like and "metamorphism" is just a fancy word for change. Since the avalanche game is played in a universe of constantly changing snow crystals, it's important to know something about the workings of the universe that will control whether you live or die. Yes, I admit, having a science background gives you a big advantage, but I've presented the information here in mostly non-science terms and kept the explanations to plain English. If you end up skipping this chapter, promise that you'll eventually come back to it when you're ready.

Homework assignment: First, before we dive in, you need to do a homework assignment, or in this case an "out-of-home" work assignment. If you have never dug into the snow before, you need to do so first. Because, unless you're a glutton for punishment, reading this chapter without having a good picture of what I'm talking about would be like listening to a protracted conversation about people you've never met. So let's meet the cast of characters. Grab your shovel and head to the mountains or the backyard. What? You don't have a shovel? You'll need one anyway to be able to dig your friend out of avalanche debris. No excuses on this one. You absolutely *must* have a shovel if you go into avalanche terrain. I like the lightweight aluminum shovels sold at outdoor shops. (Read more about shovels in the gear section of Chapter 9, Rescue.) While you're at the outdoor shop, buy a snow crystal identification book (see Bibliography) or refer to the photos in this chapter and then practice identifying what you're looking at.

Finally, buy a snow saw. You can get by without one, but you will hate digging snowpits, which means that you will soon quit digging them, which means that you will miss a big piece of the avalanche puzzle. A snow saw will make your life much easier and save you countless hours. I never leave home without mine.

Since you're still in shopping mode, pick up a cheap hand lens, too. If your outdoor shop doesn't sell one, go to the local photography shop and ask for an inexpensive "photo loupe." A plastic 8-power one costs under $20. After you get more serious about this, or if you're a gizmohead, spend about $200 on a handheld 20-power microscope. (Yep. I got one.)

Take your shovel and get out in the mountains (or your backyard, if there's enough snow). At this stage it really helps to have a friend who can teach you, or better yet, take a multiday avalanche class. Whether you're learning from someone else or teaching yourself from this book, the most important part is to get your nose in the snow and do it often. Snow and avalanches tend to be self-explanatory if you're willing to take the time to look.

Now that you have all your gear, dig down into the snow. Don't dig where the snowpack is more than about 2 meters (2 yards) deep. It's likely to be boring. Dig in shallower areas where you are more likely to see faceted crystals and other more interesting layers. Shady slopes tend to be more interesting than sunny slopes. Moving snow is easier if you're on a steep slope and in soft snow. Get down on one knee; your back will thank you. Make the snowpit big with lots of working room—about 2 meters wide—and shovel out the downhill side so you don't have to lift the snow up over the edge of the hole. This usually takes under 5 minutes.

Now that you have a hole, jump in and run your hands over the layers and *feel* them. See how the weak layers erode away when you feel them with your mitten and how the strong layers stick out, just like rock strata in the Grand Canyon. Put a thin layer of snow from a weak layer on your mitten and look carefully at the crystals. Take out the hand lens and take a closer look at them. Look in your book to see what kind of crystal it is. Take your time. After more practice, you'll do all of this very quickly.

Take a credit card and run it vertically through the snow to feel the layers. Play with your snow saw. As described in Chapter 7, Hazard Evaluation, cut out vertical columns and thump on them so you can see how weak layers fracture and how much force it takes to make slabs slide on top of weak layers. Look, feel, smell, taste, listen.

Now that you have been introduced to the cast of characters, we're ready to gossip about them in earnest.

First, for a map of where we're going: Table 5-1 is a simplified version of the international classification of seasonal snow on the ground, which is, more or less, the bible that avalanche workers throughout the world use to describe snow. (See Bibliography.)

In a typical snowpack, we can find many of these layers in various combinations. Sketch out the profile you find in your own snowpit. If you don't have any layers or if identifying the crystals is difficult, then dig in another location. Try a shallower area to find facets and try digging on a sunny slope to find sun crusts. Now let's talk about each kind of layer that we commonly find in the snowpack.

STRONG LAYERS IN THE SNOWPACK

To make an avalanche you need both a slab and a weak layer (or a weak interface). Slabs tend to be made up of strong layers of snow. A common mistake of beginning avalanche students is to concentrate on the strong layers instead of the weak ones. Strong layers are avalanches (slabs) or bed surfaces; weak layers *cause* avalanches. Thus, avalanche professionals don't spend a lot of time worrying about types and characteristics of strong layers. But here are the most common kinds.

Rounded, or equilibrium, snow is strong and deforms easily. It usually forms strong layers in the snowpack such as slabs or bed surfaces. (Yellowstone National Park, Wyoming)

TABLE 5-1. A SIMPLIFIED VERSION OF THE INTERNATIONAL		
Type	*Also Called*	*How It Forms*
New snow	There must be a hundred common names for different types of new snow.	Falls from the sky.
Rounded snow	Equilibrium snow, age-hardened snow	Small temperature gradients within the snowpack promote settlement and sintering as snow ages.
Faceted snow	Squares, sugar snow, recrystallized snow, loud powder, temperature gradient snow, or TG snow (an old term not used anymore). Depth hoar is composed of large-grained crystals near the ground.	Large temperature gradients within the snowpack causes "kinetic" metamorphism. It can form any place in the snowpack—on the surface, mid-pack, or near the ground.
Surface hoar	Frost, feathers, hoar frost.	Grows on the snow surface in calm, humid, clear conditions.
Crust	Rime, rain crust, sun crust, wind crust.	Variety of crusts are formed in a variety of ways.
Wet snow	Melt-freeze snow, clustered grains, corn snow, glop, and less flattering terms.	Free water in the snowpack.

CLASSIFICATION OF SEASONAL SNOW ON THE GROUND

What It Means Avalanche-wise	Looks Like	Snowpit Symbol
All snow starts out this way. Can be either a weak layer or a slab.		+
Strong layers—usually forms slab or bed surfaces.		●
Especially dangerous weak layer—very brittle and persistent. A common cause of avalanche accidents in intermountain and continental climates.		□ = Faceted snow ∧ = Depth hoar
Especially dangerous weak layer—very brittle and persistent. The most common weak layer involved in accidents in many areas of North America, especially in maritime climates.		∨
Can be slabs, weak interfaces, or bed surfaces.		▽ = Rime crust ⚹ = Wind crust ▬ = Rain or sun crust ⊙⊙ = Melt-freeze crust
Wet snow avalanches—both sluffs and slabs.		O

Aged, Settled Snow

I talked briefly about sintering and settlement in Chapter 2, How Avalanches Work. In the absence of a steep temperature gradient (more on this later), as snow crystals age, they become rounded and form bonds with their neighbors. We call this "equilibrium" snow or "rounded" snow or simply "rounds." In your snowpit, layers of equilibrium snow (rounds) are usually harder than the other layers and are composed of very small, hard-to-see grains. If you can't figure out what the snow is, it's probably equilibrium snow (rounds). If all snow were as well behaved as equilibrium snow, we wouldn't have to worry about most avalanches.

Wind Slabs

Wind slabs are perhaps the most common slab material and constitute an important strong layer in the snowpack. Wind grinds up snowflakes into smaller particles. Small particles bond much more quickly than larger particles and they pack together much more efficiently. Thus, wind slabs are often dense and strong. (Sintering occurs to the inverse of the fourth power of the crystal size, if you want to get technical. In other words, small crystals can bond ten thousand times faster than large crystals.)

Rime forms when supercooled water droplets in a cloud instantly freeze onto a solid surface such as the snow surface or other snowflakes. Rime grows toward the wind. (Bridger Range, Montana)

Rime

Rime is that crunchy, rough snow that looks like popcorn or Styrofoam plastered onto trees on windy mountaintops (making "snow ghosts"). Rime forms on the surface of the snow when super-cooled water in clouds freezes onto the snow surface, trees, chairlift towers, or any solid surface. It usually forms when clouds rise rapidly over a mountain range. The air rises so fast that tiny water droplets don't have time to form snowflakes (or graupel in this case), so the water droplets actually cool well below the freezing level. When they touch something solid, they freeze instantly, thus the spikes grow *into* the wind (as opposed to wind loading in which drifts form on the downwind side).

Rime usually forms a strong layer on the surface of the snowpack. A thick layer of surface rime is usually a sign of stability because, as Doug Fesler likes to say, "It's like throwing a cargo net over the snow." Is it a sign of stability within the old snow? Not necessarily. The weight of the new snow accompanying the rime, plus the weight of the rime itself, may overload buried weak layers. Watch out, however, if a thin rime crust forms on light density snow and is buried by more new snow. Avalanches can slide on or below the rime crust for a surprisingly long time.

Good News—Bad News

The good news is that, at least in the long term, the formation of a stout strong layer in the snowpack has a stabilizing effect. A good soaking rain in particular is sometimes referred to as "raising the ground level" because future avalanches seldom break below this layer. The bad news is that, in the short term, the added weight of the hard layer of snow can make the snow unstable. Example: a strong rain-on-snow event makes the snow unstable while and immediately after it occurs, but it makes the snow more stable after the instability has settled out.

WEAK LAYERS IN THE SNOWPACK

Uncohesive New Snow

"Cohesion" means how well snow sticks together. You can think of cohesion as "hardness" or "strength" if you want, but technically, "cohesion" is the more proper term. Cohesive snow makes good snowballs and you can break off blocks of snow because it holds together; uncohesive snow makes snowballs that fall apart before they hit their victims. Light, fluffy new snow tends to be uncohesive and dense new snow tends to be cohesive. You often hear avalanche professionals talk about avalanches sliding on "low-density snow" or "density inversions" in the new snow. They are talking about relatively more cohesive snow sliding on relatively less cohesive snow.

UNCOHESIVE NEW SNOW SUMMARY

Looks like: Sparkly, often star-shaped, very soft; easily confused with surface hoar.
Also called: Low-density snow, density inversion.
Distribution pattern: Falls fairly equally on all aspects and elevations (except where wind-affected).
Persistence: Stabilizes within hours to days, depending on temperature.
Forecasting considerations: Easy to miss during a storm, especially if sandwiched between denser layers when you're not looking.

Graupel

Graupel is that Styrofoam-ball type of snow that stings your face. It forms from strong convective activity (upward vertical motion) within a storm caused by the passage of a cold front or springtime convective showers. The static buildup from all these falling graupel pellets sometimes causes lightning as well.

Graupel looks and behaves like a pile of ball bearings. It is a common weak layer in maritime climates, but it's fairly rare in continental climates. Graupel is extra tricky because it tends to roll off cliffs and steeper terrain and collect on the gentler terrain at

Graupel acts like tiny ball bearings in the snowpack. They can roll off steep terrain and collect on less steep terrain below. (Wasatch Range, Utah) © Evelyn Lees

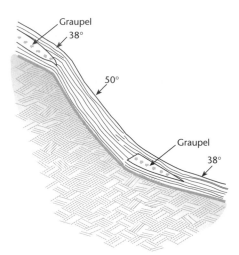

Figure 5-1. Graupel tends to roll off cliffs and steep slopes (greater than 45 degrees) and collect on gentler terrain (less than 40 degrees).

the bottom of cliffs (Figure 5-1). It sometimes takes people by surprise because avalanches aren't triggered on steep terrain (45 to 90 degrees) but are triggered on less steep terrain near the bottom of the slope (35 to 45 degrees). Graupel weak layers usually stabilize about a day or two after a storm, depending on temperature.

GRAUPEL SUMMARY

Looks like: Little Styrofoam balls.
Feels like: Stings your face.
Mechanical properties: Like ball bearings.
Distribution pattern: Rolls off cliffs and steep slopes and collects on gentler terrain and in pockets. Not dependent on aspect or elevation.
Persistence: Stabilizes about 1 or 2 days after deposited, depending on temperature and metamorphism.

WEAK INTERFACES

Most avalanche fractures occur within a distinct weak layer sandwiched between two harder layers, but sometimes the fracture occurs simply because of a poor bond between two layers—in other words, a weak interface. For instance, a hard slab might slide directly on a hard rain crust with no distinct weak layer involved. A slick bed surface combined with a very weak and persistent weak layer on top of the crust is an especially nasty combination. Often a weak interface involves two layers with distinctly different grain sizes. Like most animals, snow tends to bond better to its own kind. Small grains tend to bond poorly to large grains and especially poorly to flat surfaces like a planar ice crust. Always be suspicious of two layers that have distinctly different grain sizes.

Sun Crusts

Sun crusts form when heat from the sun melts the snow surface, which then refreezes. A sun crust sometimes forms a hard bed surface for future avalanches to run upon. However, a sun crust typically has a fairly rough texture when compared to the more slippery rain crust, and snow deposited on the crust tends to bond better than you would imagine. However, a sun crust forms a strong mechanical discontinuity in the snowpack, which tends to concentrate any shear deformation within the snowpack to the layers just above and below the sun crust. Probably more important, crusts tend to concentrate temperature gradients above and below them and they can grow a thin and almost invisible layer of weak faceted snow. (See the "Near-Surface Faceted Snow" section later in this chapter.) This probably accounts for most of the avalanches that occur on sun crusts, especially in non-maritime climates. Also, surface hoar that grows on top of a sun crust can be a very nasty weak layer.

Sun crusts, of course, form only on sunny slopes and not at all on the shady ones. So we find them mostly on southeast-, south-, southwest-, and west-facing slopes in the Northern Hemisphere (and conversely form more uniformly on all aspects in tropical latitudes and during

Sun and especially rain crusts tend to form shiny, slick layers on the surface that can be bed surfaces for future avalanches. (Wasatch Range, Utah)

spring and fall in arctic latitudes). Instabilities associated with sun crusts usually stabilize fairly quickly after a storm, depending on temperature, except if faceted snow has grown around the sun crust or surface hoar has grown on top of the crust, it can produce much more persistent avalanche activity.

HOT TIP!

When new snow falls on a sun crust, check out whether the sun crust is wet or frozen when the snow starts. If it's wet, the new snow will stick to it and you most likely won't have any immediate avalanche problem. If the crust is frozen, then the new snow does not tend to bond very well.

Caveat: *See the "Melt Layer Recrystallization" section later in this chapter.*

SUN CRUST SUMMARY

Also called: Firnspeigel (one type of sun crust).
Looks like: Shiny with slightly rough surface.
Formed by: Strong sun on the snow surface.
Distribution pattern: Forms only on sunny aspects, none on shady aspects; moderately elevation-dependent.
Persistence: Instabilities are usually short-lived, depending on temperature.
Forecasting considerations: Is it wet or frozen when the next storm comes in? If it's wet, it will bond well; if it's frozen, it will bond more poorly, except for melt layer recrystallization.

Melt-Freeze Crust

Most people know melt-freeze by its more common name, "corn," a prized commodity to skiers and boarders throughout the world for its baby-butt smooth surface and grippy texture. Melt-freeze crusts are similar to sun crusts or rain crusts in that, as the name implies, the snow gets wet and then freezes. Melt-freeze crusts differ because the snow undergoes repeated cycles of melting and freezing, which rounds the snow grains and they grow in size with each repeated cycle of melting and freezing. We usually think of melt-freeze as a springtime phenomenon because clear skies in spring produce the perfect conditions to form melt-freeze snow. During the day, the strong spring sun and warm temperatures melt the snow surface, and by night, the snow surface radiates heat away to a clear sky, which freezes the snow again. After several days of proper cooking, voilà! The snow surface turns into large-grained, supportable corn.

For corn aficionados, perfect timing counts for everything. Too early in the day and you can loosen your fillings chattering off the frozen surface; too late in the day and you sink through the unsupportable, wet crust, making for poor turning conditions and potentially dangerous wet avalanche conditions. You have to make like Goldilocks and shoot for just the right time after the sun has softened the surface and before it turns unsupportable.

HOT TIP!

As usual, terrain management comes to our rescue. Simply work the terrain to your advantage, starting on the southeast-facing slopes in the earlier morning then switching to south-facing by midmorning and finishing on southwest-facing by about noon. When you sink into unsupportable snow, it's time to either switch aspects or head home. If you linger too long, you may not only trigger wet avalanches on that slope, but you ruin the corn for the following morning's rider, which is considered not cool. Snowboarders have to be especially careful because too-soft corn is fun on a large surface area vehicle like a snowboard and you can easily find yourself triggering wet avalanches and making "canoe tracks," which gets you yelled at.

Caution—watch out for the dreaded corn slabs: A frozen, unsupportable, melt-freeze crust usually means the snow is stable, but on rare occasions it can still avalanche in what we call a "corn slab." Most of the corn slabs I have seen have occurred after several days of strong melting, which saturates the underlying snow with percolating meltwater. Then, a clear night allows a thin refreeze of the snow surface, making it feel solid and reliable. Most involve buried faceted snow, which has become saturated.

Although they are quite rare, corn slabs can easily catch experienced people. You can see a spectacular example of this in the major motion picture, *Steep*, by Sony Pictures in which my friends Andrew McLean, Matt Turley, and Dylan Freed accidentally trigger and narrowly escape a large corn slab avalanche in Iceland.

MELT-FREEZE SUMMARY

Looks like: Large-grained and rounded.

Feels like: Very abrasive, like a lemon-peel grater, which can easily make raspberries on exposed skin when you fall. (Luckily, I never fall, but I did drag my hand once back in 1972...It's an old joke, you're supposed to laugh.)

Formed by: Repeated cycles of melting and freezing—usually in spring.

Distribution patterns: Usually on sun-exposed slopes.

Forecasting considerations: Supportable, frozen crust is usually a good sign of stability; but in rare conditions with prior, strong melting and percolation of meltwater, they can avalanche as corn slabs even with a frozen, supportable surface.

Rain Crusts

Rain crusts tend to be more smooth and slippery than sun crusts except in cases of hard, drenching rain. Instabilities associated with them tend to last much longer, typically several days after a storm deposits snow on top of a rain crust and sometimes through several storms. Also, unlike sun crusts, rain crusts form uniformly on all aspects, but like rain, rain crusts are highly elevation-dependent. Typically, rain falls at lower elevations and as you ascend through the freezing level, the rain progressively turns to snow (Figure 5-2).

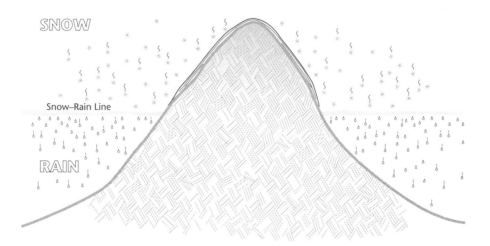

Figure 5-2. Precipitation falls as snow above the freezing level and as rain at lower elevations.

Prolonged or hard rain on new snow forms drainage channels down the fall line and makes a corrugated pattern in the surface snow. These drainage channels, also called "rill marks," are a sign of stability.

HOT TIP!

Rain crusts are not always dangerous. Like a sun crust, you have to watch closely to see whether the rain crust is soggy or frozen when the next snowstorm begins. If it's wet, the new snow will usually bond to it and you probably won't have any problems—at least in the short term. If, however, the rain crust is well frozen and the next storm begins with low density dry snow, then it's like trying to make feathers stick to a sloping pane of glass. You can expect fairly widespread soft slab activity running on the hard rain crust.

Caveat: *See the "Melt Layer Recrystallization" section later in this chapter.*

RAIN CRUST SUMMARY

Looks like: Shiny, smooth surface. Prolonged rain on new snow forms drainage channels down the fall line, making a corrugated surface pattern.
Formed by: Rain falling on snow.
Distribution pattern: Forms on all aspects, but strongly elevation-dependent.
Climates: Typical in maritime, occasional in intermountain, rare in continental.
Persistence: Instabilities of slabs deposited on rain crusts persist for several days, sometimes several storms. Faceted snow or surface hoar associated with rain crusts can produce instabilities for a very long time.
Forecast considerations: Carefully watch the rain crust when the next storm arrives. If it's still wet, the new snow will bond to it; if it's frozen, the new snow will probably bond poorly. Watch out for melt layer recrystallization if a wet rain crust gets buried by cold, new snow.

WEAK LAYERS WITHIN OLD SNOW

Faceted Snow

Faceted snow causes many of the avalanche fatalities in North America and most of the avalanches in continental and intermountain climates (Figure 5-3). And no wonder. It seems like a made-to-order villain out of a horror movie. It grows like a parasite within the snow—often out of sight—until it's too late. It becomes inexorably more and more dangerous during the seemingly most benign conditions—clear skies, cold temperatures—and it lies in wait, sometimes for weeks, until it's brought suddenly to life by a fresh load of snow or rapid warming. Then when its victim bumbles into the wrong place, it pulls the rug out from under them, rockets them down the mountain at a terrifying speed, ripping them limb

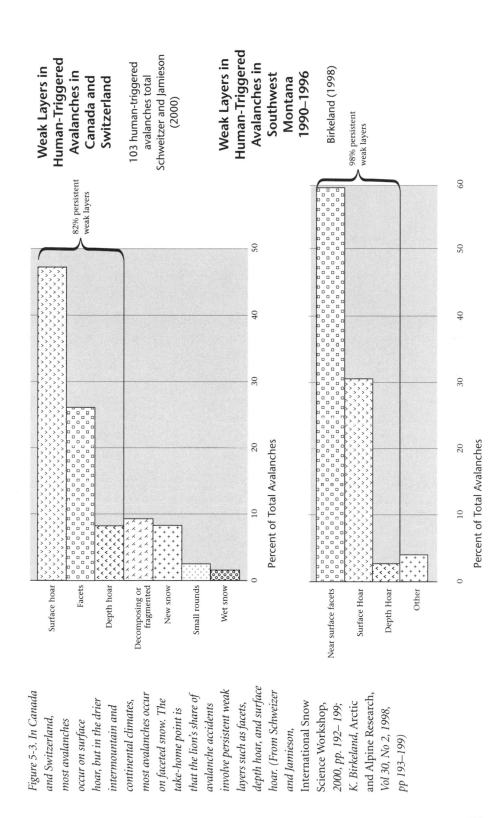

Weak Layers in Human-Triggered Avalanches in Canada and Switzerland

82% persistent weak layers

103 human-triggered avalanches total
Schweitzer and Jamieson (2000)

Surface hoar
Facets
Depth hoar
Decomposing or fragmented
New snow
Small rounds
Wet snow

Percent of Total Avalanches

Weak Layers in Human-Triggered Avalanches in Southwest Montana 1990–1996

Birkeland (1998)

98% persistent weak layers

Near surface facets
Surface Hoar
Depth Hoar
Other

Percent of Total Avalanches

Figure 5-3. In Canada and Switzerland, most avalanches occur on surface hoar, but in the drier intermountain and continental climates, most avalanches occur on faceted snow. The take-home point is that the lion's share of avalanche accidents involve persistent weak layers such as facets, depth hoar, and surface hoar. (From Schweizer and Jamieson, International Snow Science Workshop, 2000, pp. 192– 199; K. Birkeland, Arctic and Alpine Research, Vol 30, No 2, 1998, pp 193–199)

from limb as they bounce off trees and rocks, and finally entombs them under tons of icy, hard snow. Stephen King, are you listening?

How Faceted Snow Is Formed

Faceted snow forms from large temperature gradients within the snowpack. Important concept: Pay close attention to this process because it creates most of the weak layers that can kill us. A temperature gradient is simply how much temperature changes over a certain distance within the snowpack. Because warm air holds more water vapor than cold air, temperature gradients also create what we call "vapor pressure gradients"—more water vapor in one place than another. What happens when you concentrate something—especially a gas? It wants to diffuse, to move from areas of high concentration to areas of low concentration. When water vapor diffuses *rapidly,* it changes rounded crystals into faceted ones—changing strong snow into weak snow. In other words, temperature gradients create potential weak layers that can kill us. That's why we pay so much attention to them (Figures 5-4 and 5-5).

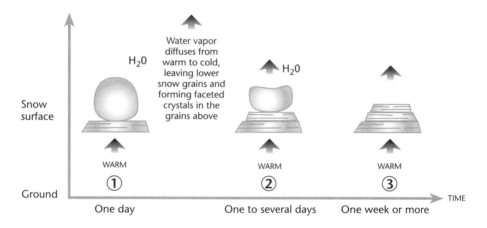

Figure 5-4 How faceted snow is formed

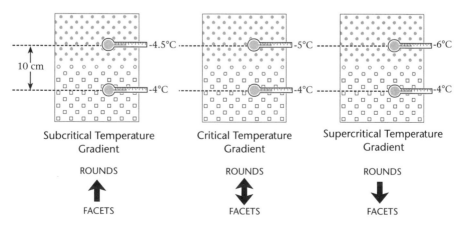

Figure 5-5. Subcritical, critical, and supercritical temperature gradients

Strong temperature gradients within the snowpack form faceted snow. Over the course of several days, the crystals grow progressively larger and more faceted. Photo courtesy of the U.S. Department of Agriculture

This process is completely reversible. A strong gradient turns rounds to facets. A weak gradient turns facets back to rounds. The process in reverse, however, occurs much more slowly, because to create a faceted crystal requires so much energy that when the energy source is taken away (the strong temperature gradient), the crystal needs a lot of time to return to its equilibrium state (rounds). In other words, it might take a week or two of a strong temperature gradient to form large faceted crystals, but after the temperature gradient is taken away, the crystals can take twice as long to stabilize, depending on the ambient temperature of the snow and how much compressive load is on top. The take-home point here is this: *small temperature gradients make the snow stronger; large temperature gradients make the snow weaker.*

How large is a large temperature gradient? For snow of an average snowpack temperature, say, around -5 degrees Celsius, the critical temperature gradient is about 1 degree celsius per 10 centimeters. In cold snow, say, colder than -10 degrees Celsius, you need a higher temperature gradient to cause faceting. In warm snow you need less.

For example, suppose we stick two thermometers into the snowpit wall, one 10 centimeters (about 4 inches) above the other. If we measure a difference of only 0.5 degree Celsius in 10 centimeters, it means that equilibrium snow is forming (snow is getting rounder and stronger). If we measure a temperature difference of 2 degrees Celsius in 10 centimeters, it means that faceted snow is forming (snow is getting weaker).

> ## HOT TIP!
> *All you have to do is find a faceted layer in the snowpack, measure the gradient, and you know whether the layer is gaining strength or losing strength. Cool, huh? This is actually a powerful forecasting tool. (Figures 5-5 and 5-6).*

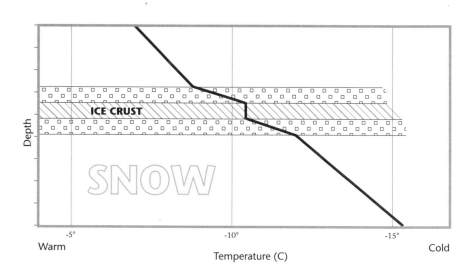

Figure 5-6. Ice crusts tend to concentrate a temperature gradient, so it is common to find faceted snow just above and below ice crusts.

Depth Hoar—Faceted Snow Near the Ground

Contrary to popular belief, as long as the ground has an insulating blanket of snow, the ground is almost always warm—near freezing—even with very cold air temperatures. Snow is a wonderful insulator and even with very cold air temperatures, it's common for the snow near the ground to remain damp for most of the season. The only exception to this is in permafrost areas (very high elevations at mid-latitudes or arctic latitudes) or in areas with a thin snow cover combined with very cold temperatures.

The top of the snow surface, on the other hand, can become extremely cold—especially when exposed to a clear sky—thus creating one of the most common temperature gradient conditions. Especially in the early winter, cold temperature often combines with a thin snowpack making the perfect breeding conditions for the dreaded faceted snow near the ground, which we call depth hoar.

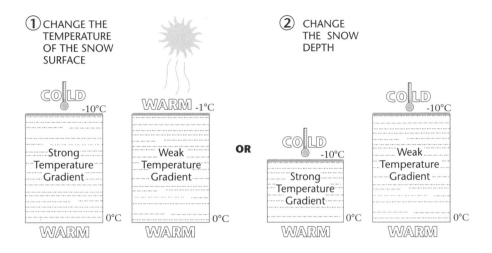

Figure 5-7. Two ways to change temperature gradient (which affects faceting, and thus strength)

Pop quiz: Since temperature gradient means a change in temperature over some distance, we can increase or decrease temperature gradient in two ways. What are they?

Answer: 1. Change the temperature. 2. Change the distance.

For instance, one way to decrease temperature gradient (which strengthens the snow) is to warm the snow surface (warmer air temperatures, sun, or clouds above shady slopes). That's obvious enough, but most people don't think about the second way to decrease the temperature gradient—increase the distance by adding more snow (Figure 5-7). Learning to appreciate the importance of total snow depth on the strength and stability of the snowpack usually takes several years of experience. That's why you often see avalanche professionals constantly probing the snow with their collapsible probes or their ski poles. They are mapping the snow depth so that they will know where the thin and weak snow exists—trigger points for future avalanches.

HOT TIP!

Bottom line: Thin snow means weak snow, and weak snow can easily be overloaded by the weight of an additional load or by the weight of a person.

Distribution Pattern

We normally think of depth hoar as an early season phenomenon. It begins to form after the first snowfall as soon as temperatures get cold or, more important, when the skies clear. As with surface hoar, radiation plays an extremely important role in snow surface temperature. (See the "Radiation and Snow Temperature" section in Chapter 4, Weather.) In most climates, it plays a more important role than air temperature. Therefore, in mid-latitudes, depth hoar grows primarily on the shady aspects, the northwest-, north-, northeast-, and often east-facing slopes. Often in midwinter when the snow is deep enough that depth hoar quits growing,

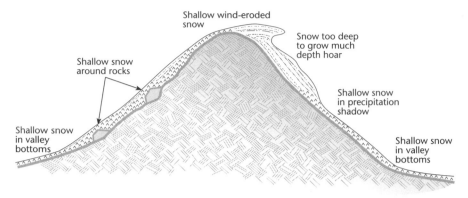

Figure 5-8. Common distribution of depth hoar

we find depth hoar on the slopes with thin snow, such as west- and south-facing slopes and near ridgelines where the wind has thinned the snowpack. In high latitudes during midwinter, such as in Alaska and northern Canada, as well as in equatorial latitudes, if depth hoar grows, it tends to do so on all aspects nearly equally.

More than most other weak layers, the strength of depth hoar varies quite dramatically from one location to another, depending mostly on the depth of the snowpack. Remember: thin snowpack means a weak snowpack. Thicker snowpacks insulate the cold air from the warm ground, have a small temperature gradient, and thus a stronger snowpack. For this reason, you usually don't find bad depth hoar under the thick layers of wind-loaded snow near the ridge tops. It's usually much weaker at mid-slope and especially near the bottom of basins, where thin snowpacks combine with cold air pooling, and around rock outcroppings (Figure 5-8). In cold climates, depth hoar usually doesn't form on top of glaciers as much as the ground because glaciers are usually colder than the ground, but depth hoar does form on warm glaciers.

Depth Hoar and Climate

In continental climates, depth hoar is extremely common; in fact, depth hoar often makes up nearly the entire snowpack until about February of each year, and then in thin snowpack years, large wet slabs fail on depth hoar in spring. Depth hoar accounts for most avalanche fatalities in continental climates and most snow stability and forecasting decisions revolve around it.

At the other end of the spectrum, in maritime climates, depth hoar usually forms only in the early season and quickly disappears after the first couple of snowstorms bury it. In very warm maritime climates you can go several years without even seeing it.

In between these two extremes, in intermountain climates, depth hoar forms in the early season during most years and depth hoar instabilities commonly last until December or January, and it is not much of a problem after that. In bad depth hoar years, large wet slabs may release in spring when meltwater saturates the old depth hoar layers.

Mechanical Properties of Depth Hoar

Mechanically, depth hoar is one nasty dude. Depth hoar behaves like a stack of champagne glasses. Although it's stronger in compression than in shear, it can also fail in a catastrophic collapse of the layer. Fractures often propagate long distances and around corners. Almost all catastrophic, climax avalanches (involving the entire season's snow cover) occur on depth hoar.

A hard wind slab on top of depth hoar is double trouble. It's like laying a pane of glass on top of a stack of champagne glasses (Figure 5-9). It bridges a person's weight out over a larger area until they either give it a hard thump, reach a place where the slab is thinner, or where the depth hoar is weaker, and then the whole slope shatters catastrophically. Fractures involving hard slabs commonly form above the victim, leaving very little chance for escape. Wind slabs on depth hoar exist throughout most of the season in continental climates, and when you add large populations to the equation, the result is many avalanche fatalities. Thus, Colorado leads the nation in avalanche fatalities.

Forecasting Considerations

As Canadian avalanche specialist Clair Isrelson once told me, "Depth hoar is like having your crazy aunt come for a visit. She stays forever and you just never know when she's going to snap."

Large-grained depth hoar persists longer than any other kind of weak layer. And as long as it does, you just tiptoe around and accumulate gray hairs. Usually the larger the grain size, the more persistent the instability. The time-honored adage among experienced avalanche professionals is "Never trust a depth hoar snowpack." Carefully watch each loading event all winter—especially the big ones. Even after you think you've seen the last of it, percolating meltwater in the spring can reactivate the depth hoar layer and produce large, wet slab avalanches. Yikes!

The best stability tests for depth hoar, listed roughly in the order of reliability, are recent avalanche activity, explosives tests, cornice drops, extended column tests or propagation saw tests, rutschblock tests, compression tests (do lots of them in representative places), and

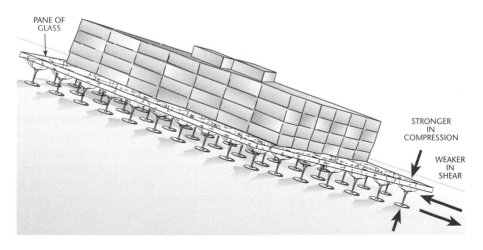

Figure 5-9. Depth hoar is stronger in compression than in shear. Mechanically, a hard wind slab on depth hoar is like a pane of glass on top of a stack of champagne glasses. When a heavy load of wind-blown or new snow is slammed down on top, it's as if the champagne glasses are trying to support a load of bricks.

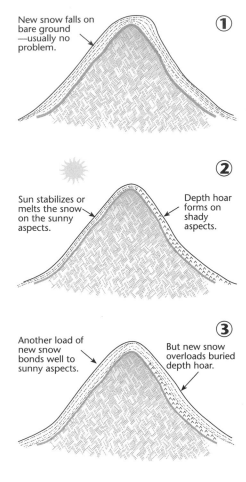

New snow falls on bare ground —usually no problem.

①

Sun stabilizes or melts the snow on the sunny aspects.

Depth hoar forms on shady aspects.

②

Another load of new snow bonds well to sunny aspects.

But new snow overloads buried depth hoar.

③

Figure 5-10. Typical early season pattern of depth hoar on shady slopes

jumping on test slopes. Weather isn't quite as reliable unless it's really obvious weather like a heavy loading or rapid warming of the overlying slab. (See Chapter 6, Stability, for more information on tests.)

If you can't use active tests, use a thermometer and carefully measure the temperature gradient across the weakest layers. As soon as the temperature gradient drops below the critical level (about 1 degree centigrade per 10 centimeters) then the snow is gaining strength. Remember that depth hoar is quick to form but takes a long time to gain strength after the temperature gradient is removed. With no additional loading and a weak layer of -5 degrees Celsius or warmer, the snow can take several days to a couple of weeks to stabilize. Cold weak layers and a lightweight overlying layer can take much longer.

Routefinding Considerations

In latitudes, say, from about the southern United States to near the Canadian border, depth hoar usually exists only on shady aspects (northwest-, north-, northeast-, and often east-facing slopes in the Northern Hemisphere). North of the Canadian border or in climates with little wintertime sun, depth hoar is found on a wider variety of aspects, a tricky situation. In very cold climates, or during arctic outbreaks, the temperatures are just too cold to grow depth hoar very rapidly and it forms instead on sunny aspects where it's warm enough to grow. Depth hoar grows best in snow temperatures between -2 to -15 degrees Celsius. No matter what aspect with respect to the sun, you usually find depth hoar in thin snowpack areas, such as windblown aspects.

At mid-latitudes, people get into trouble in the early season with the first slab that forms on top of depth hoar. The sun melts the snow away on the sunny slopes, forcing people onto the shady slopes where the depth hoar lives and they end up taking lots of rides in avalanches (Figure 5-10).

Depth hoar avalanches are frequently triggered from long distances away. Many people, including a coworker of mine, have been killed when they triggered the slope from the bottom, in this case, from nearly a quarter mile away. Triggering a steep slope is also easy by standing on a flat slope above or to the side. Sometimes the steep slope below will pull a hard slab off a flat ridge above.

Victims usually trigger depth hoar avalanches from shallow (thus weaker) snowpack areas, like a windblown ridge, a rock outcrop in the middle of a slope, or a spur ridge next to a steep slope. Most of the time we think of a rock outcrop in the middle of a steep slope to be an "island of safety," but in depth hoar snowpack, it's a trigger point.

DEPTH HOAR SUMMARY

Also called: Sugar snow, squares, temperature gradient (TG) snow (this is an outdated term), facets sometimes incorrectly called "hoar frost" by rural geezers.

Looks like: Sparkly, larger grained, sometimes cup-shaped facets 4 to 10 mm.

Feels like: Loose, runs through your fingers, granular, crunchy when chewed.

Smells like: The ground, because the rapid diffusion of warm, moist air from the ground causes depth hoar.

Formed by: Large temperature gradients between the warm ground and the cold snow surface. Usually requires a thin snowpack combined with a clear sky or cold air temperature. Grows best at snow temperatures from -2 to -15 degrees Celsius.

Mechanical properties: Collapses like a stack of champagne glasses. Relatively stronger in compression than in shear. Fails both in collapse and in shear. Commonly propagates long distances, around corners, and is easily triggered from the bottom—your basic nightmare.

Distribution pattern: At mid-latitudes, forms mainly on shady aspects (northwest to northeast) or in areas of thin snowpack. In very cold climates, forms on warmer slopes (sun-exposed, near fumaroles, non-permafrost areas). At arctic and equatorial latitudes, it shows much less preference for aspect. Doesn't tend to form as often on glaciers as on the ground.

Climates: Continental: Extremely common throughout the season. Often makes up the entire snowpack until about February. Intermountain: Common before about January. Maritime: Not as common and usually in the early season.

Persistence: Extremely persistent in the snowpack from several days to several weeks, depending on temperature. The larger the grain, the more persistent. Percolating meltwater in spring often reactivates large-grained depth hoar.

Forecasting considerations: Never underestimate the persistence of faceted snow as a weak layer. Makes large and scary avalanches, often throughout the season. Carefully measure temperature gradients across the weak layer. Large gradients mean the snow will remain weak; small gradients mean the snow is gaining strength but strengthening takes several days to several weeks depending on temperature.

Best stability tests: Recent avalanches, explosives tests, cornice drops, extended column tests, propagation saw tests, rutschblock test, compression test, test slopes.

Routefinding considerations: Easily triggered from the bottom of a slope or from an adjacent flat area. Pay attention to what your slope is connected to. Depth hoar avalanches are usually triggered from a shallow snowpack area—avoid rock outcroppings in the middle of a slope.

Near-Surface Faceted Snow

Contrary to popular belief, depth hoar is not the most common type of faceted snow. Facets form anywhere large temperature gradients develop, and there's no place in the snowpack that experiences as much temperature abuse as the snow surface. These large temperature gradients near the surface of the snow cause low-density surface snow to facet

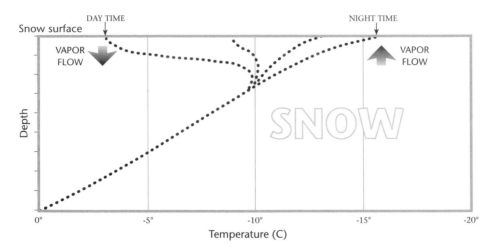

Figure 5-11. Diurnal recrystallization

very quickly. Near-surface faceted snow is caused by one of three mechanisms: diurnal recrystallization, melt layer recrystallization, or radiation recrystallization.

Diurnal Recrystallization

Each day, the sun heats up the snow surface and each night, especially with a clear sky, it cools down. These temperature extremes can be very dramatic. For instance, it's not unusual for the snow surface to be 20 degrees warmer during the day than at night and experience a temperature gradient of 20 degrees Celsius per 10 centimeters, which, as you're beginning to learn, is a steep temperature gradient (Figure 5-11). With all this monkey business going on it's no wonder that the top few centimeters of the snow surface can quickly metamorphose into weak, small-to-medium-sized faceted crystals, which we call diurnal recrystallization.

If new snow falls, followed by a clear night, the next morning people often report that the snow has "dried out" overnight. What really happened is that the clear sky allowed the snow surface to radiate its heat away and become very cold, thus producing a strong temperature gradient in the top few centimeters of the new snow. As a result, this new snow (with its interlocking arms and thus stiffer feel) metamorphosed into loose, fine-grained facets that feel lighter and fluffier than the snow of the day before, making it feel exactly like the snow dried out.

HOT TIP!

Bottom line: with the exception of very warm temperatures, as long as the sky remains clear, the surface of the snow becomes weaker and weaker.

After several days of clear skies, people often describe the snow as "loud powder." By this time the crystals have grown as large as 2 mm and the loose, granular, and angular crystals make a hissing sound when you travel through it. If clear skies keep up for a week or two, the surface of the snow can become so weak that it's difficult to ski, board, or snowmobile on a slope because the snow sluffs out from underneath, and it sometimes becomes so weak that it sluffs on its own.

These sluffs of faceted snow carry much more of a wallop than the sluffs of the powdery new snow, and they can easily knock people off their feet and bury them deeply.

Diurnal recrystallized snow is more equally distributed by aspect than depth hoar but still forms mostly on shady aspects. It seems to form best on slopes that receive some direct sun, but not enough to melt the snow surface. For instance, it can form on south-facing slopes in cold climates. At arctic latitudes in midwinter and at high elevations in equatorial latitudes, it will form on all slopes more equally.

Unlike depth hoar, which varies dramatically in thickness and strength from one part of a slope to another, diurnal recrystallized snow seems to form a layer of more even thickness and strength.

It preferentially forms within low-density snow as opposed to crusts or wind slabs, but given enough time, near-surface faceting can "eat up" crusts—like an alchemist, it can turn hard snow into soft snow. Like surface hoar, it also forms on open slopes exposed to a clear sky and not as much in the trees, but unlike surface hoar, a little bit of direct sun seems to enhance its growth, especially in cold climates.

DIURNAL RECRYSTALLIZATION SUMMARY

Looks like: Sparkly, small to medium grained (0.5 to 2 mm).

Feels like: Loose, runs through your fingers, when buried it feels like low-density new snow yet more granular and sparkly.

Sounds like: A hissing sound as you travel through it.

Distribution pattern: Mostly on shady aspects or slopes with weak sun. In extremely cold climates it occurs on the warmer sunny aspects. Forms on slopes exposed to a clear sky, and not as much in the trees. Relatively even thickness and strength across a slope. Forms mostly in low-density snow and not as much from hard layers such as wind slabs and crusts.

Persistence: Moderately persistent (one week or more depending on temperature, and up to 90 days in extreme cases).

Forecasting considerations: Carefully map layer before it's buried. The longer the sky remains clear, the weaker the snow surface becomes.

Melt Layer Recrystallization (sometimes called wet layer recrystallization)

Now here is a very tricky situation. When new snow falls on a wet layer of snow, it usually bonds well and there's no problem. However, if the temperature gets cold after the storm and stays cold for more than a couple of days—yes, that's right—we suddenly have strong temperature and moisture gradients within the new snow, and you know what that means. Moisture from warm, wet rain crust diffuses upward through the new, low-density snow and it quickly grows faceted snow, especially near the warm crust (Figure 5-12). Even though the snow bonded well initially, after 2 to 4 days under a strong temperature gradient, you suddenly start triggering avalanches on fine-grained faceted snow. Whoa! In this case, we haven't added any *weight* to buried weak layers, but instead, we've *decreased the strength* of the buried weak layer—with the same result. Like I say, tricky!

Look for this scenario any time a strong cold front blows through. Usually the stronger the front, the more it sucks up warm air from the south ahead of the front, which makes the

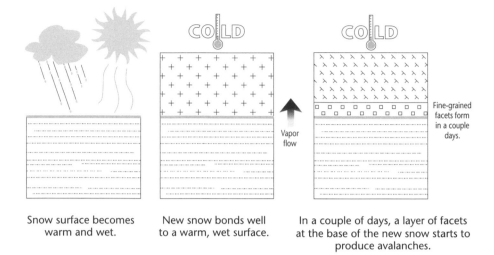

Snow surface becomes warm and wet.   New snow bonds well to a warm, wet surface.   In a couple of days, a layer of facets at the base of the new snow starts to produce avalanches.

Figure 5-12. Melt layer recrystallization

pre-storm snow wet and warm. Then new snow falls, followed by very cold temperatures. Especially if only a little new snow falls on the wet crust followed by a clear sky at night, significant melt layer recrystallization can form overnight, and even if snow begins again the next morning, you have just buried a persistent weak layer. If you don't pay close attention, it can easily surprise you.

MELT LAYER RECRYSTALLIZATION SUMMARY

Looks like: Sparkly, loose, granular, 0.5 to 2 mm. Hard to see with the naked eye.
Feels like: Granular weak layer in the snow.
Formed by: Large temperature gradients between a warm, wet snow surface and cold, dry new snow on top.
Mechanical properties: Same as other types of faceted snow. Especially with a hard and slippery bed surface, it can run on low slope angles and can be very sensitive to triggers.
Persistence: Large range of persistence, from days to months. In extreme cases can last for weeks to months. Persistent weak layers on top of a slippery rain almost always equals big, long-term trouble. Instability lasts longer than you would expect from instabilities within new snow.
Forecasting considerations: Watch for it any time cold new snow falls on a wet old snow surface, or when cold, clear weather follows a warm storm. Carefully monitor the temperature gradient.

Radiation Recrystallization

Radiation recrystallization sounds scary, and is actually fairly rare, but it forms during a very fascinating process (at least for snow geeks) common to high elevations in low latitudes, such as in Colorado, Utah, and New Mexico. I've also seen it while mountaineering in the Peruvian Andes. As you recall from Chapter 4, Weather, with a clear sky, the surface of the snow radiates heat into space very efficiently and the snow surface can become extremely cold, even on a warm day. Especially at high elevations, say, above 3000 meters (10,000 feet), there's so little atmosphere that the snow surface can remain cold and dry even with direct sun shining on it. Just below the snow surface, some of the sun's energy penetrates the snow and heats it up, but the overlying snow prevents radiation from escaping—kind of like a miniature greenhouse—and the sun can warm it to the melting point, even though the snow surface stays cold and dry. The result is an extremely steep temperature gradient in the top 1 to 2 centimeters of the snow surface (Figure 5-13).

Radiation-recrystallization crust looks like a thin sun crust with fine- to medium-grained facets on top and sometimes on the bottom. When buried, it forms a fairly persistent, thin weak layer in the snowpack and, if you're not looking very carefully, you could mistake it for a surface hoar layer. It forms mostly on high-elevation, sun-exposed slopes on sunny days when there is a balance between incoming and outgoing radiation.

RADIATION RECRYSTALLIZATION SUMMARY

Looks like: Thin, weak sun crust with small-grained (0.5 to 2 mm) faceted snow on top and bottom—sometimes mistaken for surface hoar.

Mechanical properties: Behaves like a thin layer of surface hoar—makes a nasty weak layer.

Distribution pattern: High-elevation sun-exposed slopes, none on shady slopes.

Climates: Common in continental, somewhat common in intermountain, and rare in maritime except at higher elevations.

Persistence: Forms a persistent weak layer that can last for days or weeks, depending on temperature.

Forecasting considerations: Although at mid-latitudes sun-exposed slopes tend to be more stable than shady ones in midwinter, they can still form a nasty and persistent weak layer that commonly surprises people.

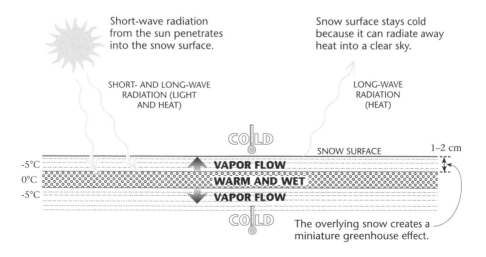

Figure 5-13. Radiation recrystallization

Surface hoar–like millions of tiny potato chips. When buried, they are extremely weak, fragile, and hard to detect. (Wasatch Range, Utah)

Surface Hoar

Surface hoar is just a fancy name for frost. It doesn't fall from the sky, it grows on the surface of the snow on clear, calm, and humid nights. Surface hoar is probably the trickiest weak layer on the planet. Based on Canadian and Swiss statistics, it accounts for more human-triggered avalanches than any other kind of weak layer (Figure 5-3). Surface hoar on a slippery ice crust is probably the scariest situation of all. When buried, it's extremely persistent, very sensitive, and can produce avalanches on surprisingly gentle slopes. The take-home point here is that surface hoar is thin, hard to detect, pockety, long-lasting, and very scary.

How It Forms

If you've forgotten the discussion on radiation and snow surface temperature in Chapter 4, Weather, flip back and reread it because radiation is what causes surface hoar and you need to have a firm grasp of the concepts. During a clear sky, the snow in the shade or at night radiates a tremendous amount of heat and the snow surface becomes very cold. Since we know from earlier in this chapter that warm air holds more water vapor than cold air, the vapor from the warmer air above the snow will condense onto the surface of the snow and, voilà, we have surface hoar. Surface hoar is simply the winter equivalent of dew.

Next, we need humid air and, finally, we need the last ingredient, calm air. Too much wind will destroy the fragile surface hoar crystals, plus, too much wind doesn't allow the cold air to pool and become humid. Actually about 5 km/hr (3 mph) is best for surface hoar production because it's just fast enough to bring a continuous supply of humid air to the snow surface but not too fast to destroy it (Figure 5-14).

Distribution Pattern of Surface Hoar

With this knowledge of both radiation and humidity in mind, let's see where we will most likely find surface hoar after a clear, calm night. First, the snow must be exposed to a clear sky. This means that surface hoar doesn't grow under a canopy of thick evergreen trees, which disrupt the back-radiation process. However, surface hoar grows just fine in a sparse grove of aspen trees because they don't block much radiation.

What about humidity? We know that cold air sinks and with cold, clear conditions, cold air will pool in the bottom of a valley or a mountain basin. When air cools it becomes more humid, thus, surface hoar tends to form more at lower elevations or especially in the bottom of mountain basins and not nearly as much on mountaintops or ridges. We also find thick layers of surface hoar near open streams because they provide such a constant vapor source.

Normally we expect more avalanche danger the higher we go on a mountain because there's more snow and more wind. But with surface hoar as a weak layer, counterintuitively, often more danger exists at lower elevations, which commonly surprises people who aren't accustomed to surface hoar.

What happens if the air in the valley bottom becomes so humid it turns into fog? (Remember, the snow surface has to be exposed to a clear sky to form surface hoar.) If the fog is thick enough, it prevents surface hoar from forming. With a thin fog, surface hoar grows like crazy. Let's say the fog is thick, perhaps 100 meters (300 vertical feet), which is usually thick enough to prevent surface hoar from forming on the valley floor. It can form along the top of the fog layer, though, where we still have the perfect conditions for surface hoar. So like a bathtub ring, in the morning we often see a thick layer of surface hoar along

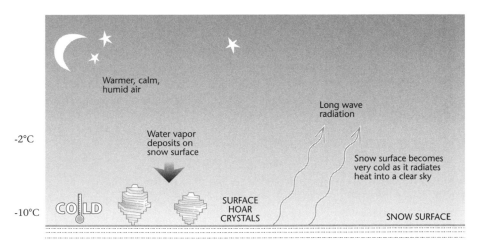

Figure 5-14. Surface hoar formation

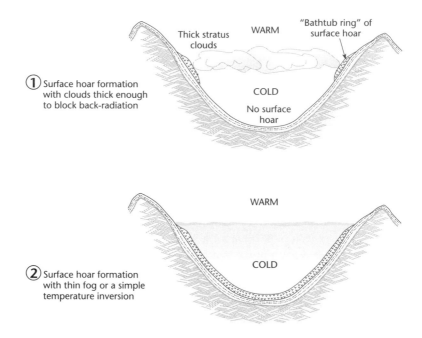

Figure 5-15. Example of surface hoar growing under an inversion layer

the top of the fog layer. Often you see this same bathtub-ring effect along the top layer of stratus clouds that are low enough for the mountaintops to rise above them (Figure 5-15).

Once formed, surface hoar is very fragile, and even a light wind can blow it away. Because the wind can remove surface hoar from some areas and leave it in others, once buried, it can be devilishly difficult to detect. A snowpit in one place might show nothing suspicious while one 3 meters away might show a very fragile layer. We don't find as much surface hoar on mountaintops, not only because of the aforementioned humidity differences but also because the wind blows more on mountaintops and ridges than in valleys.

Surface hoar forms much more commonly in maritime climates than in continental climates because it needs humid air. In arctic and subarctic latitudes, surface hoar grows all day long since the sun is so weak in midwinter. I have seen widespread areas of 10- to 20-centimeters-tall surface hoar crystals in Alaska, in the bottom of mountain basins, especially near streams.

Mechanical Properties of Surface Hoar

Surface hoar makes perhaps the perfect avalanche weak layer. It's thin, very weak, notoriously persistent, and commonly forms on hard bed surfaces, which are also slippery. Finally, thin, weak layers tend to fail more easily because any shear deformation within the snowpack is concentrated into a small area.

Surface hoar can fail either by collapse or in shear. It can fail in collapse if the new snow is added slowly and the surface hoar crystals remain standing up like columns. When critically loaded, just one thump and all the columns collapse catastrophically, like the old

A typical avalanche on surface hoar. This one was slightly wind-affected snow overloading very weak surface hoar. It was very sensitive to triggers and so unstable it broke up onto the gentle part of the ridge, which could easily take someone by surprise. (Alaska) © Doug Fesler

college trick where you can stand on an upright, empty beer can without crushing it, but one tap of a finger and—crunch!—ready for the recycle bin. In fact, this is probably the most common scenario for surface hoar, as well as other persistent weak layers: often the first or second storm on top of a surface hoar layer doesn't weigh enough to overload it, but the third or fourth storm finally adds up to the critical weight. Whamo! Just like the college beer can experiment.

Surface hoar can also fail in shear when the first snowfall lays the surface hoar crystals over on their side; they remain as a paper-thin discontinuity in the snowpack with very poor bonding across that layer. These laid-over crystals, however, tend to bond up more quickly than the ones that remain standing on end.

HOT TIP!

Today's snow surface is tomorrow's weak layer. Be sure to carefully map the snow surface conditions before each storm. Weak layers are much easier to see before they are buried than afterward. This is especially true for a sneaky, thin layer of surface hoar.

Forecasting Considerations

Surface hoar crystals are notoriously persistent in the snowpack. Instabilities commonly last for a week or two and up to months in cold snowpacks.

Here is another tricky situation with surface hoar. During a snowstorm, it might be snowing and cloudy when you go to bed and still snowing and cloudy when you wake up. But during the night, unbeknownst to you, the winds died down, the sky cleared for a few hours, and a thin layer of surface hoar formed. The next day, you'll notice sensitive soft-slab avalanches within the new snow. You'll expect them to calm down after a day, as usual, but instead, they last for several days. You dig to investigate and find the culprit. Darn that sneaky surface hoar!

SURFACE HOAR SUMMARY

Also called: Hoar frost, frost, feathers.
Looks like: Sparkly, flat, featherlike or wedge-shaped or platelike, stepped, striated crystals—sometimes mistaken for facets or stellar snow that falls from the sky.
Formed by: Clear sky, light to calm wind, humid air.
Distribution pattern: Open areas without thick trees or sparse trees exposed to a clear sky; lower elevations as opposed to upper elevations; the bottoms of mountain basins; beneath thin fog layer, the top of a thick fog layer, or stratus cloud layer; shady, calm areas; near streams.
Persistence: Extremely persistent weak layer—one week to months depending on temperature. Especially persistent and dangerous when on top of a firm ice crust.
Best snowpit tests: Extended column test, propagation saw test, shovel shear test, or compression test. Look at the bottom of the block to see the crystals.
Forecasting considerations: Carefully map the distribution of surface hoar *before* it is buried by subsequent snow. Be suspicious of it with each loading event.

Snow subjected to strong rain or strong melting forms vertical percolation columns where water drains to lower levels. These frozen columns were then exhumed by wind erosion, giving us a rare view of percolation columns. (Alaska) © Doug Fesler

WET SNOW

Most professionals make a hard distinction between dry snow and wet snow. Although dry snow and wet snow avalanches exist on a continuum from dry snow to damp snow to wet snow, it's only natural to draw a distinct line between them because they are such different beasts altogether. Wet avalanches are triggered differently, they move differently, they're formed by different conditions, you forecast for them differently, their deposits are different, and the scars they leave on the vegetation are different.

First, let's start with how wet avalanches form, fail, and fracture. Recall from Chapter 2, How Avalanches Work, the main difference between wet and dry avalanches is that dry avalanches are caused by *overloading the strength* of buried weak layers while wet avalanches are caused by *decreasing the strength* of buried weak layers.

To understand the difference between dry snow and wet snow, go to the store and buy a bunch of grapes. In this analogy, the grapes are the snow grains and the grapevines are the crystalline bonds between them. When water percolates through the snowpack, it dissolves the bonds between crystals—the more saturated the snow, the more it dissolves the bonds, thus, dramatically decreasing the strength of the snow. In our grape analogy, when you wash the grapes, imagine that the grapevines dissolve, leaving you with nothing but loose grapes.

Why doesn't all saturated snow instantly avalanche? Part of the reason comes from the bonding power of water itself. In the Lilliputian world of snow crystals, a tiny bead of water clinging between the grains serves as a weak "glue" because of the "surface tension" of water. In the grape example, you can see the tiny bead between the grapes. Surface tension means that water tends to cling to itself, kind of like gravity, which is why rain comes down as discrete drops instead of falling as a fog. The surface tension of water can hold wet snow together even after snow grain bonds dissolve, but it's only a very weak glue.

Try this experiment: Go to a slushy pond and grab a handful of completely wet, soggy snow, but don't make a snowball. The loose snow sticks together because of the force of the surface tension of water. Now squeeze the snow into a snowball. Squeezing together melts the snow where the grains touch each other, and releasing the pressure instantly freezes the snow at these points of contact. In other words, most wet snow is held together not only by tiny beads of water but also by snow grain bonds between the grains, which can dissolve very easily, which brings us to the final part of the experiment.

Put the snowball back in the puddle of slush, and notice that it doesn't take long for the water to dissolve the ice bonds between the grains. When you flood the caverns in the pore spaces between the grains, there's no more surface tension because there's no more surface. As a double whammy, the water quickly dissolves the bonds between the grains, and as a triple whammy, the ice particles have suddenly become buoyant—floating in the water like tiny icebergs. The take-home point here is that, when snow becomes saturated, it quickly loses strength and can no longer hold up the weight of overlying snow. A wet sluff or a wet slab avalanche fractures out and heads down the mountainside like a giant margarita.

Note on glide avalanches: Glide occurs when the entire snowpack slowly slides on the underlying ground—similar to a glacier—usually over the course of several days. These glide slabs can release catastrophically more or less at random. Paradoxically, they seem to show a slight preference for releasing during colder temperatures or freezing following a protracted period of melting. You should treat glide cracks like icefalls—don't linger beneath them.

What Causes the Snow to Become Saturated?

First, water must percolate through the snowpack. The water comes from either rain or melting of the snow surface (warm temperature or strong sun). When water percolates through the snowpack, it can either pool up above a less permeable crust or it encounters a fine-grained weak layer that acts like a sponge and soaks up the water. Fine-grained new snow and buried wind slabs especially tend to have a spongelike quality (Figure 5-16).

Rain on Snow

Rain on snow does not always cause avalanches. It depends on the preexisting snow. Fine-grained snow soaks up rain like a sponge, quickly loses strength, and causes almost instant avalanching. Old, larger-grained snow, especially snow that has already been rained on, is more permeable and the water tends to flow through it instead of pooling up. Older melt-freeze snow is especially permeable.

The first water that percolates through a cold, dry snowpack comes as quite a shock, which is the snowpack equivalent of when you take a cold shower. The first time cold, dry snow warms up it often produces "rollerballs," "pinwheels," or "snow snails" that roll down the slope, sometimes so big that they can bowl a person over. As melting continues, water begins to percolate through the snowpack. When it encounters ice layers or spongelike layers of finer-grained snow, the water pools up, which causes wet slab avalanches or wet loose snow avalanches. After some time, ranging from hours to days, the layers begin to dissolve,

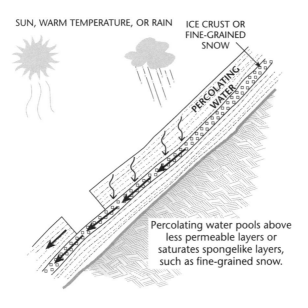

SUN, WARM TEMPERATURE, OR RAIN   ICE CRUST OR
FINE-GRAINED
SNOW

PERCOLATING WATER

Percolating water pools above
less permeable layers or
saturates spongelike layers,
such as fine-grained snow.

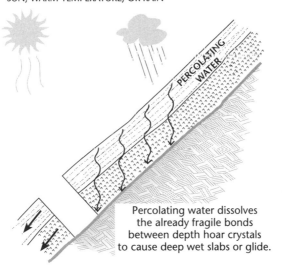

SUN, WARM TEMPERATURE, OR RAIN

PERCOLATING WATER

Percolating water dissolves
the already fragile bonds
between depth hoar crystals
to cause deep wet slabs or glide.

Figure 5-16. Two common examples of wet slab avalanches

snow grains grow in size, and drainage channels form so that water can more efficiently drain through the snow. The snow begins to stabilize. When rain- or sun-melted snow percolates through old melt-freeze snow that has *already* been subjected to percolating water the snowpack says, "No problem. Been there. Done that. I can handle it."

The bottom line: The first few hours of rain on new snow are the most dangerous. By the second day, most likely the snow will have stabilized or already slid.

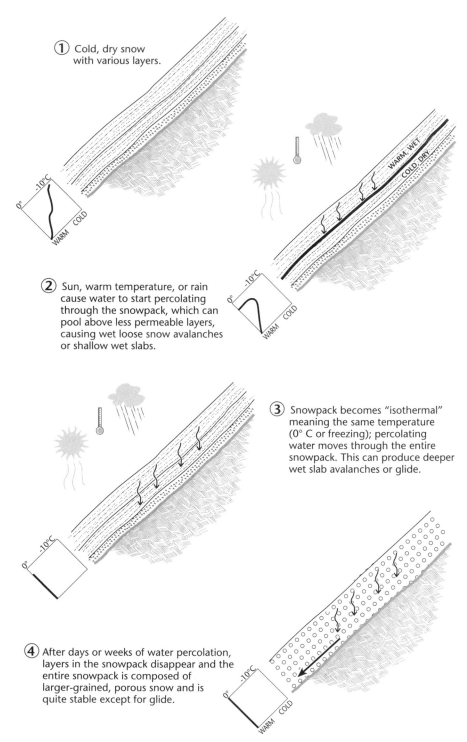

① Cold, dry snow with various layers.

② Sun, warm temperature, or rain cause water to start percolating through the snowpack, which can pool above less permeable layers, causing wet loose snow avalanches or shallow wet slabs.

③ Snowpack becomes "isothermal" meaning the same temperature (0° C or freezing); percolating water moves through the entire snowpack. This can produce deeper wet slab avalanches or glide.

④ After days or weeks of water percolation, layers in the snowpack disappear and the entire snowpack is composed of larger-grained, porous snow and is quite stable except for glide.

Figure 5-17. A typical life-cycle of a cold, dry, snowpack that transforms into a stable, summer snowpack

Sun on Snow

In continental and intermountain climates, rain on snow thankfully occurs very rarely, so most wet avalanches occur from heating by the sun, usually in spring.

A typical spring wet avalanche cycle often plays out like this: Warm sun on new snow makes the usual round of pinwheels and shallower wet snow sluffs off steep cliffs, especially off rocks that warm up in the heat of the sun. As the melting continues, the water reaches impermeable ice layers or saturates weak layers; then larger, wet loose snow avalanches, wet slab avalanches, or glide avalanches begin breaking out. This can take several hours to several days, depending on conditions. After several days of meltwater percolating through the snowpack, the snowpack stabilizes because of the aforementioned establishment of drainage channels; the development of more porous, large-grained snow; and the dissolving of ice layers (Figure 5-17). In temperate climates, the south-facing slopes are usually the first to slide in a springtime wet avalanche cycle and the first to stabilize afterward. As spring progresses, the east- and west-facing slopes go through the wet slide cycle, until late in the spring, the north faces finally warm up enough to go through a wet slide cycle. Sun-induced wet slide cycles tend to start on one side of the mountain, work their way around to either side, and finally end up on the cold side of the mountain over the course of a month or two each spring. (See also Chapter 6, Figure 6-12.)

WET SNOW SUMMARY

Also called: Melt-freeze, corn snow, clustered snow, mashed potatoes (when new snow gets wet).

Looks like: Shiny, forms damp or wet snowballs.

Formed by: Liquid water in the snowpack caused by rain, sun, or warm temperatures.

Distribution pattern: Below rain-snow line, on sunny slopes, on all slopes in warm temperatures.

Persistence: Usually short-lived, within a day or two. Longer for glide avalanches.

Forecasting considerations: What is the porosity of the snow? Percolation through new snow or fine-grained old snow causes avalanching, while percolation through snow that has already been subject to free water usually doesn't cause avalanching.

Best stability tests: Snowpit tests don't work very well since wet snow is so transient. Best to closely watch the weather and other clues (how far are you sinking in?).

chapter six

STABILITY

Nature does not reveal its secrets. It only responds to a method of questioning.

—Werner Heisenburg

In this chapter, we try to answer Atwater and LaChapelle's second question in their risk evaluation checklist—will the snow slide (see Chapter 7, Hazard Evaluation)? In other words, where do we sit in the continuum between stress and strength? Everything in the universe, including the snowpack, exists in a constant state of conflict between opposing forces. In the universe of the snow avalanche, the opposing forces are stress and strength. Everyone comes home healthy and happy when the snow is stronger than the stress exerted upon it. When stress nearly equals strength, people can trigger avalanches. When stress equals strength, avalanches occur naturally (Figure 6-1).

When we do stability analysis, our job is to figure out where the snowpack sits in the conflict between stress and strength. The bad news is that not only are we dealing with hundreds of different combinations of slabs and weak layers, we're dealing also with something that's invisible. The good news is that most of the time the invisible becomes visible through observations and tests; though only as long as you know how to ask the questions and listen for the answers.

Judging snow stability is a lot like playing a giant game of Concentration. You never, ever get all the pieces of the puzzle in front of you at one time—you have to fill in the missing pieces with your imagination. The more knowledge and skill you have, the easier the game becomes. In other words, stability evaluation means _integrating_ a lot of different pieces of information—putting the pieces of the puzzle together in an organized way. You should never make your entire stability evaluation based on just one piece of information, which would be like deciding to get married on the first date. Bad mistake. You need to shop around, do some homework, meet the in-laws, take a trip to a third world country, paddle a canoe together for a month. Then you'll have a lot better idea whether to invest the most valuable of all your possessions—your life.

Also, just like in the game of Concentration, research clearly shows that the most powerful way to make decisions about the stability of the snowpack is to continually reevaluate your belief as more information comes in. This is an iterative process. You get a new piece of information; you challenge your preexisting belief and decide whether your belief fits the facts; if it doesn't you change your belief, and you repeat this process over and over throughout the day. In this way, you force yourself to make evidence-based decisions and overcome "belief inertia" (see Chapter 10, The Human Factor). The power of snow stability assessment lies in the integration of the information and, even more important, the willingness to update your preconceived notions when the facts change, which is often the hardest part of all.

In this chapter, I describe a number of different, time-tested methods to answer the question: will the snow slide? Most of the methods don't take much time or work, but they do require awareness and discipline.

THREE CRITICAL SNOWPACK CHARACTERISTICS

For many years, avalanche professionals have used various snowpit tests to figure out the strength of the weak layer, yet many were still frustrated by their poor ability to predict human-triggered avalanches. In the 1980s, researchers Conway and Abrahamson, who published a snow stability index, found quite a bit of "spatial variability" in the strength of the weak layer, meaning that the strength varied significantly from place to place. The

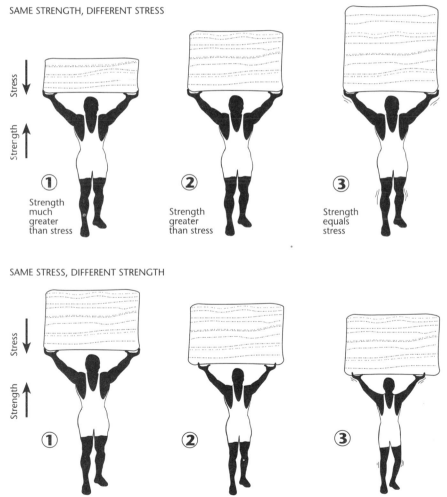

Figure 6-1. Strong snowpacks can support large amounts of stress, but weak snowpacks are easily overloaded by the same stress.

Luckily for us, when the snowpack is unstable there are many clues. Here, two feet of dense snow fell on very fragile depth hoar. The snow continually collapsed as we traveled on flat slopes. I was able to easily trigger this avalanche by jumping on the flat part of the ridge above the breakover. Then my wife and I could safely get onto the bed surface to examine the fracture, which is the best way to learn about avalanches.

weak layer often exhibited "deficit zones" where it was thought avalanche fractures
This matched experience, since it was common for people to trigger avalanches
tracked with earlier ski cuts that hadn't triggered avalanches. And ski patrollers often talk
about finding the "sweet spot" when triggering avalanches with explosives; while explosives
in other areas on the slope failed to trigger the avalanche. So avalanche workers began to
think of avalanche slopes as minefields. Snowpit tests and explosive tests were fine as long
as you did enough of them to find the critical trigger points.

Despite the poor predictive ability of strength measurements in snowpit tests, almost
all avalanche professionals agreed that digging snowpits and snowpit tests gave them a tremendous amount of information and most say they would feel completely naked without
regularly digging snowpits. So what gives? In quizzing all the frontline avalanche workers, it
became clear that they paid just as much attention to other snowpack qualities revealed by
the snowpit, namely shear quality and snowpack structure, although many of them did this
intuitively and had a hard time explaining why. In recent years, many researchers, including Karl Birkeland, Bruce Jamieson, and Juerg Schweizer, found that shear quality (how the
snow fails or fractures) and snowpack structure not only exhibit less spatial variability than
do tests of snow stability but they are actually better predictors of avalanche activity than
the traditional stress tests.

Finally, engineering consultant and avalanche educator Ian McCammon helped to
explain these properties to practitioners as standard engineering concepts using as an example how the U.S. built the Liberty Ships during World War II. Although the Liberty Ship

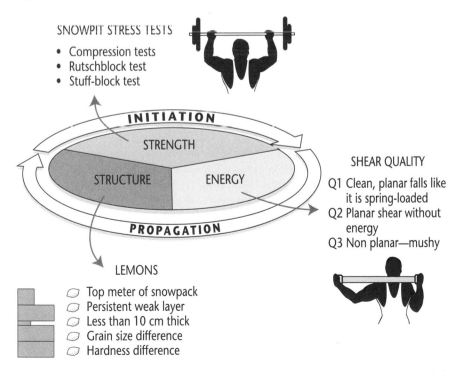

Figure 6-2 . Three critical snowpack characteristics. Strength controls initiation of a fracture while
energy and structure determine whether that fracture can propagate. Your stability analysis is not
complete unless you take all three into account. (From Ian McCammon)

engineers designed the ships with steel and welds many times stronger than the expected stresses, many ships unexpectedly broke in half, with disastrous consequences, due to special variability in weld strength. The solution? Although strength was the property that controlled initiation of a fracture, propagation of that fracture was equally important, and propagation was controlled by both the stored elastic energy in the system and the structure of the materials. When engineers controlled for all three properties—strength, shear, and structure—they could finally build large, welded steel ships that were very safe.

By focusing on only one leg, strength, of a three-legged stool, avalanche forecasters make the same mistake the Liberty Ship designers made. When used in combination, the three snowpack qualities of strength, shear, and structure represent an extremely powerful predictive tool. Fracture initiation is controlled by strength; fracture propagation is controlled by energy and structure (Figure 6-2). The latest thinking among avalanche researchers is that the traditional stress tests, such as the compression and rutschblock tests, are good indicators of strength (fracture initiation), while snowpack structure and tests for shear quality are indicators of the potential for fracture propagation.

In this chapter, I will describe tests for all three factors and present a method for integrating the results. I will also present tests that do this integration automatically.

This all sounds complicated but, luckily, we don't have to dig snowpits to get the quickest of answers. Despite all of our theories, the best sign of avalanches is still avalanches. Plus, there are a number of other simple observations and tests that are excellent indicators of levels of strength, energy, and structure in the snowpack. Therefore I have separated this chapter into three sections: observations, active tests, and snowpit tests, and we will start with the easiest and most reliable of the three—observations.

OBSERVATIONS

You can tell a lot about the stability of the snowpack by simply observing—being aware of your surroundings. Here are some of the important clues.

Recent Avalanches

The best sign of avalanches is avalanches. The absolutely best, bull's-eye, top-of-the-list clue that a particular slope is dangerous is if you see a recent avalanche on a similar slope. It's such an obvious clue that most people miss it. Time after time, we investigate avalanche accidents in which the victims walk right past a recent avalanche, then get caught on a slope exactly like it.

My wife will be more than happy to tell you I'm dangerous when I'm driving in avalanche terrain because I'm always rubbernecking in search of the most important clue of all. So we've agreed that either she drives while I watch or she watches while I drive. I keep binoculars in my glove box and I use them often. I also travel in the field with a lightweight monocular, which doubles as a microscope for snow crystals. For me, it's an essential tool and I use it for spotting fracture lines far more often than I use it for looking at crystals. Don't forget to look for small fractures on the road cuts as well as big fractures on the usual slopes.

Collapsing

Collapsing snow (sometimes mistakenly called settlement) is when the snowpack collapses under you with a loud WHOOMPH. (Actually, "whoomph" has been adopted as a

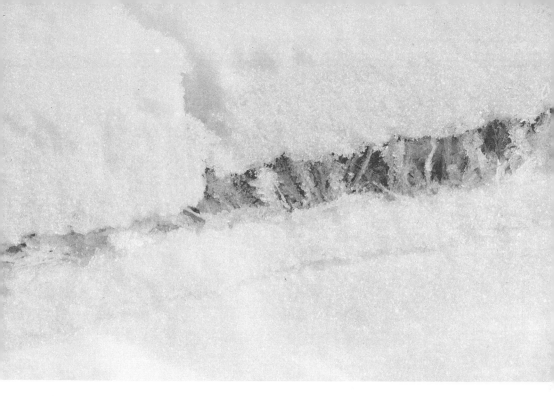

Collapsing snow is an obvious sign of instability. Here the left side of this surface hoar layer has collapsed. (Canada) © Bruce Jamieson

technical term to describe collapsing snow.) As Alaska avalanche expert Jill Fredston says, whoomphing is the sound of Mother Nature screaming in your ear that the snowpack is unstable and if you got a similar collapse on a slope that was steep enough to slide, it wouldn't hesitate to do so. Collapsing snow occurs when your weight is enough to catastrophically collapse a buried weak layer, which is most commonly depth hoar or surface hoar. You can easily bring avalanches down from above in collapsing snow conditions. When the weak layer is already holding up the weight of a significant amount of snow and just the wimpy addition of your weight can collapse all the snow in sometimes a very large area, most people intuitively recognize this for a very dangerous situation. Whoomphing almost always elicits a heart-thumping, wide-eyed look of terror. It's interesting that seeing the scar of a recent avalanche doesn't produce the same response, yet it's a much better indicator of danger.

Cracking

Cracking is another buzz from the avalanche rattlesnake. It means don't take another step; stop and take stock of your surroundings. Cracking snow means that all the ingredients for an avalanche are present: your weight is not only overloading a buried weak layer but the snowpack is also storing enough elastic energy to propagate a fracture. Once again, Mother Nature is hollering in your ear. Generally, the longer the crack, the worse it is. Stop. Poke around and see how well the slab is bonded to the underlying snow.

We see cracking usually in fresh wind slabs, but it can occur with most other kinds of instabilities. I like to take students to small test slopes that have been recently wind loaded, like a 10-foot-high road cut, and let them jump on the wind slabs to get a feel for them. It's

an important skill to develop—recognizing wind slabs, knowing the feel of them, knowing how they crack, recognizing that cracks mean danger. (See Chapter 3, Terrain Management, for details on how to recognize wind slabs.)

Hollow Sounds

Similar to cracking, hollow sounds usually mean that you are standing on a slab (the drum skin) and there's not much underneath. Wind slabs on top of soft snow usually sound hollow. Dig down and investigate or jump on test slopes to test the sensitivity of the wind slab. Unlike cracking, hollow sounds do not always indicate danger, but you should definitely put on your avalanche goggles.

Volunteer Stability Testers

The mountains are increasingly filled with volunteer stability testers—snowmobilers, skiers, climbers, snowboarders, snowshoers, hunters, hikers, helicopter skiers, film crews, and Boy Scout troops, as well as falling cornices, falling seracs, and sluffs. If these handy volunteer stability testers make it down without triggering an avalanche, then the chances are better that you will too—not guaranteed, remember—but tracks are almost always better than no tracks. Also, how old are the tracks? The older the better, since that much time has passed since the slope was loaded by new or windblown snow and tested by volunteers. (The snowpack has had time to adjust to its load.)

There are not too many rules of thumb in the avalanche business, but one of them is this: If Joe Gnarly Powder Pig wants first tracks, let him have it. I always try to go last—never first. I have a million excuses—eating my lunch, fiddling around with my equipment, or getting on the cell phone to "call in a report." This is your life we're talking about here. Never go first.

Avalanche Weather

Weather that creates dry slab avalanches includes rapid changes to the mechanical or thermal energy state of the snowpack, such as wind loading, loading of new snow, or rapid temperature rise of the slab. Also, larger changes and higher rates of change will create worse avalanche conditions. (See Chapter 2, How Avalanches Work, and Chapter 4, Weather, for more details.)

For wet avalanches, look for conditions that will produce free water in the snowpack. Rain, sun, or warm temperatures can make cold, dry snow damp and start pinwheels or rollerballs. With continued or stronger melting of surface snow, water percolates through the snowpack and can cause shallow wet sluffs and wet slabs. With continued percolation, deeper wet slabs can occur. (See Chapter 4, Weather, and Chapter 5, Snowpack, for more details.)

ACTIVE TESTS

As an avalanche professional, I spend most of my career never getting a good look at the one thing I want to see—the buried weak layer. Why? Because it's invisible, hidden beneath the perfect façade. So we have all kinds of artifice to make the stability of the snow reveal itself.

Opposite: Cracking snow is an obvious buzz from the avalanche rattlesnake. Don't take another step! Here, a 40-foot crack shoots out from my wife's skis. She was able to crack the fresh wind slab by safely standing on the flat of a ridge and watch the crack propagate below her. Luckily, the slope below is barely 30 degrees and is a good, small, test slope. (Wasatch Range, Utah)

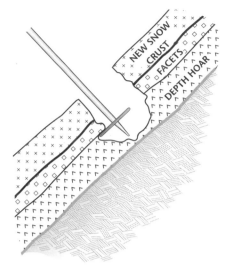

Figure 6-3. Ski pole probing

Rollerballs (also called "pinwheels" or "snow snails") occur when dry snow becomes wet for the first time. They are usually a precursor to more serious wet avalanche danger. It's time to get off steep slopes. (Wasatch Range, Utah)

Counting all the usual tests, the unusual ones, and their variations, I have heard of at least a hundred ways to test snow stability.

Here I'll list only those tests that fit my criteria. First, the test has to actually work. Second, in the winter I invariably have twice as many things to do as I can possibly get done, so the test has to be quick—5 minutes maximum. Third, it must be simple and lightweight. No gizmos. I like to go fast, cover a lot of ground, and do a lot of tests in a lot of places. Plus, snow stability tests can't resemble drudgery or no one will do them.

Ski Pole Test (1 to 5 seconds)

Push your ski pole or ice ax into the snow, feeling the unseen layers below. Most avalanche professionals do this hundreds of times per day. With hard snow, use the handle-end of the ski pole. Remember that you are dealing with the invisible here, so you are like a blind person. Use your white cane to "see" the unseen (Figure 6-3). Simply push your pole down and feel for weak layers buried in the snow. If you feel a lot of resistance in the surface layers and suddenly your pole drops through a layer that feels like mostly air, this usually means that a slab overlies a layer of faceted snow, which is an especially dangerous combination. When you feel this, it's time to dig down and investigate further. Remember that this test only gives you a general feel for snowpack layering. It misses thin layers or subtle weak layers, such as surface hoar.

When riding a snowmobile you can often feel the same thing by paying attention to the track bogging down or punching through surface layers into weaker layers below. Realize, though, that it will not be nearly as sensitive or reliable as stopping and feeling with your hands.

Advantages
- You can perform hundreds of tests per day.
- Works well with depth hoar and faceted snow, especially in shallow snowpacks.
- Works well for density inversions within the new snow.

Disadvantages
- Doesn't detect surface hoar well because surface hoar is usually quite thin.
- Doesn't work well for deeper weak layers, thin layers, or weak interfaces.
- Snowmobilers and snowboarders don't carry ski poles, but you can as you travel feel the layers with your feet or the snowmobile, though with less sensitivity.

Hand Shear Test (also called Armpit Test) (5 to 20 seconds)

After a storm, I will do this dozens of times as I'm traveling along. Dig out a small hole with your hand, and then on the uphill side, saw out a small square of snow with either your hand or the handle-end of a ski pole. Pull to see how well the surface slab is bonded to the underlying snow.

Advantages
- You can perform dozens of tests per day.
- Works well with new snow instabilities.
- Works well with shallow weak layers.

Disadvantage
- Only good for shallow weak layers.

Stepping Above the Track (5 to 20 seconds)

When following a diagonal or horizontal track, travel above the trail and try to knock some surface snow onto the trail below. Or kick the snow at the apex of each switchback and look for little slabs that pop out between the tracks. If the lower track penetrates through the slab, it can also be a quick way to test the bridging ability of the slab. You can also do this on a snowmobile.

Advantage
- You can perform dozens of tests per day.

Disadvantages
- Only works on shallow weak layers.
- Not as effective with snowmobiles.

A quick test of surface layers: Cut out a small block and tug on it. (Wasatch Range, Utah)

Test slopes—my favorite test: Don't pass by these sources of valuable information. By jumping on small, safe slopes, you can get an idea of whether the big slopes are likely to kill you.

Slope Cuts (also called Ski Cuts) (5 to 20 seconds)

Ski cuts have been a standard technique among ski patrollers and helicopter ski guides for decades. But snowboarders and snowmobilers can do them as well, so instead I call them slope cuts. The theory is if you do trigger an avalanche, your momentum will help to carry you off the moving slab, which helps minimize the chances of getting caught. (See Chapter 8, Routefinding and Safe Travel Rituals, for more details.)

Advantages
- Quick.
- Good for soft, new snow with shallow weak layers.
- Snowmobilers, snowboarders, and skiers can do them.

Disadvantages
- Not very effective on hard slabs or deep weak layers. Dangerous if done improperly or without a belay rope on paths with bad consequences.
- Climbers and snowshoers can't do them.

Test Slopes (5 to 30 seconds)

This is my favorite backcountry test. Find a small, steep slope where the consequences of a slide are small, such as a road cut, or a small breakover in the slope. Then jump on the slope to see how it responds. If you get an avalanche on the test slope, what does that tell you about the big slope you were headed for with exactly the same steepness and aspect? A test slope is a gift from the avalanche gods. Don't ever pass a test slope without jumping on it.

Remember that even on small slopes, it's possible to get buried. Always have your partner watch from a safe spot.

Advantages
- Easy-to-interpret results.
- Relatively safe.
- Quick.
- Everyone can do them—snowmobilers, skiers, snowboarders, climbers, and snowshoers.

Disadvantages
- Dangerous if done on slopes with bad consequences.
- Not a good test of deep weak layers, especially ones overlain by hard slabs because of the compressive support from the bottom.
- Hard slabs are especially hard to trigger on small slopes and may not be representative of larger slopes.

Tilt Test (20 to 60 seconds)

This has long been a standard test for new snow instability at study plots, such as for highway avalanche forecasters, but I regularly use it in the backcountry as well. Simply cut out a square of new snow the same dimensions as the blade of your shovel. Slide the shovel blade under the block and pick it up. Tilt the shovel blade on edge progressively steeper and steeper while tapping lightly on the bottom of the shovel until the snow fails. Hold the bottom of the column with your hand so that the column doesn't just slide off the shovel. The steeper the tilt, the more stable the snow. You can measure the angle with an inclinometer if you want an exact number.

Advantage
- Works well with new snow instabilities.

Disadvantage
- Doesn't work as well for deeper weak layers and depth hoar.

Tilt test: Take a sample of snow and tilt the shovel steeper and steeper while tapping on the bottom until it shears off. (Wasatch Range, Utah) © Howie Garber/Wanderlust Images

Trundling a cornice down the slope is an excellent stability test. 1) make sure no one is below, 2) wear a belay rope, 3) cut something that weighs more than you (refrigerator size or larger), 4) cut on a steep angle. You can use a snow saw mounted on the end of a ski pole, the other end of your belay rope, or a parachute cord with knots tied every foot or so.

Cornice Test (5 seconds to 5 minutes)

This is a test for advanced users only. As you can well imagine, cornice tests can be very dangerous if done improperly. But they have been standard techniques for decades among ski patrollers, helicopter ski guides, and especially climbers. Cornices are the "bombs of the backcountry." First, do this test *only* if you are certain that no one is below you—very important. It is often very hard to see the entire slope below you while standing at the top so you should look at the slope from another angle or use a spotter. Imagine how you will feel if you are responsible for someone's death or injury. To my knowledge, no one has been sued yet for triggering an avalanche on top of someone else, but it's only a matter of time.

Find a cornice that weighs significantly more than a person and knock it down the slope. A cornice the size of a refrigerator or a small car bouncing down a slope provides an excellent stability test. The smaller the cornice, the less effective the test. Look for small, fresh cornices, not the large, old hard ones. You can kick the cornice, shovel it, or best of all, cut it with a snow saw mounted on the end of a ski pole. With larger cornices you can use either your belay rope or a parachute cord with knots tied in it every foot or so, which acts like teeth on a saw. Throw the cord over the cornice or push it over the edge with an avalanche probe. You can saw off a fairly large cornice in under 5 minutes. Make sure your cut with the snow saw or cord is at least 40 degrees off the vertical plane. If you make your cut too flat, you will do a lot of huffing and puffing for nothing. The cornice will just sit there. This is also a great way to create a safe descent route during very unstable conditions. In other words, make an avalanche and use the slide path to descend. (See Chapter 8, Routefinding and Safe Travel Rituals, for more discussion on cornices and cornice-triggering techniques.)

Caveat: It doesn't take much imagination to see that knocking cornices down avalanche paths can be very dangerous. *Always* use a belay rope on slopes with bad consequences and practice your cornice techniques on safe slopes until you get the techniques worked out. Cornices have a nasty habit of breaking farther back than you think they should. And finally, once again, do this test only if you can be certain no one is below you.

Advantages
- Probably the best test of a slope; it's similar to using explosives.
- Easy to interpret, as long as the cornice is large enough.

Disadvantages
- Very dangerous if done improperly.
- Small cornices don't stress the slope enough for a reliable test.
- Cornices aren't always available.

SNOWPIT TESTS

Most of the time we can gather enough information about the snowpack without ever taking out the dreaded shovel. But sometimes the only way to get good information about deeper weak layers is to grease up the elbows and do some honest work. I always dig at least one snowpit in a representative location to get the general picture of what's going on in the snowpack.

If you are going to get serious about making standardized tests and observations, you should own a copy of the "Bible" for observations, what has become known as SWAG (*Snow, Weather and Avalanches: Observational Guidelines for Avalanche Programs in the United*

Stop along your route on a convenient slope to dig a snowpit before you get to the dangerous slopes. (Ron Johnson of the Gallatin National Forest Avalanche Center, Montana) © Lance Reik

States, 2004) published by the American Avalanche Association. In Canada, you should own a copy of OGRS (*Observation Guidelines and Recording Standards, 2002)* published by the Canadian Avalanche Association. These publications include descriptions of standardized tests and how to notate them using abbreviations.

Where to Dig a Snowpit

Where to dig a snowpit is probably more important than how to dig one. Choosing a representative location is an art, and art is difficult to describe, but here are some pointers.

Dig your pit on a slope most representative of the slope you are interested in but without putting yourself in danger. Often you can find a small test slope—one that won't kill you if it does slide. Or you can work your way into progressively more dangerous terrain. For instance, if a snowpit on safe terrain gives you a green light, then it gives you the confidence to dig another one on more dangerous terrain. Green light there? Then move on to even more dangerous terrain, and so on. *Never dive into the middle of a dangerous avalanche path without first gathering lots of additional data about the stability of the slope.*

Don't dig a snowpit along ridgelines where the wind has affected the snow—a common mistake. Although sometimes the crown face of an avalanche may break right up to the ridge, the place where we most often trigger avalanches is down off the ridge. Avoid areas of densely spaced trees or under a single tree because conditions are often quite different than on open slopes. Trees tend to shed their loads of snow onto the snow directly below them, thereby compacting that snow. Avoid compression zones at the bottom of the slope. Avoid places where people have compacted the snow.

Use an avalanche probe to find a representative place with at least average depth. Don't dig in deep areas but in areas of average or below-average depths, because shallow areas are often trigger points. Poking around with a probe can save time from digging in stupid places like on top of a rock or tree or where a previous party had their lunch.

Many cagey avalanche professionals dig their snowpits above a tree so they can grab it if the slope does slide. Better yet, tie a belay rope onto that tree and dig below the tree, but of course well away from the tree. People don't tend to ski, snowboard, or snowmobile just below trees. I often carry a lightweight belay rope and use it on a regular basis. Most important, dig lots of snowpits in lots of different areas because the snow can vary quite a bit from place to place. Look for the *pattern* of instability.

Probably the best place to do snow profiles is on the flank wall of a recent avalanche. You get to see the beast up close and personal. If you dig in along the fracture line, you can see the exact layer that fractured just minutes, hours, or days ago. Don't pass up these opportunities. Also, with some exceptions, it's usually safe to go into an avalanche path after it has slid. (See Chapter 9, Rescue, on how to judge.)

Caveat: Remember that you won't find the *exact* conditions that caused the avalanche because much of the time, all the unstable snow is now in the debris pile. The stable snow tends to get left behind. In my experience, you will almost always find more stable conditions in the crown and the flank wall than you would expect. I've found that flank walls give much more representative information than crown faces. You can probably find the most representative conditions in the next avalanche path over—the one with the same aspect and elevation as the one that just slid—and yes, that should set off alarm bells in your head because that slope is extremely dangerous. Good news—bad news.

Bottom line: *Look for neutral, open areas at mid-slope without wind effects.* Better yet, dig on the flank wall of a recent avalanche.

How to Dig a Snowpit

Contrary to popular belief, snowpits don't have to take a lot of time. My philosophy is that if your feet get cold, you're doing something wrong; I almost never spend more than 10 minutes in a snowpit. Since snow can sometimes vary quite a bit from place to place, I would much rather dig several quick pits and average the results than spend 30 minutes in one pit documenting every detail. We're trying to get the *big picture* here. Dig one pit, and then move on to another location. Often I dig the hole without even taking off my skis or board, but it usually helps to at least take off the uphill ski or take one foot out of the board binding.

First, the shoveling: Get down on one knee when you shovel. It's easier on your back. Make the hole wide—about the width of a ski length. Don't dig a vertical hole like you're digging to China, but instead shovel out the downhill side so you have room to work, which actually takes less time in the long run. Just slide the chunks of snow downhill on your shovel without lifting it. This takes only a couple of minutes if you're on a steep slope (where you should be) and in soft snow.

After digging the snowpit, which gives you a lot of information in itself, I like to just dive in and *feel* with my hands. Some people like to use a paintbrush to gently brush the wall to reveal the layers, but I'm a kinesthetic person and I like to feel it with my hands along the layers, preferably on the side wall so you don't ruin the uphill wall. Just like an eroded rock outcropping, notice how the weak layers crumble away while the strong layers remain sticking out. Then stand back and *see* the layers. Remember that this is not just an academic exercise. This is your life we're talking about here. Just looking and thinking will not work.

Crawl around, shove your arms into the weak layers. Feel it, see it, chew on it, smell it—live it. Use as many pathways as possible—*be* the snowpack. Dust yourself off (if you're not getting snow on you, you're doing something wrong) and carefully smooth the upper snowpit wall in preparation for the various stress tests you will perform. Make sure it's smooth and vertical. This is important because only good tests will give you good answers. Whatever tests you do, they must be done exactly the same each time so that you can accurately compare one snowpack to another.

> ## HOT TIP!
> *When I'm traveling with a partner, I prefer to split up and each person dig their pit in separate locations instead of collaborating on one pit. The advantage is that you get information from two locations (more data points). Two people in one snowpit tend to just get in each other's way anyway, kind of like two cooks in a kitchen.*

How Deep to Dig

Since it's difficult for humans to trigger avalanches more than about 1 meter (3 feet) deep (unless they are triggered from a shallower spot), I seldom dig snowpits deeper than about 4 feet unless I know that a deeper weak layer may cause problems. Each situation is a little different and in time you will get a feel for it. In general, keep your snowpits less than 1.5 meters deep (4 feet) unless you know of a good reason to go deeper.

Some Final Details

For almost all of these snowpit tests you need to be on a slope of at least 30 degrees in steepness. The optimum steepness is 38 degrees, since that's the most dangerous slope steepness for slab avalanches. Finally, using a snow saw makes all these tests go much faster. I suppose you could get by without a snow saw, and rely on using the handle end of a ski pole or the edge of your ski, but you will quickly learn to hate digging snowpits. Buy a snow saw and use it often.

The times listed for these snowpit tests don't include the time of digging the hole. Most snowpits dug in reasonably soft snow, with a good shovel, and on a steep slope take only a couple of minutes. Hard snow may take twice that time. If you live in a place with perpetually very hard snow you should think about moving to a nicer climate, but not to Utah, please.

Finally, you can find video tutorials for many of these tests on our website, www. utahavalanchecenter.org.

Extended Column Test (1 to 2 minutes)

This is a wonderful, ingeniously-simple new test invented by Ron Simenhois, an Israeli physicist who currently spends his winters ski patrolling in the U.S. and his summers patrolling in New Zealand. He and Karl Birkeland of the Forest Service National Avalanche Center recently published their work on this test. It was inspired by Ian McCammon and others who illuminated the importance of both initiation and propagation in avalanche fractures. As I discussed near the beginning of this chapter, many of these snowpits tests only indicate the propensity of the snowpack to initiate a fracture and they are less effective at addressing the propagation potential of the fracture, which recent research indicates is

Cutting the column for an extended column test two different ways, with a cord running around a probe and with a snow saw on the end of a ski pole. For an extended column test, you isolate a 30 cm x 1 m column from the back snowpit wall so it runs horizontally across the slope. For a propagation saw test, you cut using the same technique with the same dimensions, but isolate a column from the side wall of the snowpit so the column runs vertically up the hill.

even more important. The extended column tests for both initiation and propagation of a fracture. As of this writing, the test has only been used for a couple of years, but the results seem very promising and the test is quickly gaining popularity.

On the uphill wall of the snowpit, isolate a column of snow about 30 centimeters deep by 1 meter wide (1 foot by 3 feet). You can either use a snow saw mounted on a ski pole or saw with a cord and probe pole. (See photo.) On one end of the column, place your shovel on top, just like a compression test as described later in this chapter, and start tapping harder and harder until you get a fracture. Now comes the important part: when you get fracture initiation, watch carefully to see if the fracture propagates all the way across the column. The statistics indicate that if the column both initiates and propagates a fracture at the same time, it is an excellent indicator of instability regardless of how hard you have to tap on the column to initiate the fracture. In this way, it's an either/or test. Either it propagates a fracture or it doesn't. You don't have to interpret any shades of grey. Results from two seasons of field testing indicate that it only has about a 3 percent false stable rate compared to around 10 percent for other tests. ("False stable" means that the test indicates that the slope is stable, yet the slope is actually unstable.)

Advantages
- Preliminary results suggest that it may be much more effective at predicting human-triggered potential than other tests.
- Tests for both initiation and propagation potential.
- Easy to interpret.
- Semi-quantifiable, meaning that different testers should be able to repeat the test with the same results.
- Works for any type of weak layer, especially effective with faceted snow or surface hoar.
- Seems to work well on flat slopes especially with faceted snow as the weak layer.

Disadvantage
- Takes a little longer than a compression test since it is larger.

Propagation Saw Test (1 to 2 minutes)
This is very similar to the extended column test and it is currently being developed and evaluated in Canada. It's meant to be done after the compression test so that you have some sense of where the snowpack's weak layer lives. Isolate a column the same size as the extended column test (1 foot by 3 feet) except you cut the column out of the side wall of the pit, running vertically up the hill instead of horizontally across the slope like the extended column test. Again, you can cut with a snow saw on a ski pole or with a cord running around a proble pole. Next, use your snow saw to cut upslope along the snow's weak layer from the downhill side of the column until you get a propagation along the weak layer. It's easier to cut with the dull side of the snow saw because it's easier to stay in the weak layer instead of wandering around. Similar to the extended column test, keep track of whether a fracture propagates. If a fracture propagates through the entire column by cutting less than 50 percent of the weak layer then it indicates unstable conditions. The distance you need to cut does not seem important. In the preliminary results from the past two seasons of testing, the propagation test seems to differentiate very well between stable and unstable slopes. The advantages and disadvantages are the same as the extended column test.

Compression Test (1 to 2 minutes)

This test and its cousin, the stuff-block test, have become standard fare in most parts of the world for testing the strength of the weak layer. It's quick, easy to interpret, and works for most kinds of weak layers. However, it does not test for propagation potential of the fracture unless you combine it with the shear quality of the fracture (see "Shear Quality," below) and the snowpack structure (see "Snowpack Structure," below). You should only use the results of this test in combination with shear quality and snowpack structure as described in the introduction.

Start by isolating a column about the same size as the blade of your shovel, in other words, about 30 by 30 centimeters (1 foot by 1 foot). Be sure to completely isolate the column. Take the blade of your shovel and lay it flat on top. Now tap on the shovel blade with your hand, tapping progressively harder until the column fails. Start with 10 taps by articulating from your wrist, then 10 more taps by articulating from your elbow,

Compression test or tap test. Tap 10 times by articulating from the wrist, 10 from the elbow, and 10 from the shoulder. (Wasatch Range, Utah)

then 10 more from your shoulder using the full weight of your arm. Don't push your arm into the snow, but let it fall with its own weight. In this way, the test is somewhat quantifiable. In other words, it doesn't depend on "feel" or the opinion of the tester, but it has a reproducible number, and can easily be communicated to others. For instance, perhaps the column failed on an easy tap from the elbow, or it failed on a moderate tap from the elbow or a hard tap from the shoulder. It's also common to rank with a number from 1 to 30. Since snow stability is dependent on the size of the trigger required to make it fail, this test is especially easy to interpret. **Note:** If you have an unusually light arm or an unusually heavy one, you need to take that into account when comparing to the table below or to other people's test results. You can describe these tests as easy, medium, or hard. They don't yield a good stability evaluation unless you combine them with shear quality and snow structure and integrate the results with all your other tests and observations.

TABLE 6-1	
Results	*What It Means*
Breaks when articulating from the wrist (1–10 taps)	Easy
Breaks when articulating from the elbow (11–20 taps)	Medium
Breaks when articulating from the shoulder (21–30 taps)	Hard

Stuff-Block Test (Variation on the Compression Test)

Karl Birkeland and Ron Johnson of the Gallatin National Forest Avalanche Center in Bozeman, Montana, have developed an excellent test they call the stuff-block test, which is a more quantifiable version of the compression test. After isolating the column, take a stuff sack, fill it with 4.5 kg (10 pounds) of snow (weigh it with a lightweight fishing scale), place the shovel blade on top of the column, and drop the stuff sack onto the column from progressively greater heights until the column fails. Attach a string on the bottom of the stuff sack marked in 10 cm increments to take the guesswork out of the drop heights. This version is similar to the compression test. Table 6-2 ranks the snow danger.

Stuff-block test. Fill the stuff sack with 10 pounds of snow and drop it from a progressively higher point until the column fails. (Wasatch Range) Photo courtesy of the U.S. Forest Service

TABLE 6-2	
Results	*What It Means*
Breaks with drop from 20 cm or less	Easy
Breaks with drop from 20 to 40 cm	Medium
Breaks with drop from over 40 cm	Hard

Advantages for Compression Test and Stuff-Block Tests
- Quick.
- Easy to interpret.
- Semi-quantifiable.
- Works for any type of weak layer, especially effective with faceted snow or surface hoar.
- Works well for non-skiers since you don't need skis.
- When combined with shear quality and snowpack structure, these are very powerful tools.

Disadvantages of Compression Test and Stuff-Block Tests
- Small sample size. You need to do several tests for consistent results.
- Don't work as well on flat slopes.
- Do test for propagation potential unless combined with shear quality and snowpack structure.

Rutschblock Test (3 to 5 minutes)
The rutschblock (pronounced ROOTCH block) test has been a standard snowpit test of choice for avalanche professionals for many years but it seems to be losing in popularity to the compression and extended column tests because it takes longer. The main advantage to the rutschblock is that it uses a larger sample size, which tends to smooth out any local variations in the snow. Second, the test is semi-quantifiable and easy to interpret. Finally, it duplicates the kind of shock to the snowpack when a skier or snowboarder crosses the slope.

First, on a slope of at least 30 degrees, completely isolate a block of snow about a ski length across, and a ski-pole length up the slope (2 meters wide by 1.5 meters upslope). Remember to completely isolate the block, including cutting out the back. If you don't cut the back, it's not a rutschblock test. (See discussion below.)

If you use a snow saw mounted on the end of a ski pole, you can usually cut the block in a minute or two. If you're with a partner, you can also insert two probe poles at the upper corners and run a parachute cord or a snowpit cable (made by some manufacturers) around the outsides of the probes. Two people can grab each end of the cord and saw out the block. It goes pretty quickly but you need two people. You can also use the tail of a ski to saw out the block, but it takes longer. Finally, you can shovel out the block, but this takes a very long time, especially in hard snow. I personally think cutting with a cord works best, but for a single person, the snow saw mounted on a ski pole is the best option.

Next, simply step onto the upper third of the block while wearing your skis or snowboard and jump progressively harder until the block fails. Pay special attention to how the

block fails (shear quality). You should only pay attention to fractures in which the whole block fails at once on a clean plane.

Most people rank the test on a scale of one through seven (Table 6-3). Quality 2 or 3 shears are generally not significant but quality 1 shears are very significant—the clean shears that pop out like they are spring-loaded.

TABLE 6-3	
Number	What Happens
1	Fails while isolating the block
2	Fails while stepping onto the block
3	Fails with an easy weighing
4	Fails with one easy jump
5	Fails with one hard jump
6	Fails with several hard jumps
7	Doesn't fail

Advantages
- Large sample size makes the test more reliable.
- Duplicates what happens with a person on the slope.
- Easy to interpret.
- Semi-quantifiable.
- When combined with shear quality and snowpack structure, it's a very powerful tool.

Disadvantages
- Takes more time, but with a cord or snow saw not much more time.
- Climbers and snowmobilers have to jump on the block on foot, which though it skews the results, can still be very useful.

Note on Cutting the Back of the Block
Some people don't cut out the back of a rutschblock and they call it a "three-sided rutschblock." Some people feel that it's more realistic to not cut out the back because, after all, the slab properties are just as much a part of the avalanche equation as the characteristics of the weak layer. Hence, testing the strength of the slab and the weak layer at the same time better duplicates how the weight of a person may trigger an avalanche.

Keep in mind that if you don't cut the back, you are testing the strength of both the slab and the weak layer at the same time—mixing apples and oranges, as it were. If you don't cut out the back, the results will often be dramatically different than those with a rutschblock test. The stronger the slab, the more difference between tests. This makes the test harder to interpret.

My main pet peeve with not cutting the back is that you can't call it a rutschblock, because it's not. If you don't cut out the back, call it another name. Name it after your

Opposite: Rutschblock test. Isolate a column a ski length across and a pole length uphill. Jump on it progressively harder until it fails. (Wasatch Range, Utah)

dog or something, but don't call it a rutschblock, because that causes no end of confusion when you try to communicate your results to others. Sharing avalanche information is an extremely powerful tool but it only works when everyone uses standardized tests and nomenclature. (You can also reference the *Snow, Weather, and Avalanche Guidelines* issued by the American Avalanche Association, downloadable for free at www.americanavalancheassociation.org.)

Shovel Shear Test (30 seconds to 1 minute)

The good-old shovel shear test has been taught in almost every avalanche class since the dawn of time and its popularity has waxed and waned through the years. Nevertheless, I still do it for two reasons: First, if you need to remove a block of snow to perform other tests, then you might as well get some information from it. Second, it's a good way to identify weak layers in the snowpack. You should not, however, use the shovel shear test to determine the stability of the snowpack or the shear quality. Other tests are much more reliable. The shovel shear test usually leads you to believe that the snowpack is much more unstable and sensitive than it actually is. As one prominent Canadian avalanche forecaster told me once, "The shovel shear test is a trendy, little, easy test that has ruined more good skiing than anything else we have ever taught students."

Shovel shear test. A good test for identifying weak layers but a poor test for stability evaluation. (Wasatch Range, Utah)

Figure 6-4. Shovel shear test

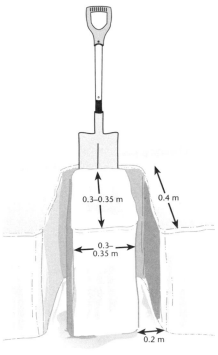

Make vertical cuts with your snow saw in the snowpit wall about the same distance apart as the width of your shovel and 1 to 1.5 meters deep. Then turn your snow saw vertically and cut behind the column about 30 to 60 centimeters (1 to 2 feet) down. Do *not* cut the whole column. Now insert your shovel behind the column and pull it toward you until it fails (Figure 6-4). Don't lever on the shovel, but pull it straight toward you. Then remove the block and cut another 30 to 60 centimeters (1 to 2 feet) down, and pull again, and so on, until you reach the bottom of the column. Don't pay too much attention to how easily the blocks pull out or the shear quality but for all the clean shears, turn each block upside down to see what weak layer was involved.

Advantages
- Works on a flat slope.
- Good test for identifying weak layers, especially surface hoar.
- Anyone can do it—snowmobilers, climbers, skiers, snowboarders, and snowshoers.

Disadvantages
- Hard to interpret—do not use for stability evaluation
- Subjective.
- Small sample size.
- Snow seems less stable than it actually is.

SUMMARY OF STABILITY TESTS

Best Active Test for Deep Slab Instability
   1. Cornice test (as long as it's a large cornice)

Best Active Tests for New Snow Instabilities (in order of reliability)
   1. Cornice test
   2. Test slopes
   3. Slope cuts (ski cuts)
   4. Hand shear test
   5. Ski pole test

Best Snowpit Tests for Deep Slab Instabilities
   No snowpit test works very well for deep slab instabilities. Better to use observtions, cornices, or explosives. But extended column test, propagation saw test, and rutschblock test are often useful.

Shear Quality
All of the above snowpit tests indicate the strength of the weak layer, which is a good indicator of whether a fracture can be initiated. But, unfortunately, with the exception of the extended column and propagation saw tests, these tests do a poor job of addressing the other two legs of the stool—energy and structure—which determine whether the fracture will propagate. Researchers believe that shear quality does a good job of determining energy in the snowpack.

So what do we mean when we talk about energy or shear quality? High quality shears break on a clean, planar surface and pop right out with "energy" like they're spring-loaded. Canadians

Snowpack structure and shear quality are more important than snow strength, but it's important to integrate all three pieces of information.

describe them as "pops and drops," meaning they pop out with energy or they collapse. It's difficult to describe, but you'll know it when you see it. Lower quality shears are not planar and they kind of mush out like a limp rubber band. It's really just that simple. When you do your favorite snowpit tests, simply pay close attention to shear quality.

Recent research has clearly shown the importance of shear quality; in fact, shear quality is more important than strength in predicting human-triggered potential. Finally, shear quality exhibits less spatial variability than strength, making it a more reliable indicator. Shear quality is a big deal. Ignore it at your own peril.

TABLE 6-4	
Shear Characteristics	*Shear Rating*
Breaks on a clean, smooth break like it's spring-loaded	Q1
Breaks on a smooth plane, but not like it's spring-loaded	Q2
Breaks on a rough or broken plane	Q3

SNOWPACK STRUCTURE

The above tests indicate two out of the three important factors for human-triggered avalanches—strength and energy. The final, third leg of the stool is snowpack structure. In a study published in 2002, avalanche researchers Ian McCammon and Juerg Schweizer studied the database of human-triggered avalanches from Switzerland and Canada and identified five critical characteristics of weak layers that produced human-triggered avalanches. McCammon refers to these critical factors as "lemons" and the term has caught on, though you will sometimes hear them referred to as "yellow flags" as well. For instance, someone might say that the weak layer had four lemons, meaning that it had four out of the five critical characteristics. Below are the weak layer characteristics common in human-triggered avalanches:

1) Persistent grain type (depth hoar, faceted snow or surface hoar)
2) Grain size difference between weak layer and surrounding layers greater than 1 mm
3) Hardness difference between weak layer and surrounding layers greater than 1 step
4) Less than 10 cm thick
5) In the top meter of the snowpack

INTEGRATING THE SNOWPIT INFORMATION

Next, we have to integrate the three types of information gathered in our snowpit: strength, shear quality, and structure. It's extremely important to use all three. Don't get lazy here or skimp because we would be back to getting married on the first date. Schweizer, McCammon, and Jamieson in a 2006 study determined the critical criteria for these three categories, which I list below:

CRITICAL CRITERIA FOR HUMAN-TRIGGERED AVALANCHES	
Critical Range	
Shear Quality	Quality 1 shear. Whole-block failure on rutschblock.
Propagation on extended column test or propagation saw test	
Strength of Weak Layer	Rutschblock 3 or less. Compression test 15 or less. Stuff block 20 cm or less.
Snowpack Structure	4 to 5 lemons

THE BOTTOM LINE	
Red Light	2-3 predictors in critical range, especially shear quality and structure
Yellow Light	One predictor in critical range
Green Light	No predictors in critical range

A common "false positive" scenario that fools experienced avalanche people is getting a green light on strength tests but failing to notice that shear quality and snowpack structure are both in their critical range. We often hear stories of people digging a snowpit and pronouncing the slope safe, only to trigger an avalanche. In these cases, they have usually considered strength alone before heading downslope. The bottom line is that you *must* pay attention to all three of the critical snowpack characteristics.

HOW TO GRAPH A SNOW PROFILE

If you're going to get serious about avalanches, sooner or later you'll want to document what you find in the snowpack. You'll want to keep a field notebook and track changes over time—to have some systematic way to compare what you find in the snowpack with avalanche activity.

Most people like to use a small waterproof field notebook and a pencil. Some people like to write data down in columns and later enter the data into a snowpit graphing computer program or into a PDA at the snowpit site. (See Bibliography for a list of software.) Although computers work well for sharing data with others in a computer network, it's an unnecessary step if you do snow profiles only for your own edification. Avalanches are something you just have to get a *feel* for and I think that analog information works best for that. I would suggest that you start out by simply sketching a graph of the snowpack in a field notebook.

First, as described before ("How to Dig a Snowpit"), run your gloved hands along the layers and get a nice tactile feel for the way weak layers easily crumble away while the strong layers remain sticking out. Then stand back and sketch the layers in your pit book.

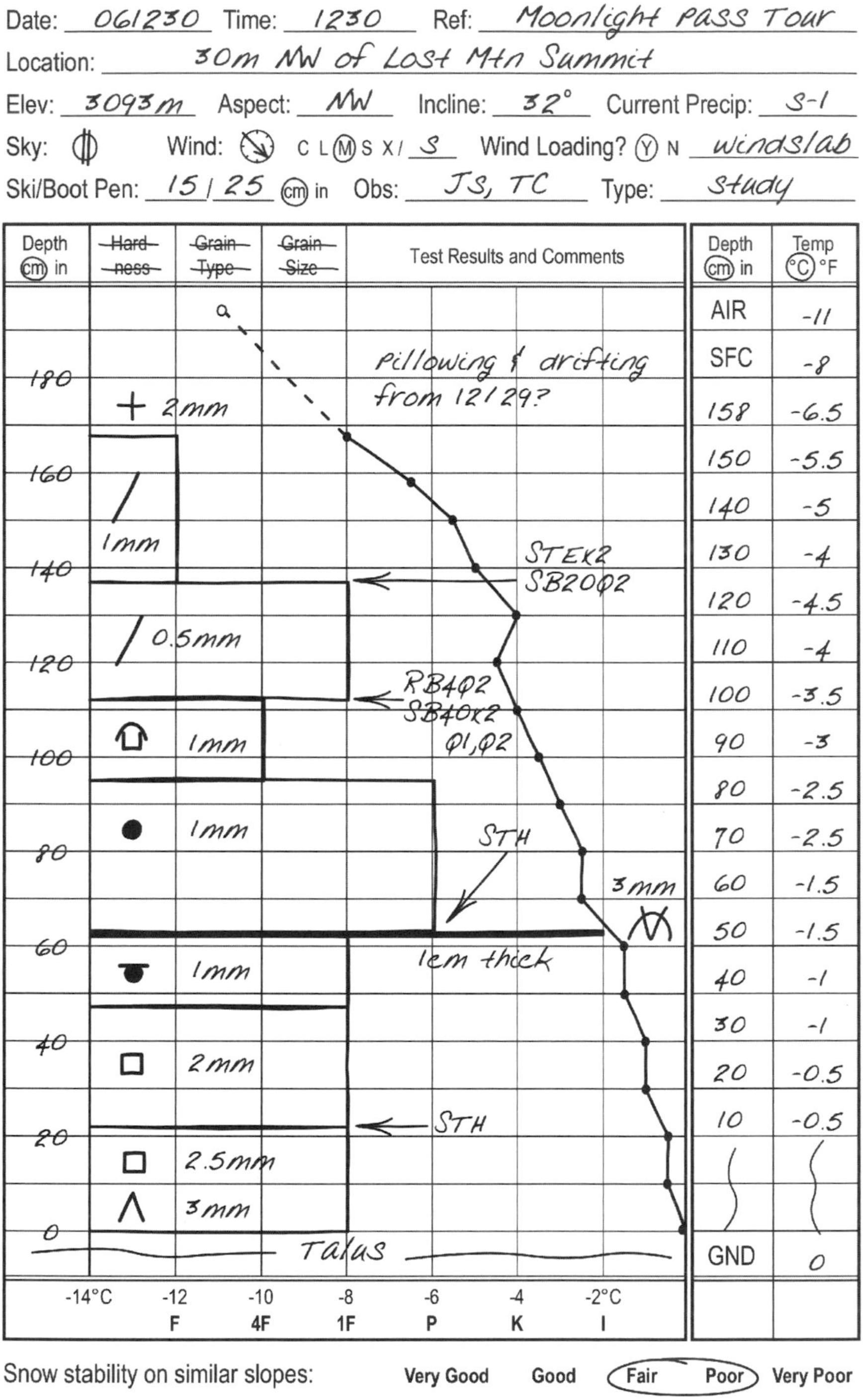

Date: **06/23 0** Time: **1230** Ref: **Moonlight Pass Tour**

Location: **30m NW of Lost Mtn Summit**

Elev: **3093m** Aspect: **NW** Incline: **32°** Current Precip: **S-1**

Sky: Ⓧ Wind: Ⓧ C L Ⓜ S X / **S** Wind Loading? Ⓨ N **windslab**

Ski/Boot Pen: **15 / 25** Ⓒ in Obs: **JS, TC** Type: **study**

Depth (cm) in	Hardness	Grain Type	Grain Size	Test Results and Comments	Depth (cm) in	Temp (°C) °F
		a			AIR	-11
180				Pillowing & drifting from 12/29?	SFC	-8
	+ 2mm				158	-6.5
160					150	-5.5
	/				140	-5
	1mm			STEK2	130	-4
140				SB20Q2	120	-4.5
120	/ 0.5mm				110	-4
				RB4Q2	100	-3.5
	⬆ 1mm			SB40x2 Q1,Q2	90	-3
100					80	-2.5
80	● 1mm			STH	70	-2.5
				3mm	60	-1.5
60					50	-1.5
	▼ 1mm			1cm thick	40	-1
40	□ 2mm				30	-1
					20	-0.5
20	□ 2.5mm			STH	10	-0.5
	∧ 3mm					
0				Talus	GND	0

-14°C	-12	-10	-8	-6	-4	-2°C
	F	4F	1F	P	K	I

Snow stability on similar slopes: **Very Good   Good   (Fair   Poor)   Very Poor**

Figure 6-5. This is an example from a field snowpit profile. (From Snow and Avalanche Field Notebook *by Ian McCammon, www.snowpit.com)*

By learning to identify the crystals in the weak layer, you can discover a powerful piece of the avalanche puzzle—what kind of avalanche dragon you are confronting. (Wasatch Range, Utah)

Determining Snow Hardness

Do a quick hand hardness test: Push your hand into the snow and feel how much resistance you encounter. Push just hard enough so that you feel the pressure in your wrist bone. Rank it on the scale shown in Table 6-6. Be sure to do this using a gloved hand, not a bare hand for two reasons, 1) snow is *cold*, you silly; wear your gloves and 2) the tests are calibrated for a gloved hand. I usually wear mittens instead of gloves so I have to take that into account.

Graph the snowpit like that shown in the example (Figure 6-5). Notice that your graph looks similar to the snowpit wall after you've run your hands over it. The strong layers stick out and the weak ones erode away. Remember to include the date, location, aspect, elevation, steepness, and weather.

Identify the Crystal Types

Now identify the crystal types in the layers of snow. This takes some practice and patience at first, so make sure you're dressed warmly. The best way to learn to recognize the layers is to take an avalanche class and have the instructor show you what they look like, or consult the photos in Chapter 5, Snowpack, and use your loupe to identify the crystal types for yourself. You don't really *need* to identify the crystal types. But if you want to push into the realm of avalanche forecasting, then you'll need to know what kind of avalanche dragons are lurking. If you're going to get serious about avalanches, eventually, you'll want to move up to the next level—into the nerdy realm of snow crystal identification. Why? Because crystal structure can tell you a lot about the snowpack. And knowledge is power—the power to stay alive and play safely in places where others fear to tread. (See Table 5-1 in Chapter 5, Snowpack, for more on crystal identification.)

TABLE 6-5. SUMMARY OF ACTIVE TESTS AND SNOWPIT TESTS

Test	Time	Used for (S=Surface D=Deep)	Semi-quantifiable: Yes or No	Advantages	Disadvantages
Active Tests					
Cornice	5 seconds–5 minutes	S, D	N	• Delivers big shock to the slope • Easy to interpret • Tests for all kinds of weak layers • Can create a safe way down	• Dangerous if done improperly • Cornices aren't always available
Tilt Test	20–60 seconds	S	Y	• Works well with new snow instabilities	• Doesn't work as well for deeper weak layers and depth hoar
Test Slopes	5–30 seconds	S	N	• Safe if done properly • Easy to interpret	• Dangerous if done improperly • Test slopes aren't always available
Slope Cuts	5–20 seconds	S	N	• Good technique for minimizing the odds of getting caught • Good for surface instabilities • Can do them on skis, snowboard, or snowmobile	• Dangerous if done improperly • Not effective on deep instability or on hard slabs • Doesn't work for climbers or snowshoers
Ski Pole	1–5 seconds	S	N	• Quick, can do hundreds of tests • Good for faceted snow or density inversions	• Difficult to detect surface hoar • Does not test shear strength • Snowboarders and snowmobilers don't carry ski poles
Hand Shear	5–20 seconds	S	N	• Quick, can do dozens of tests per day • Good for surface instabilities	• Not effective for deep instabilities
Ski, Board, or Snowmobile Above Track	5–20 seconds	S	N	• Quick, can do dozens of tests per day • Good for surface instabilities	• Not effective for deep instabilities

TABLE 6-5. SUMMARY OF ACTIVE TESTS AND SNOWPIT TESTS (CONTINUED)

Test	Time	Used for (S=Surface, D=Deep)	Semi-quantifiable: Yes or No	Advantages	Disadvantages
Snowpit Tests					
Extended Column Test or Propagation Saw Test	1–2 minutes	S, D	Y	• Semi-quantifiable • Quick • Easily communicate results to others • Easy to interpret	• None
Compression	1–2 minutes	S, D	Y	• Semi-quantifiable • Easy to interpret • Quick • Easily communicate results to others	• Must combine results with shear quality and structure to determine stability • Small sample size
Rutschblock	3–5 minutes	S, D	Y	• Large sample reduces uncertainty • Semi-quantifiable • Easy to interpret • Easily communicate results to others	• Takes more time than other tests
Shovel Shear	30 seconds–1 minute	S, D	N	• Can identify surface hoar • Can perform on a flat slope	• Hard to interpret • Not quantifiable • Takes time to develop feel • Small sample size • Can't determine stability

TABLE 6-6		
Rating	*Hardness*	*Examples*
Fist	Very soft	• New snow, mature depth hoar
Four fingers	Soft	• Settled new snow or near-surface facets • Common soft slab material
One finger	Medium	• Hard, old snow • Common hard slab material
Pencil	Hard	• Sun crust or a stout wind slab
Knife	Very hard	• Rain crust or melt-freeze crust

Perform Some Stability Tests

Now it's time to perform your favorite stability tests. Write the results in your notebook. Also note the quality of the shear for each stability test. Take notes, writing down other snow stability clues you see (avalanche activity, collapsing, cracking, etc.) so you can compare what you find in the snowpack with the observable snow stability.

Finally, remember that a snowpit gives you information only for the place where you dug the snowpit. The snow 100 meters (110 yards) away may be completely different and snow on other aspects is almost always completely different. I usually dig several quick snowpits in representative areas and then I sketch out what I feel is an average snow profile for that particular aspect and elevation.

Remember: Never get married on the first date; never base your whole stability evaluation on just one piece of information.

A large, wet avalanche like this typically flows like concrete and makes the track look like the chute of a concrete truck, gouging down to the dirt and destroying everything in its path. (Wasatch Range, Utah)

WET SNOW AVALANCHES

All of the above stability tests work nearly as well for determining the stability of wet snow as they do for dry snow. However, the stability of wet snow is very transient, changing from minute to minute, compared to dry snow, which changes day by day, so these tests end up being not nearly as useful.

The best way to determine the stability of wet snow is to carefully watch the weather and test your theories by jumping on test slopes or watching for avalanche activity. See Chapter 4, Weather, and Chapter 5, Snowpack, for details on weather that produces wet snow avalanches. For wet melt-freeze snow, such as spring, sun-induced wet instability, use how far you sink into the snow as a guide (see Table 6-7).

TABLE 6-7		
When Walking on Foot	*What It Means*	*What You Should Do*
Walking on top of a thick supportable crust	Green light (unless it's a thin refreeze on a wet, recently isothermal snowpack, which may be yellow light)	Good conditions to do most anything.
Sinking in to your ankles	Yellow light	Switch aspects or head home.
Sinking in to your calves	Red light	Get off and out from underneath steep slopes.
Wallowing up to your knees	Red light with siren	Get off and out from underneath steep slopes.

PUTTING IT ALL TOGETHER

Now let's put the pieces of the stability puzzle together in an organized way.

Confidence versus Information

As we evaluate snow stability, the more information we gather and analyze, the more confident we become in our assessment of the stability. This is good. On the flip side of the coin, when we don't know squat, our confidence should also be squat. Unfortunately, this is not always the case, and I think it's important to regularly do exercises to combat this.

For instance, Doug Fesler and Jill Fredston have devised a checklist that helps you get a handle on what you know and what you don't know and how it affects your opinion of the stability of the snowpack. In the left column, you rank what you think is the stability of the snowpack from one to five. In the right column, you rank how confident you are in your opinion, once again on a scale of one to five. When teaching students, we poll the class early in the day, in the middle of the day, and at the end of the day. Early in the day, they still haven't gathered much information; their opinions about the stability of the snowpack are usually scattered all over the chart and their confidence in their opinions is usually low. In the middle of the day, they have begun to zero-in on the actual stability and their confidence rises. By the end of the day, they have all pretty much nailed the stability right on the money and their confidence is quite high.

I usually do the same exercise in my head when I'm evaluating the snowpack on my own tours or when I'm forecasting for public avalanche advisories. It's a good checklist to keep in your head.

At Beginning of Tour (x = each student's vote)

Opinion of Stability		Confidence in Stability Assessment	
Extreme	xx	Very confident	
High	xxxxxxx	Confident	
Considerable	xxxx	Medium confidence	
Moderate	xxx	Not too confident	xxxxxxxxxxx
Low	xxxx	Not confident at all	xxxxxxxxxx

At Lunch Time

Opinion of Stability		Confidence in Stability Assessment	
Extreme	x	Very confident	
High	xxxxxxxxxx	Confident	xxxxxxxxx
Considerable	xxxxxx	Medium confidence	xxxxxxxxxx
Moderate	x	Not too confident	xxxxxxxxxxx
Low		Not confident at all	xxxxxxxxxx

At End of Tour

Opinion of Stability		Confidence in Stability Assessment	
Extreme		Very confident	xxxxxxxxxxxxxxxxxx
High	x	Confident	xxxx
Considerable	xxxxxxxxxxxxxx	Medium confidence	
Moderate		Not too confident	
Low		Not confident at all	

Here is another very basic checklist to use in determining snow stability.

Stability Checklist—Dry Snow

Observation	Red Light	Yellow Light	Green Light
Recent avalanche activity on similar slopes	Widespread activity	Localized activity	No activity
Collapsing snowpacks	Widespread collapsing	Localized collapsing or collapsing only on flat or shallow snowpacks	No collapsing
Cracking	Widespread cracking	Localized cracking	No cracking
Cornice fall tests (use refrigerator size or larger)	Sensitive, widespread avalanching	Localized "stubborn" avalanches	No avalanches
Loading (addition of new or windblown snow)	Heavy and rapid loading on a weak snowpack	Moderate loading on a moderately stable snowpack	Light to moderate loading on a strong snowpack
Rapid warming	Rapid warming of cold, unstable snow with persistent weak layer	Rapid warming of moderately stable snow on a less persistent weak layer	Rapid warming of stable snow

Snowpit Tests	Red Light	Yellow Light	Green Light
Extended column or propagation saw test	Propagates	Some tests propagate, others don't	No propagation
Rutschblock test	Breaks with easy jump or less and with planar, complete break	Breaks with one hard jump; complete or incomplete break	Breaks with several hard jumps or no break or with partial break
Compression test	Breaks with taps articulating from the wrist (1 to 10 taps) with Q1 shear and 4–5 lemons	Breaks with taps articulating from the elbow (11 to 20 taps) with Q2 shear and 3–4 lemons	Breaks with taps articulating from the shoulder (21 to 30 taps) with Q3 shear and 0–3 lemons
Stuff-block test	Breaks with drop from 20 cm or less with Q1 shear and 4–5 lemons	Breaks with drop of 20 to 40 cm with Q2 shear and 3–4 lemons	Breaks with drop of over 40 cm with Q3 shears and 0–3 lemons

Stability Checklist —Wet Snow

Observation	Red Light	Yellow Light	Green Light
Sinking into wet snow	Sinking in past your shins	Sinking in to your ankles	Not sinking in
Rain	Rain on cold, dry, new snow	Rain on old, dry snow	Rain on mature melt-freeze snow
No overnight freezes	Three nights without a freeze on a recently isothermal snowpack	One night without a freeze on a recently isothermal snowpack	No overnight freezes on a mature, well-drained (summer) snowpack
Rollerballs	Widespread	Localized or only off very steep slopes	No rollerballs

RANKING THE SIGNIFICANCE OF TESTS AND OBSERVATIONS

The power of stability evaluation comes not from latching onto one test or observation, but through the *integration* of the information. This sounds like a great idea on paper, but it's hard to do in practice. How do we know which tests and observations are important and which ones are not, and in which situations? Well, funny you should ask because much of the rest of this book deals exactly with that question.

We need to focus on the information that does the most to eliminate uncertainty. Ed LaChapelle describes it as going for "low-entropy" information. Doug Fesler describes it as going for "bull's-eye" information. Separate the wheat from the chaff, and all that.

To get some idea of the significance of clues, I have ranked various observations and tests on a scale from zero to 100, with 100 meaning very significant. This ranking is based on an average, cold, dry, midwinter snowpack in a temperate latitude. Other avalanche situations will vary from this example. Remember, the following lists give a *general* idea of how to rank the significance of clues.

The best signs of avalanches are avalanches.

Signs of Instability for Dry Snow

Significance	Signs of Instability
100%	• You trigger an avalanche—can't get better than that • Recent avalanche activity on similar slopes
90%	• Cornice tests produce sensitive avalanches • Long shooting cracks as you cross the slope
80%	• Collapsing of the snowpack as you travel across it • Several representative snowpit tests show unstable snow
70%	• Hollow, drumlike sound • Recent heavy loading of new or windblown snow on unstable snowpack
60%	• One snowpit in a nonrepresentative spot showed unstable snow
50%	• Rapid warming of a cold, dry snowpack with unstable snow on a persistent weak layer
40%	• Two-day-old avalanche activity
30%	• Good snowpit in a nonrepresentative spot showed unstable snow
20%	• You got an "easy" shear on a shovel shear test • The TV anchorman says it's "extreme danger out there"
10%	• Just not your lucky day
0%	• Someone got killed on that slope last year

Signs of Stability for Dry Snow

Significance	Signs of Stability
100%	• Sorry, there's no such thing as 100 percent. Let's say 95%.
95%	• You just rolled an Oldsmobile-sized cornice down the slope without triggering an avalanche • A skilled avalanche specialist digs several representative snowpits combined with other tests and observations and determines the snow is stable • Two hundred snowmobilers just climbed the slope without incident
90%	• Several good snowpits from representative areas show stable snow
80%	• Five big skiers who fall a lot just descended the slope without incident
70%	• Ten smooth skiers just descended the slope without incident
60%	• One good snowpit from a representative spot showed stable snow
50%	• Two snowboarders made it down without incident
40%	• Settlement cones around trees and bushes
30%	• A good snowpit in a representative spot but using poor technique showed stable snow
20%	• One skier made it down without incident
10%	• It's your lucky day
0%	• One good snowpit from a nonrepresentative spot shows stable snow

Signs of Instability for Wet Snow

Significance	Signs of Instability
100%	• You trigger an avalanche • Recent avalanche activity on similar slopes
90%	• Heavy rain on cold, dry, new snow • Sinking in to your knees in wet snow • Rapid melting of new snow
80%	• Snowpack collapses as you travel across it • Three nights without a freeze on a recently isothermal snowpack
70%	• Sinking in to your ankles in wet snow
60%	• Heavy rain on old, dry snow
50%	
40%	• One night without a freeze on a recently isothermal snowpack
30%	
20%	• Heavy rain on old, well-drained, corn snow
10%	• The TV anchorman said it was "extreme danger out there"
0%	• Newsstand tabloid says we'll have "monster avalanches" this year

Signs of Stability for Wet Snow

Significance	Signs of Stability
100%	• Sorry, nothing is 100% sure in the avalanche game, but a solid, multiday freeze on a mature corn snowpack is close.
90%	• Solid multiday freeze on a recently isothermal snowpack
80%	• Much cooler weather following rain or strong melting
70%	• Solid, one-day freeze on a recently isothermal snowpack
60%	
50%	
40%	• Thin freeze on a recently isothermal snowpack that experienced strong melting the previous day
30%	
20%	• Your psychic said it was OK (well, maybe 50% for a good psychic)
10%	• The TV weatherman said the snow was stable
0%	• The real estate developer didn't mention anything about avalanche hazard to your dream home

So far in this chapter, we have learned how to judge snow stability on a particular slope at a particular time — a two-dimensional view, if you will. Now we will expand snow stability into a three-dimensional, 360-degree view. In other words, we learn to judge the pattern of snow stability by aspect and elevation.

Warm temperatures and prolonged melting soften up cornices that drop off randomly. Not a good place for a picnic. (Beartooth Mountain, Montana)

AVALANCHES IN THREE DIMENSIONS

Most people need many years of experience in the mountains to gain a good intuitive feel for how avalanche hazard varies by aspect and elevation. It's hard enough to figure out if one particular slope is dangerous and it's even harder to develop a good 360-degree pattern, i.e., how stability varies with aspect, plus how it varies with elevation. The tool I like to use for this is a graphic I call an aspect-elevation diagram or an avalanche rose. Most avalanche centers have now adopted this avalanche rose graphic in their avalanche forecast products.

To understand the aspect-elevation diagram, pretend you are floating in a balloon directly over the peak of a conical-shaped mountain and looking straight down. The outside circle in the aspect-elevation diagram represents the base of the mountain and concentric circles represent the elevation contours as you go higher on the mountain. In other words, the center of the circle is the top of the mountain and the edge of the circle is the base of the mountain. Align the north-south-east-west on the map with real terrain below your balloon and you're ready to start sketching snow conditions and avalanche hazard onto your aspect-elevation chart. You can put specific elevations on the diagram for your local area if you want (Figure 6-6).

Let's work through a few examples, starting in the early season and finishing in spring. Refer to Chapters 3, 4, and 5 for the details of exactly how avalanche conditions change with various combinations of terrain, weather, and snowpack.

Example 1: You are in the Northern Hemisphere at mid-latitudes, in an intermountain climate with the mountaintops around 3000 meters (10,000 feet) in elevation. The first couple of snow storms of the season have laid down 1 meter (3.5 feet) of new, low-density snow. Over the course of the next two sunny weeks, the 1 meter (3.5 feet) of snow settles to 60 centimeters (2 feet). Then another storm arrives and lays down 60 centimeters (2 feet) of dense snow. What's the weak layer? Where will you find it? What's the pattern?

Answer: During the sunny two weeks, depending on temperature, much of the snow will melt off the sun-exposed slopes, or at least settle down into more stable snow (farther north

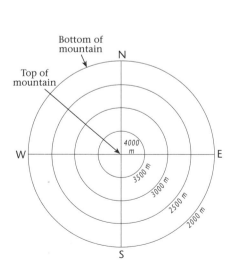

Figure 6-6. A sample aspect-elevation diagram

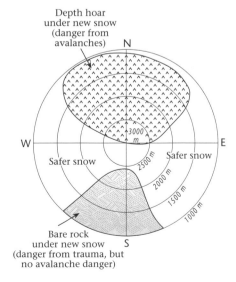

Figure 6-7. Aspect-elevation diagram for Example 1

or at higher elevations, this might not occur). On the shaded slopes, it's a different story. The clear skies have kept the snow surface very cold. Combined with a thin snow cover, we now have a thick layer of the dreaded depth hoar on the northwest- through northeast-facing slopes, and possibly on east-facing slopes (since east is always colder than west). Plus, we may also have surface hoar on the snow surface. (See Figure 6-7.)

The new load of dense snow will almost certainly overload the depth hoar and begin a cycle of soft slab avalanches on the northeast- through northwest-facing slopes, possibly extending onto east-facing slopes as well. The southwest- through southeast-facing slopes will tend to stay in place because the new snow has either fallen onto more stable snow or directly on the rocks, which provide good anchoring. This is a lose-lose situation. Either you stay on safe terrain and get banged up on the rocks or you trigger avalanches where the snow is better. Human factors are always nightmarish because powder fever runs amok in the early season. These kinds of conditions usually claim several lives in North America each fall. Remember, as avalanche educator Lynn Wolf puts it, that today's snow surface is tomorrow's weak layer.

HOT TIP!

Before the storm arrives, carefully memorize the pattern where you find depth hoar and surface hoar, which with this thin snowpack will be on or near the surface and easy to detect. Where is it thick? Where is it weak? Which elevations? Which aspects? It's usually worst on mid-slope shady aspects at high elevations. If you wait until after the storm arrives, the only way to map the preexisting snow is to dig a gazillion more snowpits. You want to make life easy, don't you? Watch the weather forecast. Be proactive.

Example 2: It's now January with about 2 meters (80 inches) of settled snow on the ground and the snow is mostly stable. After a moist storm, the skies clear as the moisture lingers for several days. There's a strong temperature inversion and you have to scrape frost off your windshield each morning. The next morning, a south wind blows and that afternoon, a foot of snow falls. What kind of avalanche dragon will you be dealing with? What's the pattern? Where will you go to find safe snowmobiling and why?

Answer: The weak layer will most likely be surface hoar. Scraping your windshield is an easy clue. Most likely, the humid, calm conditions combined with a clear sky quickly laid down a thin layer of surface hoar on all aspects. Strong sun may have melted the surface hoar on the sunny aspects, but what about elevation? Surface hoar tends to form more at lower elevations than on the mountaintops, especially basin bottoms where cold, humid air pools during clear nights. How about the wind? The wind most likely destroyed the surface hoar on the windward slopes, especially along the high-elevation wind-exposed ridges. So where does that leave surface hoar still existing? At mid- and lower elevations and basin bottoms on shady slopes. (See Figure 6-8.)

Where can you safely go snowmobiling? First, jump on lots of test slopes and/or dig lots of quick hand shears to test your theory. If correct, then head for sunny slopes or slopes that got scoured by the pre-storm winds. Avoid shady, wind-sheltered slopes, especially at mid-slope or in basin bottoms.

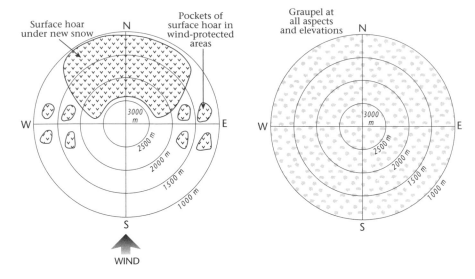

Figure 6-8. Aspect-elevation diagram for Example 2

Figure 6-9. Aspect-elevation diagram for Example 3

HOT TIP!

Once again, before the storm arrives, take a reconnaissance trip and carefully map where you find surface hoar and where you don't.

Example 3: A strong cold front passes followed by cold, unstable air with lots of convective showers. There's even lightning. When you head out the next day to do some extreme snowboarding, you dig down and notice a layer of graupel buried a foot deep in the snowpack, and it still seems sensitive to your hand shear tests. (See Figure 6-9.) Where will you go to find safe snow?

Answer: The avalanche dragon in this case is probably graupel. Strong cold fronts and highly convective storms tend to precipitate graupel, especially at the beginning of the storm. These storms also tend to have wild wind and rapidly changing snow densities, so there will likely be other weak layers within the new snow. You'll find them quickly with a hand shear test. Graupel is like little Styrofoam balls and it tends to roll off steep terrain and collect on gentler slopes below. By steep, I mean about 45 degrees or more. It will also fall equally on all aspects. This might be a good day to abandon your plans for extreme terrain. It's never a good idea to head for the steeps the day after a storm. Even if the graupel isn't producing avalanches, a wild storm like this will surely have produced some other weak layers within the new snow. Even if you've done some very thorough fact-finding and determined that everything is stable, you will probably get some big sluffs going on the steep slopes. If you don't know how to manage sluffs, they could knock you off your feet and send you over a cliff or bury you in a terrain trap.

Graupel usually stabilizes in a day or two so, like I say, you really ought to forget about today. Tomorrow will always be there unless, of course, you blow it today.

Example 4: It's March, with a deep, stable snowpack. You have just climbed a big mountain along the Pacific Coast and you return to your camp in a blizzard in a couple of feet of new snow. As you break your camp to descend steep slopes to your car, you notice that the snow has turned to light rain. (See Figure 6-10.) What do you do?

Answer: The freezing level has risen. Rain is now falling on new snow, which almost always causes instant avalanching. If you have to cross avalanche terrain or cross beneath avalanche terrain on the descent, you are walking into a trap. The choice is simple. As long as you're in a safe spot, set your camp back up and stay put. Rain falls equally on all aspects, so you can't find a safe aspect. Rain usually falls more at lower elevation than high elevation, so going down is stupid in this case. Relax and enjoy. Even if it keeps raining for a week, it's usually better to cross a slope on the second day of rain than the first day. Perhaps you will discover that the steep slope you need to cross has already avalanched, giving you a safer route. Also, by the second day, perhaps the snow will have developed drainage channels and be more stable after enduring 24 hours of rain.

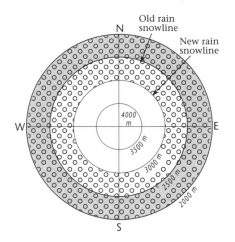

Figure 6-10. Aspect-elevation diagram for Example 4

Example 5: It's May in Colorado and you've had lots of big avalanches down to the depth hoar for most of the winter. So what else is new in Colorado? Warm weather has finally arrived and after a week of melting and freezing, it has finally created passable corn snow on the south-facing slopes. After a record-warm day, you wake up early to catch some good corn, but you notice that

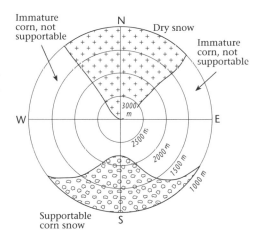

Figure 6-11. Aspect-elevation diagram for Example 5

it didn't freeze very well the night before and you notice some high clouds. While walking on foot up an east-facing slope, you sink in to your knees in punchy, thinly refrozen snow. What do you do?

Answer: First, you're on the wrong slope. You need to find a south-facing slope to see if it's got a supportable crust. The south slopes will turn isothermal first and produce the most percolating meltwater because they catch the most sun, therefore, after they refreeze, you'll find the thickest crust on south-facing slopes. (See Figure 6-11.) If it's still supportable on south, then go fast, get in a run, and get the heck off the slope and head home when you start to sink through the crust when walking on foot. You won't have much time in these conditions.

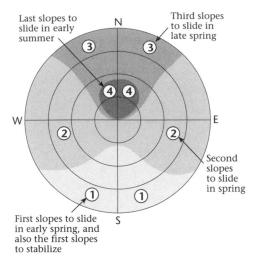

Last slopes to slide in early summer

Third slopes to slide in late spring

Second slopes to slide in spring

First slopes to slide in early spring, and also the first slopes to stabilize

Figure 6-12. A typical example of a spring wet slide cycle. It begins on lower-elevation south-facing slopes and ends on high-elevation north-facing slopes.

If it's not supportable, abandon your plans and head home. With yesterday as a record-warm day, you can bet that the buried depth hoar got thoroughly soaked and there's not much holding the entire snowpack together. You can sometimes trigger full-depth wet slabs to depth hoar even with a thinly refrozen crust on top. You can never trust depth hoar, especially freshly saturated depth hoar. On a day like this you're probably safer on a north-facing slope that still has cold, dry snow.

The usual pattern for spring, sun-induced, wet avalanches is that they often occur first on south-facing slopes, starting at lower elevations and working to upper elevations through time. After meltwater has percolated through the snowpack for several days, it destroys all the layers and the snowpack becomes denser, more homogenous, and much more stable. Often, after the south-facing slopes have "cooked down" and become stable (combined with a good refreeze overnight), wet avalanches begin on east- and west-facing slopes. Then wet avalanches work their way around the mountains, ending on the north-facing slopes in late spring. Finally, they will stabilize as well. (See Figure 6-12.) It's important to know this pattern and adjust your terrain accordingly.

You can keep track of snow stability distribution patterns in your field notebook. Figure 6-13 is an example of one method.

The Danger of Unusual Loading Patterns

Looking for unusual loading patterns is important because unusual weather makes unusual avalanches.

Example 1: During the middle of winter, the high elevations usually have a deep snowpack while the lower elevations, and the lee sides of mountain ranges, usually have a shallower snowpack. Suppose a cold front without much wind comes through that lays down 60 centimeters (2 feet) of dense snow in a very even blanket over all the terrain—high elevation and low elevation alike. Where will the avalanches occur?

Answer: Low elevations and on the lee side of the mountain range. Why? Because as we have learned, shallow snow tends to be weak snow (see Chapter 5). Therefore, 60 centimeters of new snow on top of thin, weak snow is much more dangerous than 60 centimeters of new snow on top of deep, strong snow. Also, remembering our mantra that unusual weather makes unusual avalanches, 60 centimeters (2 feet) of snow on top of an already-deep snowpack is not unusual. But 2 feet of snow in the valleys is unusual. The snowpack becomes unstable when subjected to unusual or rapid changes.

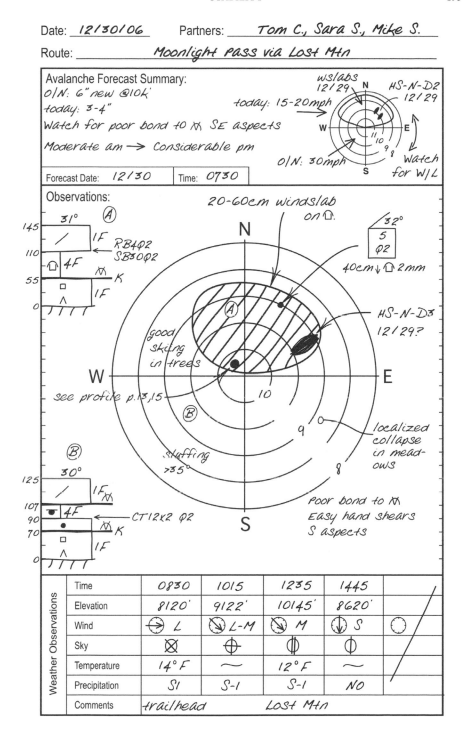

Figure 6-13. *An example of field notes for the distribution patterns of snow stability (From* Snow and Avalanche Field Notebook *by Ian McCammon, www.snowpit.com)*

Example 2: For the previous month, storms have come from the west, which, in this case, is the prevailing wind and storm direction. Then a storm comes in on an easterly flow. Where can you expect to find avalanches?

Answer: Once again, in the places that receive an unusual or disproportionate amount of new snow. In this case, the eastern side of the mountain range will get more snow than the west, and the wind will deposit fresh wind slabs along the west-facing slopes along the crest. The snowpack in both of these areas is not used to getting much snow accumulation and it's likely to be dangerous. Also, people tend to get habituated to, say, always being able to climb a certain slope safely because it's usually wind scoured. Unusual patterns will take them by surprise.

AVALANCHE FORECASTING—PROJECTING AVALANCHE HAZARDS INTO THE FUTURE

Now for the final step. Here we take snow stability from three dimensions to four dimensions—how stability changes through time.

When I forecast avalanche hazard, I boil it all down in my head to three questions: (1) What kind of avalanche dragon am I dealing with? (2) Is the rubber band stretched? (3) What's next?

Let's take a look at each one of them in turn. First, always, start with the preexisting snowpack.

1. **What kind of avalanche dragon are we dealing with?**
   a. Is it dry snow or wet snow? These are two radically different beasts altogether. They are caused by different processes, we forecast for them differently, they behave differently, and they're triggered differently.
   b. What type of weak layers? Persistent weak layers (facets and surface hoar)? New snow? Wet snow? Weak interfaces? Each has its own characteristics.
   c. What kind of slab? How thick? How stiff? Is it uniform or does it vary in thickness? What is its temperature?
   d. How slippery and continuous is the bed surface? Slick and continuous bed surfaces produce avalanches more easily than rough or discontinuous bed surfaces.
   e. What is the distribution pattern? Almost all instabilities vary dramatically by aspect, elevation, steepness, terrain type. What's the pattern?

2. **Is the rubber band stretched?** In other words, have there been recent, rapid, or large changes to the snowpack? Snow does not like rapid changes. Snow can adjust to slow or small changes much easier than to rapid or large changes. Rapid or large changes introduce elastic energy into the system—stretching the rubber band—which makes the snowpack especially sensitive to failure and fracture from triggers such as the additional weight of a person (a *very* rapid change).
   Symptoms include:
   a. Recent avalanche activity.
   b. Sensitivity to triggers.
   c. Cracking and collapsing.
   d. Stability tests show unstable snow and/or shears pop out like they're spring-loaded.
   These are caused by:
   a. A rapid or large addition of new or windblown snow or rain (loading).

b. Rapid warming of a cold snowpack.

c. Rapid or prolonged melting or rain especially on snow that has not been subjected to percolating water.

Important questions as you assess the rubber band:

a. What kind of avalanche dragon are you dealing with? Rapid changes do not always cause avalanching. Stable snow can withstand a lot of abuse before it gets cranky. Unstable snow can withstand only a small amount. Persistent weak layers produce avalanches for a long time.

b. How much change and how fast? A meter of dense new snow is a whole lot different than a meter of fluff. And a meter of new snow added over 3 weeks is a whole different story than a meter added over 3 hours.

c. Time since changes occurred? Wind loading a week ago pales in comparison to wind loading an hour ago. Has the snowpack had enough time to adjust to changes?

d. What is the distribution pattern? Aspect? Elevation? Terrain type? Avalanche danger is almost never the same on all slopes. There's always a pattern.

3. **What's next? (Weather forecast)** This is the "forecasting" part of it—where snow stability goes into the fourth dimension—into the future. Take what you know about the present avalanche conditions and imagine how the future weather will affect it. Will it make it more stable, less stable or stay the same? And what's the pattern?

a. Expected loading and loading rate (snow, wind loading).

b. Expected temperature trend.

c. Expected rain.

STABILITY VERSUS TIME

Stability varies dramatically through time and each setup is slightly different. Here are some

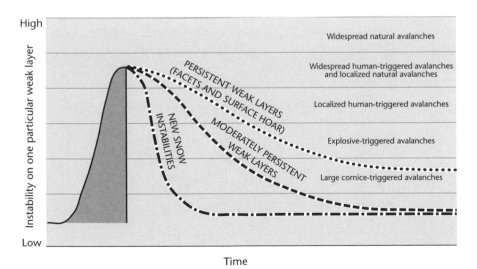

Figure 6-14. A conceptual diagram of the stabilization over time of various kinds of weak layers

conceptual illustrations of how stability may vary through time with different situations. These examples tend to be true in Utah, but they may be slightly different for other areas. Pay close attention to how stability changes through time in your local area and come up with your own characteristic patterns.

Some of these examples came from back-of-the-napkin sketches by my friend Roger Atkins, a helicopter ski guide in Canada, over a number of protracted avalanche discussions we have had over the course of several river trips, climbing trips, bike rides, and late night ramblings (Figures 6-14 through 6-22).

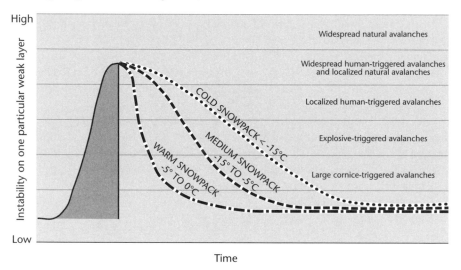

Figure 6-15. A conceptual diagram of the stabilization over time of weak layers at various temperatures

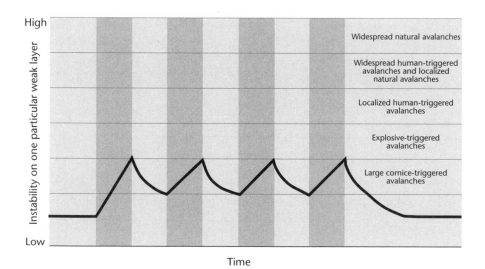

Figure 6-16. A conceptual diagram of small storms with no persistent weak layer

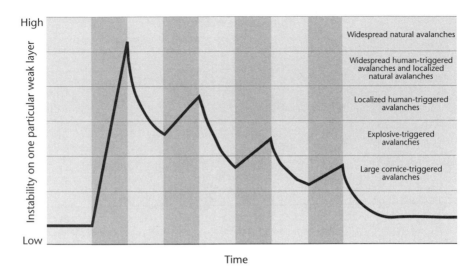

Figure 6-17. A conceptual diagram of large storms on a moderately persistent weak layer. After the first storm, the snowpack on a particularly weak layer becomes generally more stable over time.

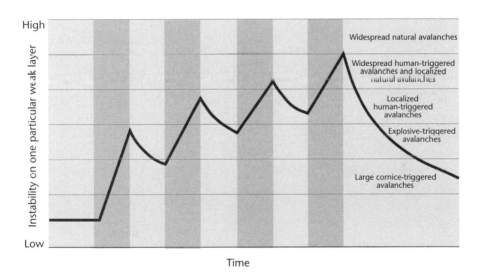

Figure 6-18. A conceptual diagram of small storms on a very persistent weak layer. The snowpack on that weak layer becomes less stable with each incremental loading.

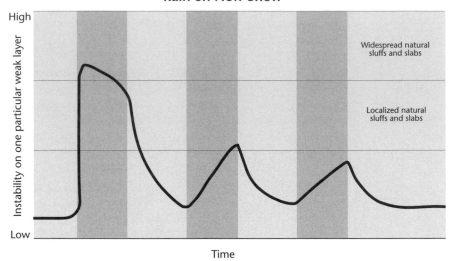

Figure 6-19. Rain on new snow usually causes nearly instant widespread avalanching. Subsequent rains cause much less avalanching because the snow has become more permeable and has formed drainage channels.

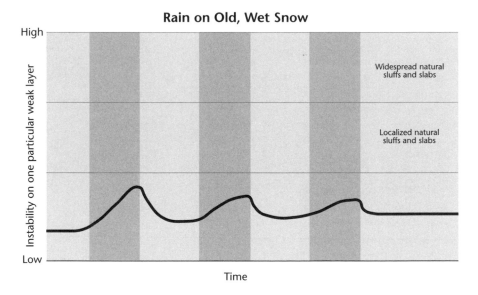

Figure 6-20. Rain on old, wet snow does not usually produce avalanches because the snow has no more porosity and has already formed drainage channels.

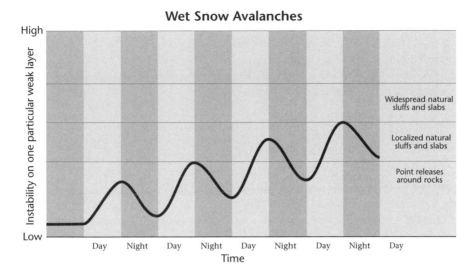

Figure 6-21. A conceptual diagram of a wet, recently isothermal snowpack with a deeply buried, persistent weak layer subjected to strong daytime melting with no overnight freeze

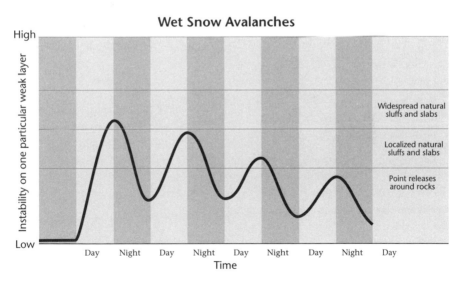

Figure 6-22. A conceptual diagram of a wet, recently isothermal snowpack with either a non-persistent weak layer or a shallowly buried weak layer subjected to strong daytime melting with no overnight freeze

AVALANCHE BOOT CAMP

Maybe all this sounds confusing to you, and it should, because only time and work will make all of this intuitive. So now for the time and work part of it! We're off to avalanche boot camp where you have to work and toil, learning about avalanches by doing—and doing and doing—over and over until it's second nature. Hut, hut, hut, off we march for a two-week crash course in how to be a mighty avalanche hunter.

Day 1

First, we have a relatively easy day. Today we make our seasonal history chart. Go get a large piece of graph paper and make it look like the example, Figure 4-11, in Chapter 4, Weather. If possible, get on the internet, find a site with data from an automated station, and fill in all the data from the first snowfall to the present time. If you're starting at the beginning of the season—great—that's the best time to start. That's when all avalanche professionals begin their charts and do a mind-meld with the snowpack, a bond not to be broken until the snow melts and heads to the ocean in spring. The snowpack is like a child. You watch it change each day. You wake up in the night to check the weather. You watch the snowpack crawl, then take its baby steps, then run, then mature, then go through its life changes, and then it finally dies and goes back to where it came. Each season is unique and so is each snowpack, each with its distinct personality and characteristics. I know it sounds crazy but I go through a grieving process each spring when it's all over—every single year. It may take all day to construct this chart so enjoy your rest day while you can.

Day 2

Now we get serious. Today, we start the daily routine—a routine most avalanche junkies do every day, all winter. First, call or browse to the recorded avalanche advisory to get the big picture of what's going on, what kind of avalanche activity happened yesterday, what they think is going to happen today. If there's no forecast for your area, check the internet and bring up the closest one and extrapolate the best you can. Check the weather radio to get the latest forecast. Then, get on the internet for the latest weather data, or better yet, keep your own weather station in the mountains in a place you can visit each day. Take the latest data and update your seasonal history chart. Every avalanche professional I know gets completely out of touch with the snowpack if they take a vacation in the winter for more than a few days. When they get back it takes several days to get back in the rhythm of the weather and snowpack. If you're a weekend warrior who lives away from the mountains, then you are already at a disadvantage, but not an insurmountable one. Call the forecast each day. Keep it on your speed dialer at home or work or check the internet each day, like when you're away from your family for a week, call every day to keep up. Otherwise when you return home, you're just another stranger.

Now, it's time to head for the mountains. You'll need all your gear—snow saw, hand lens, compass, inclinometer, thermometer, rope, beacon, shovel, probe, Avalung™, field notebook. Head for your favorite place—someplace you go often and know well, someplace where there are avalanches, someplace interesting. Notice everything. How much new snow? How long since it snowed? What kind of snow is on the surface? Temperature? Wind? Humidity? Cloud cover? How many tracks are on the slopes? Are people triggering avalanches? Do you see any avalanches, and if so, how old are they, how deep, how wide, what aspect, what elevation? Write it all down in your field notebook.

Whatever you do, don't go jump on a steep slope. Now is the time to gather information. Head for a small, safe, test slope that's as close to 38 degrees as possible. How does the snow feel on the way to the test slope? Do you notice collapsing, cracking, or a slabby feel, or is the snow right side up and solid underneath? On the test slope, position yourself at mid-slope at the steepest part. Dig a snowpit with lots of working room and perform all the tests in Chapter 6, Stability. Today is the day to go slow and pay attention. Write down everything, including date, time, elevation, aspect, steepness, weather, snow surface conditions, snow profile, temperature profile, results of stress tests, and crystal types. What's the weakest layer? How weak is it? How much force is it going to take to rip it out of there? And most important, does the fracture propagate? Plan to spend the entire day refining your snowpit techniques, so dress warmly and try to pick a warm, sunny day so you will be comfortable. Make sure your pit wall is smooth and vertical. Do all the tests properly and do them over and over until you can do them correctly every time. Spend time identifying all the snow crystals and all the layers. Look at them carefully through your hand lens. Dig other snowpits on the same slope to see how the snow varies from place to place, especially from shallow areas to deep areas.

OK, enough for today. When you head home, watch for recent avalanches, wind, clouds, new snow, and recent tracks. Are people triggering avalanches or are they crossing the slopes without incident? Write all of this down in an organized way.

Day 3

Morning routine: Consult the avalanche report. Did avalanche control work produce any avalanches? Were there any human-triggered or natural avalanches in the backcountry? Check your weather radio. Check the internet. Update your seasonal history chart. Head for the mountains, back to your favorite spot. This time, find another test slope with another aspect, a place where the snowpack is shallower or deeper (use your probe to find a good snowpit spot). How is the snowpack different? What changed and why? Then go to another part of the test slope with yet another aspect or go to another test slope at the same elevation with a different aspect. Dig again, notice everything, write everything down. How is it different and why is it different? Do you find the same layers in all the pits or different ones? How widespread is the weak layer? Is there a lot of variability of the weak layer from one place to another or is it similar? Why? Is there a lot of variability in your stress tests or are they all about the same? Keep digging more snowpits until you can't stand it anymore. Hey, who said that boot camp would be easy?

What patterns have you noticed? How does the snow change by aspect, by depth, by steepness? Keep doing this until you have a good 360-degree map of the snowpack, north, south, east, and west. What's the pattern? Write everything down and begin to construct an avalanche rose (aspect-elevation diagram), or at least the aspect part of it. We will get to elevation tomorrow.

Day 4

You know the morning routine: Avalanche report—weather radio—internet—update your seasonal history chart. Head for the mountains. Now that you have a good two-dimensional view it's time for the third dimension: go to a higher elevation—perhaps 1000 meters (3000 feet) higher—and dig more pits. How does the snowpack change by elevation? Work your way around the compass, digging snowpits again to see how it changes with aspect at this new elevation. Now you are starting to develop a good three-dimensional view of the snowpack. Sketch out the pattern on an aspect-elevation diagram. If you can comfortably sketch the snowpack on an avalanche rose, then you are already ahead of 90 percent of the general public who go into the backcountry. You're doing well. It may take a week of work to arrive at this point, but once you have arrived, you should celebrate a little. Go for some well-deserved play on the slope you have determined is safe.

Now that you know what you're talking about, leave a message on the avalanche recording telling the forecasters what you found. They can't be everywhere at once and they depend on feedback from people like you. Your information could save someone's life.

Day 5

Sore muscles? Bummer. Sorry, this is boot camp. Same routine again today. Consult the forecast, listen to the weather radio, get on the internet, update the weather chart. Do you notice any weather chart patterns? How do they affect the snowpack? After a week of sunny, warm weather, do you notice sun crusts on sunny slopes and faceted snow on shady slopes? If the weather hasn't changed much, then the snowpack probably didn't change either (unless it's very cold or very warm). If so, you can take the day off to reread this book because now it will all make more sense. But no such luck today. A big storm came in last night. Aren't you glad that you mapped the snowpack yesterday—*before* the storm arrived?

Now for the payoff. Lots of avalanches today, so no time for rest because this is an extremely valuable opportunity. Find a test slope that's safe and dig more snowpits. Now the weak layers that you saw yesterday have been loaded. Are you getting different results on your stress tests? Do your columns fall out when you isolate them or when you just tweak them a little? Great. That's what unstable snow feels like. Memorize this and count it as a great gift. Go to other safe slopes. Dig more, test more, notice everything, write it all down. How does the data vary by aspect, steepness, depth, and elevation? Do you notice that yesterday's snow surface is today's weak layer?

If you can find a recent avalanche and get onto it safely, then go to the fracture line (flank walls work best) and dig more snowpits. What was the weak layer? How does the weak layer and slab thickness vary from one spot to another? How steep is the starting zone? Where do you think the trigger point was? Wow, this is great experience. See what fresh avalanche debris feels like and imagine what it would be like to be caught in it or to have to search for others in it.

These are great days to practice triggering avalanches. But only on very safe little test slopes where you won't get hurt if something goes wrong, say a 3-meter-high (10 foot) road cut that is getting wind loaded. With your partner watching you, jump on it or do a slope cut to see if you can kick something off. Triggering tiny avalanches teaches you to get a feel for them—to learn what sensitive wind slabs feel and look like and learn what slabby snow feels like. Remember to practice on *small*, safe slopes. These are also good days to practice using your belay rope. Today is definitely *not* the day to be on or underneath larger, steep slopes, so don't be tempted. Days like this are for learning, not for taking risks. When you get home, leave a message for the local avalanche center telling them what you found.

Day 6

Up early again to follow your usual morning routine and head back out in the mountains again. Now that it's the day after the storm, the snowpack has had a little time to adjust to

Here I am hard at work in my office. My avalanche boot camp lasts all winter.

its load. How are the stress tests different? Do you have to tap harder on the columns to make them initiate and propagate, jump harder on the rutschblocks? Is the snow still collapsing or cracking? If the visibility is better, perhaps you can see all the avalanches that occurred. What was the pattern? Aspect, elevation, steepness, terrain type—where did the avalanches occur, how far did they run? Notice everything and write it all down. Sketch out your aspect-elevation diagram. How has it changed from yesterday? What's the pattern of the snow surface texture and what does that tell you about stability? Did the winds before the storm blow from a different direction than winds during the storm? This means that the old wind slabs are covered up and hard to see. Once again, when you get home, leave a message for the avalanche forecasters about what you found.

Day 7

Same routine, but today it's sunny and beautiful. Two days after loading and the snowpack has had even more time to adjust to its load. Do you notice that the persistent weak layers like facets and surface hoar are taking a lot longer to adjust to their load than the other layers? Great. There are extremely valuable lessons here. Do you notice that the avalanches may be harder to trigger but the ones that are occurring are larger and more dangerous? Another good lesson. Do you notice that sunny days put people in a good mood and make them more confident even on slopes where the snowpack is still in a foul mood? Wow! That's the best lesson of all—how human factors cause most avalanche accidents. Don't you just love avalanche boot camp?

These are the kinds of days on which most avalanche accidents occur—the first sunny day after a storm. So don't be tempted to follow all the other people who are headed to the upper-elevation, steep, shady slopes because that's where the best powder is, because that's also where there's likely to be lingering avalanche danger from buried persistent weak layers. Head for a safe slope instead. You already know where they are because you have been doing your homework. If someone triggers an avalanche today, help with the rescue because that's absolutely the best avalanche education you can get—learning about the consequences of mistakes on unstable days. Don't be condescending because you could be next.

Week Two

Same routine. Dig snowpits on the slopes with persistently weak layers and see how fast they are gaining strength. Do you notice that the larger crystals gain strength more slowly than the small-grained crystals? What other patterns do you notice? Is the weak layer buried beneath a thick slab gaining strength faster than the same weak layer buried beneath a shallow slab where the temperature gradient has remained strong? Are low-elevation areas gaining strength faster than upper-elevation areas? Have the wind slabs and new snow gained strength faster than the persistent weak layers? Avalanches are self-explanatory if you take the time to ask the right questions in the right way.

Congratulations!

You have completed two weeks of boot camp and are well on your way to becoming safe in avalanche terrain. You already know how to avoid 90 percent of the problems that White Death will throw at you. Now all you have to do is keep abreast of changing conditions. Even on the days when you can't get out, keep the same morning routine: call the avalanche report, update the seasonal history chart, check the internet for past and future weather, listen to the weather radio, sketch an aspect-elevation diagram of what changes you imagine are going on in the snowpack, and the next time you go out, check your answers. You are a natural detective and your job is to gather evidence, make educated guesses, and systematically test your theories. Remember the overarching theme of this book—use a system to evaluate avalanche danger to stay alive in avalanche terrain? Working through this book together with your own practice has trained you to do it.

When I first started learning about avalanches, I must have dug thousands of snowpits and filled up dozens of field notebooks and updated many seasonal history charts. After doing this for a few years, I noticed that I didn't dig nearly as many snowpits because, if I was watching the weather closely, I pretty much knew what I was going to find before I even dug the pit. Getting to that point takes some hard work. Remember that gut feelings don't mean very much unless they're based on a lot of experience, so the bottom line is this: Learn to make evidence-based decisions and be very suspicious of beliefs.

You have started your journey down the road to becoming an avalanche warrior. Poor warriors charge into battle without enough preparation. Good warriors not only know where the battlefield is but they also choose when to show up, they know their enemy and how to fight the battle, they know what to do if something goes wrong, and most important, they have mastered themselves.

Reading this book, however, doesn't make you an avalanche master. This is just the first step in a long journey. The journey takes time and work, but luckily, the work is pleasant, the workplace is stunningly beautiful, the rewards—recreating safely in glorious snow—are exhilarating, and the coworkers are some of the finest people in the world. I feel very blessed to have lived the life I have and I hope to someday become an avalanche master myself. I hope to see you along the way.

chapter seven

HAZARD EVALUATION

If avalanche decisions were easy, thirty years ago we would have come up with one of those box diagrams—a step-by-step way to make decisions. We would tape it to our forehead, hold up a mirror and everything would be simple. But avalanches aren't that way.
　　　　　　—Chris Stethem, Canada's leading avalanche consultant

[To make good business decisions] you have to assume that humans are capable of looking at facts, finding root causes and formulating solutions. On my planet there's not much evidence to support this assumption.... If humans had the ability to look at the facts and make good decisions, think how different the world would be. There would be only six kinds of cars on the market and nobody would buy a car that was second best in its price range. There would be no such thing as jury selection since all jurors would reach the same conclusion after viewing the facts, and all elections would be decided unanimously. That's not the world we live in. Our brains are wired backwards. We make decisions first—based on irrational forces and personal motives— then we do the analysis. The facts get whittled until they fit into the right holes.
　　　　　　—Scott Adams, creator of the Dilbert cartoon

EMOTIONAL VERSUS LOGICAL DECISION MAKING

The central theme of this book is that in order to stay alive in avalanche terrain, we need to use a system of organization and analysis to make evidence- not emotion-based decisions. But as countless studies have shown, for whatever reasons, people do not naturally make logical decisions, especially evaluating risk, and most especially, evaluating risk to themselves. Anyone who has ever followed the stock market, or worked in sales or politics knows this already. We are emotional creatures, often lazy when it comes to logic, so fact-based decision making doesn't come easily. Therefore, the avalanche game is much more of a people problem than an avalanche problem. So what is the answer?

　　Luckily, we are not the first people to have to figure this out. Airline pilots, engineers, soldiers, and stock traders, all come to mind. Similar to us, they survive only by keeping bad decisions to an acceptably small number. They do this systematically, using various kinds of procedures, decision-making algorithms, computer automation, and checklists. Similarly, if you look at avalanche statistics, professional avalanche workers enjoy a very low accident

Checklists, protocols, procedures, and rules. To err is human but errors in the mountains can kill. Thus, we need a system. This is the list I keep taped to the dashboard in my car all winter. My wife is asking me if I forgot my boots—AGAIN.

rate compared with recreational users because we operate in a very controlled environment, and we use systems for gathering data, for making hazard evaluations, for safe-travel protocol and for rescue in case something goes wrong.

Of course, systems save you from making bad decisions only if they are actually used. Among professionals, adherence to the system occurs through the master-apprentice relationship and also through the motivation of the almighty paycheck. Either you follow the rules, or hey, don't let that door hit you on the way out.

For recreational users, however, there is little motivation to follow any kind of system and the backcountry ends up being a nerve-wracking, free-for-all of foolish behavior and bad decisions. Since snow is stable most of the time, people think that their methods work just fine but eventually they discover otherwise. Consequently, the vast majority of avalanche accidents occur to backcountry recreationists.

That's what hazard evaluation is all about—providing ways to organize information so that it makes some sense to us and helps us make evidence-based decisions based on facts. Like it or not, we will not do this instinctively. We must be forced. That's why airline pilots use checklists and follow procedures, stock traders have trading systems, and lawyers draw up contracts and agreements. They don't do this for their pleasure; they do it because it's the only thing that works. Recently, medical researcher Peter Pronovost was featured as one of *Time* magazine's 100 most influential people. He instituted a simple checklist in intensive care units that helped prevent infections. His checklist has saved 1500 lives so far. Systems like this don't have to be complex to work. In most cases, the simpler they are, the more effective they are, because they will be used.

USE THE LOCAL AVALANCHE BULLETIN

The first step in a comprehensive avalanche system is to consult the local avalanche bulletin. Many avalanche-prone areas in the world, including the United States and Canada, have either a local or regional avalanche center that issues regular avalanche advisories for the public. (See Bibliography for a current list.) It's cool because professional avalanche forecasters do much of your work for you. Acting as a central clearinghouse for avalanche and mountain weather information, they closely follow avalanche conditions throughout the season. Yet, there is wide variability in avalanche centers; unfortunately, many are chronically underfunded. Some avalanche centers issue weekend-only bulletins while the major regional centers not only issue daily bulletins but have websites overflowing with useful information. The avalanche bulletins give you a good overview of the avalanche conditions; but to evaluate local slopes, you will be on your own.

Avalanche Danger Ratings Explained

Advisories throughout the world use a standardized 5-point scale of avalanche danger (See Appendix for United States Avalanche Danger Descriptors.) In English, the ratings are called "Low, Moderate, Considerable, High, and Extreme," and they have equivalents in other languages. Especially in Europe where tourists routinely cross language boundaries, the danger ratings are more commonly referred to by their number, 1, 2, 3, 4, or 5 and you may see many North American avalanche bulletins change to numbers or use numbers in conjunction with names because of widespread confusion over the meaning of the words, especially the often criticized and confusing, "Considerable."

These are "hazard" or "danger" ratings; in other words, they rate the potential for harm and they do not describe "risk," which includes the amount of exposure (the number of people exposed to the harm). Here, we will use the word danger instead of hazard because they mean the same thing and, historically, the word danger has gained widespread use. Determining an avalanche danger level is not as simple as it looks. Avalanche danger depends on two factors: the likelihood of an avalanche and the severity of that avalanche should it occur. For instance, there may be only localized places where a person could trigger a large and unsurvivable avalanche, or there may be widespread places where people can trigger small and relatively harmless avalanches.

The standard definitions of these danger ratings were written many years ago and nowadays most people find that they are not particularly useful, nor accurate, because they are defined only in terms of the likelihood of an avalanche and do not address avalanche severity. I am today on a committee of North Americans who have regular meetings to rewrite the hazard descriptors and also come up with a standard "technical model" that provides guidance to forecasters when determining hazard ratings. This committee also meets with Europeans to come to some sort of consensus. Be sure to monitor www.avalanche.org and www.avalanche.ca for the latest developments as they occur. For now, I have included a diagram (Figure 7-1) I think is useful in helping people conceptualize the factors that go into an avalanche hazard rating. As you can see, it's a complex interaction of several variables. Figure 7-2 illustrates more on risk, slope steepness, and danger rating. How do we determine danger ratings at the Utah Avalanche Center? Yes, we consult the "technical model" when we're confused, but most of the time it just comes down to the pucker factor (see Table 7-1)—what kind of terrain would each of us be willing to cross and under which particular conditions?

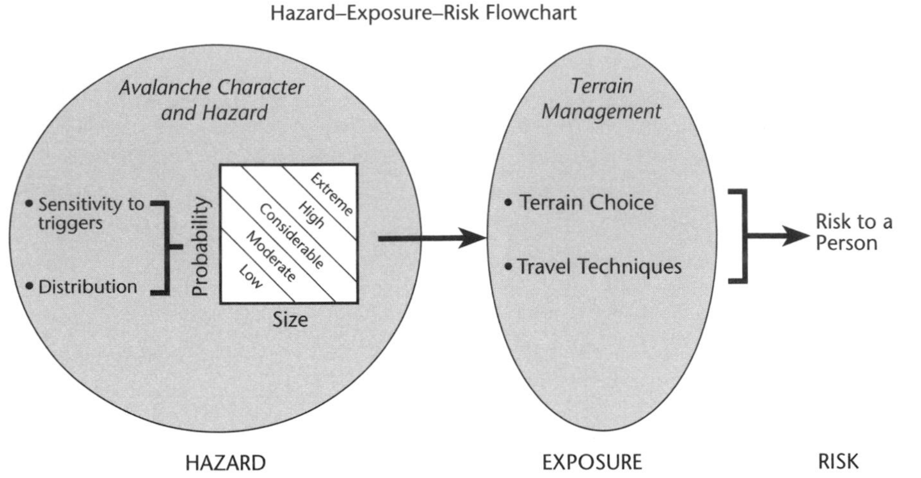

Hazard–Exposure–Risk Flowchart

Figure 7-1. A conceptual diagram of avalanche hazard, exposure, and risk. This comes from preliminary work by a U.S.–Canadian committee, of which I am a member, to determine a conceptual model for avalanche hazard and to rewrite the public definitions of avalanche hazard. Please consult www.avalanche.org or www.avalanche.ca for the latest developments from this committee. Also see Appendix for the preliminary Public Danger Scale.

TABLE 7-1 PUCKER FACTOR	
Low danger	Generally comfortable on all slopes.
Moderate danger	Willing to cross most slopes, but watch for localized booby traps.
Considerable danger	Would avoid crossing many slopes but willing to cross some slopes under special circumstances and after careful evaluation.
High danger	Would avoid crossing all slopes, and most runouts.
Extreme danger	Would avoid all slopes and stay well away from all runouts.

Finally, remember that most avalanche accidents happen on slopes rated as Considerable Danger (3) because that's where people and avalanches interact most. (See Figure 7-3.) People perceive that "Considerable" does not sound too dangerous, yet "Considerable" is exactly when human-triggered avalanches are possible on many slopes—and most recreationists don't know how to tell the difference between safe and unsafe slopes. High and extreme ratings sound, well, extreme; when these warnings are issued most people obligingly avoid these slopes.

SYSTEMS FOR MAKING EVIDENCE-BASED DECISIONS

I have always been amazed at how much checklists and diagrams help to organize the pieces of the puzzle—any puzzle. When faced with an overwhelming deluge of sometimes contradictory information, the best way for the human brain to sort it all out is to put it on paper in some sort of matrix or diagram. I actually learned this from my mother.

I know it sounds like I'm bragging (because I am), but my mother is no ordinary woman. After degrees in both English and Math, she raised six children, then earned a CPA and an

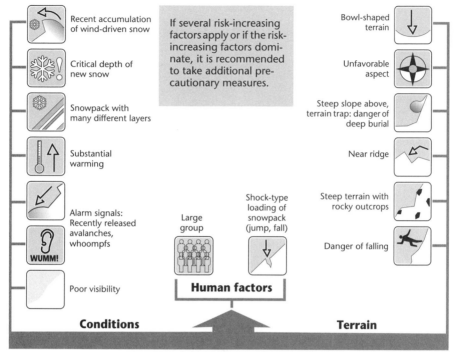

AVALANCHE RISK

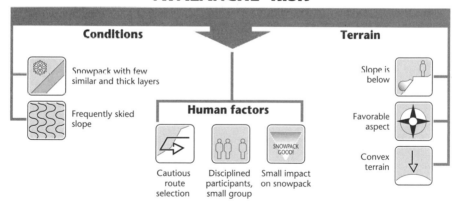

Figure 7-2. Of all the simplified, rule-based decision-making methods from Europe, I like this one the best. (From the Swiss Institute for Snow and Avalanche Research, www.slf.ch/info/Caution_ Avalanches.pdf)

MBA, was a university professor, then earned a law degree and worked as a lawyer until she retired a few years ago. One day when I was maybe ten years old, I had some hard decision to make—I just *couldn't* figure out what to do. She said, "Let the facts make the decision."

"How do I do that?" I asked.

"Make a matrix," she replied. "It's a way you can get the facts out in front of you and, like magic, the facts make the decision for you."

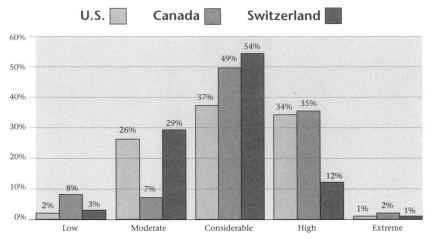

Percentage of Avalanche Fatalities by Danger Rating

Figure 7-3. *Most avalanche fatalities occur at the "considerable danger" rating because it is the maximum interaction between people and avalanche hazard.*

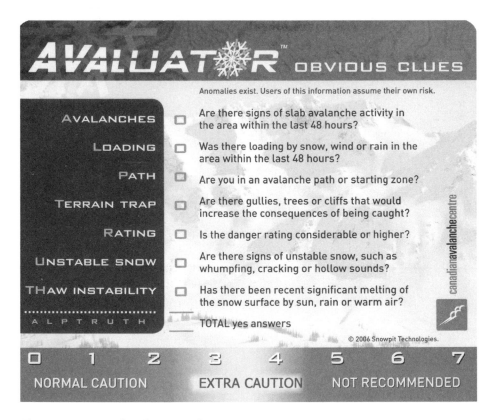

Figure 7-4. Front of Avaluator card

Across the top of the paper, she listed my three choices for the decision I was trying to make. Down the left side of the paper, she listed all the factors I thought were important about the decision. Then she drew horizontal and vertical lines to make a matrix. Finally, for each of the three decisions, I ranked each factor on a scale from one to ten. When I added up the columns under each decision, the numbers told me which was the best. Magic!

I've used this method dozens of times since, from deciding what career to follow to what kind of car to buy, and we use it every time we hire someone new at the Utah Avalanche Center. Luckily, they didn't use this method when hiring me.

RULE-BASED DECISION-MAKING METHODS

The world is a complicated place. As Ian McCammon likes to point out in his avalanche classes, we all like to think that we make decisions by looking at the facts and analyzing all the combinations. But if you add up all the parameters mentioned in an avalanche book—take this book as an example—wind, snow, steepness, anchors, precipitation rate, temperature, etc., etc., you would come up with a very long list. And if you looked at all the various

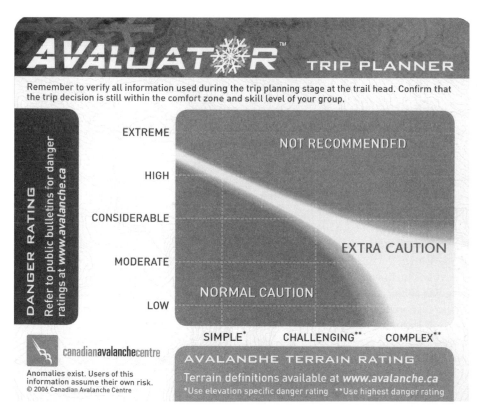

Figure 7-4. Back of Avaluator card. The "Avaluator" is a great rule-based decision-making card with accompanying booklet published by the Canadian Avalanche Centre. The Obvious Clues come from the work of Ian McCammon and the Trip Planner is derived from terrain ratings pioneered by Grant Statham and Parks Canada (www.avalanche.ca). Refer to Chapter 3, Terrain Management, for an explanation of simple, challenging, and complex terrain © Canadian Avalache Centre.

combinations of those factors it would add up to more than the grains of sand on all the beaches in the world! Obviously, to help us make a decision we have to have reliable ways to zoom in on the important information and organize it.

A number of rule-based decision-making methods have been invented to help evaluate avalanche hazard. During the late 1990s, avalanche experts in the European countries created and published cards that people could carry with them in the backcountry and consult when they had a decision to make. Most prominently, there was Werner Munter's Reduction Method from Switzerland, the Stop/Go card from Austria, and the Nivo Test card from France. I won't present all those methods here because they are all available on the web, but I have reproduced my favorite one from Switzerland. (See Figure 7-2.)

The ALPTRUTh Method

In recent years, an American, Ian McCammon, took another stab at the problem. Based on methods that worked in other fields, he came up with a rule-based decision-making method that was simple, portable, and reliable—three essential elements in successful rule-based systems. First, he analyzed the American avalanche accident database and came up with the seven most obvious clues people missed when they were in an avalanche accident. He found that 93 percent of avalanche accidents occurred when three or more obvious clues were present. So that's it. It's that simple.

What has become known as the Obvious Clues or the ALPTRUTh method (a mnemonic for the obvious clues) is not only the simplest method he could find, but it's also relatively easy to memorize (making it portable and useful once you're familiar with it even if you left the card back in the car) and when compared statistically against all the European methods, it outperformed them all. Ian worked with the Canadians to come up with a card suitable for North America, which resulted in the Avaluator card (Figure 7-4) and booklet, which you can view or purchase from the Canadian Avalanche Centre's website. On the flip side of the card is the Trip Planner, which allows you to decide where to plan your outing based on the avalanche hazard rating as well as the rating for the terrain. I encourage all beginning and intermediate students to purchase the booklet (which includes the card) and use it on a regular basis until it becomes second nature.

As pointed out in the Avaluator, technically this is not a rule-based decision-making method as are the European methods. Instead, the total number of obvious clues tells you how your situation compares to the conditions of past accidents. Also, obviously, this does not cover all the conditions that can cause avalanches, it's simply a way to identify the conditions that produced the past accidents. Finally, when anyone learns a new skill, beginners generally learn best with a rule-based method. Intermediate users will graduate to methods that help to partition or organize the information and prompt them to consider certain important factors (hence the two methods presented below). Experts tend to make decisions intuitively and the more advanced sections of this book will help the advanced user to gain knowledge about how avalanches work and thereby develop an intuitive feel for unsafe and safe conditions.

Obvious Clues Method (ALPTRUTh)		
A	Avalanches	Has there been avalanche activity in the past 48 hours?
L	Loading	Has there been loading of new or wind-blown snow in the past 48 hours?
P	Path .	Is it an obvious avalanche path?
T	Terrain Trap	Does the avalanche path terminate in a gully, trees, cliff, or crevasses?
R	Rating	Is the avalanche hazard rated Considerable or higher?
U	Unstable Signs	Did you notice collapsing or cracking of the snow?
Th	Thaw	Has there been a rapid or prolonged thaw of the snowpack?

Presence of three or four clues is a warning to make your next decision very carefully.

Presence of five or more clues means that you should not continue unless you have expert knowledge to evaluate and manage the avalanche hazard. Even then, your best option may be to choose a safer slope.

You can also organize the obvious clues chronologically as you gather information throughout the day:

Obvious Clues Method (in chronological order)	
Rating	The big picture, decide on the general area.
Path	Decide on specific slopes.
Avalanches	Look for the most obvious clue in the area.
Loading	Look for the next most obvious clue.
Thaw	In springtime or wet conditions look for obvious clues for wet avalanches.
Unstable Signs	Look for obvious signs as you travel.
Terrain trap	What will happen if it slides?

HOT TIP!

Notice that with all the methods presented in this chapter your choice of terrain determines your hazard. You have no control over weather or snowpack but you always have a choice when it comes to terrain. In other words, the only way to turn four checkmarked obvious clues into two or three is either to avoid obvious avalanche paths or to avoid ones with a terrain trap—or both.

HAZARD EVALUATION CHECKLIST BY DOUG FESLER AND JILL FREDSTON

For intermediate users, here's a popular checklist developed by Alaska avalanche educators Doug Fesler and Jill Fredston. To use this, you will need to have some basic skills for evaluating terrain, snowpack and weather. This checklist seems deceptively simple, but they have put a lot of thought into it and refined it through hundreds of multiday classes over the past 30 years. The checklist is an easy way to organize the information and get it in front of you so that you can take a step-by-step approach to determining hazard on a particular slope at a particular time. They use the analogy of a stoplight: red means stop, yellow means caution, green means go.

Hazard Evaluation Checklist

TERRAIN—IS THE SLOPE CAPABLE OF PRODUCING AN AVALANCHE?			
	Red	Yellow	Green
Steepness (Is it steep enough to slide? Is it prime time?)			
Aspect (Leeward, shadowed, extremely sunny?)			
Configuration (Anchoring and shape)			
Subtotal			

SNOWPACK—COULD THE SNOW SLIDE?			
	Red	Yellow	Green
Slab configuration (Slab? Depth? Distribution?)			
Bonding ability (Weak layer, tender spots?)			
Sensitivity to triggers (How much force? Shear tests? Clues?)			
Subtotal			

WEATHER—IS THE WEATHER CONTRIBUTING TO THE INSTABILITY?			
	Red	Yellow	Green
Precipitation (Type, amount, intensity, weight)			
Wind (Snow transport? Amount and rate of deposition?)			
Temperature (Storm trends? Effects on snowpack?)			
Subtotal			

HUMAN FACTORS—WHAT ARE THE ALTERNATIVES AND THEIR CONSEQUENCES?			
	Red	**Yellow**	**Green**
Attitude (Toward life? Risks? Goals? Assumptions?)			
Technical skill level (Traveling? Evaluating avalanche hazard?)			
Strength/Equipment (Strength? Prepared for the worst?)			
Subtotal			
Overall			

Using the Hazard Evaluation Checklist

Let's work through some specific examples using the checklist.

Example 1: The weather is storming like crazy. Six feet of new, dense snow has fallen in the past two days. You can hear avalanches roaring down in the mountains. You want to go skate-skiing on a road that crosses a 20-degree slope that has no steeper slopes above or below. (You have measured the runout angle when the visibility was good.) Go or no-go?

Terrain . . . . Green
Snowpack . . . . . . Red
Weather . . . . Red
Human . . . . Doesn't matter

Answer: It's a go. It's nearly impossible to trigger an avalanche on a 20-degree slope. If you stay out from underneath slopes of about 30 degrees or steeper, you will be quite safe. This is a good day to stick to green-light terrain. Watch out for poor visibility because you might bumble into dangerous terrain, in which case you could easily get slaughtered on a day like today—a good day for a map and GPS.

Example 2: You are a producer of extreme snowmobile videos and you want to film hill climbing in steep, mountain couloirs. You head to a 45-degree chute below a large funnel-shaped avalanche path. The weather has been sunny and warm for the past week, including today. From all of your tests and observations, you determine that the snow is very stable. Go or no-go?

Terrain . . . . Red
Snowpack . . . . . . Green
Weather . . . . Green
Human . . . . Yellow

Answer: It's a go. Yes, you are in very dangerous terrain, but this is the time to do it; in fact, it's the only time to do it—during times of good weather and stable conditions. This is the time to follow your dreams. Watch out for human factors, though. Kodak Courage will elicit stupid behavior in even the saintly, but at least you won't have to worry about most avalanches.

Example 3: The weather is finally beautiful and sunny after four days of storms. You head for your favorite bowl for a day of skiing. On the way, you notice collapsing of the snowpack on a deeply buried layer of depth hoar. You see several avalanches that have run during the storm. You plan to ski on a 35-degree north-facing slope.

Terrain. . . . . Red
Snowpack . . . . . . Red
Weather. . . . . Recent weather: Red; present weather: Green
Human. . . . . Red

Answer: Definite no-go. These are precisely the conditions that kill most avalanche victims—the first sunny day after a storm. The sunny weather and fresh powder makes us feel great, but the snowpack does not necessarily share our opinion. In this case, the snowpack is obviously unstable and doubly dangerous since it has some fluffy "sucker snow" on top. Human factors run rampant because everyone desperately wants to ski great powder in the beautiful sunshine, and we tend to rationalize nearly anything to do so. This is the time when avalanche experts become very unpopular in a group because they spoil everyone's fun. Even knowledgeable groups sometimes start cautiously on gentle slopes, then when nothing happens, they keep working up to steeper and steeper slopes until catastrophe strikes.

HOT TIP!

Look for a slope that avalanched during the storm and now has a little fresh powder on it. Often you can play on it perfectly safely while you wait for the yet unslid slopes to stabilize or slide. Also, if only north-facing slopes are unstable, perhaps you can find safe conditions on south-facing slopes or vice versa. Check them out. Be sure to get a good 360-degree view of snow stability.

Example 4: You want to go ice climbing on a north-facing frozen waterfall beneath a large funnel-shaped avalanche path. The weather has been cold and clear for the past week, which has kept the 50 centimeters of powder snow light and dry. The weather forecast calls for a warm front to push into your area today. You notice increasing high clouds and warmer temperatures as you approach the climb.

Terrain. . . . . Red
Snowpack . . . . . . Green turning to Red
Weather. . . . . Green turning to Red
Human. . . . . Doesn't matter

Answer: Depends on timing. You may be able get away with it if you go quickly before the temperature starts to seriously warm up. But you could just as easily be too late already, and it's hard to evaluate slopes far above you. The warming temperatures, wind, and high clouds will warm up the cold, dry snow on the north-facing slope above and cause loose sluffs that may knock you off the ice climb. It's probably best to choose a route without overhanging hazards.

THE ATWATER-LACHAPELLE RISK EVALUATION CHECKLIST

Here is a checklist that is similar to the Fredston-Fesler checklist, but this one adds the factors of consequences and alternatives. In other words, risk to an individual equals the likelihood of something bad occurring times the consequences of that something bad taking place. Once people know the consequences, they are much more likely to consider the alternatives.

In the late 1950s, Monty Atwater and Ed LaChapelle came up with four simple questions to ask yourself when you travel in avalanche terrain. The questions have been slightly refined through the years, mostly by Doug Fesler, to their now-familiar state. The four questions are:

- Is the terrain capable of producing an avalanche?
- Could the snow slide?
- What will happen if it does?
- What are the alternatives?

Whether you're managing avalanche hazard at a ski resort, guiding clients, or recreating in the backcountry, you should always run through these questions with every slope you cross. Do it over and over until it's second nature.

I have fleshed out the questions into the following checklist, in which you can color each factor red light, yellow light, or green light, and integrate them together into a no-go or go decision. Many people also add the human factor to this list, so I have as well, since human factors not only color all of our decisions, but without the skills and knowledge, you won't be able to evaluate any of the rest of the factors anyway. Refer to Chapters 3, 4, 5, 6, and 10 for more details on evaluating each question. The bullets under each question are the factors I consider.

Human: Are you prepared for the job?
- Attitude, judgment, communication, awareness
- Skills and knowledge
- Equipment and strength

Terrain: Is the terrain capable of producing an avalanche?
- Steepness
- Configuration (shape, aspect)
- Anchors

Snowpack: Could the snow slide?
- Observations (recent avalanches, cracking, collapsing, etc.)
- Tests (test slopes, snowpits, etc.)
- Past and present weather

Consequences: What will happen if it does?
- Avalanche size
- Terrain consequences (terrain traps, shape, size, escape routes, etc.)
- Number of people involved

What are the alternatives?
- Back track
- Find another slope or route
- Dig in and wait it out

Finally, we can also make the above list into a flowchart (Figure 7-5).

With the Risk Evaluation Checklist in mind, let's look at some photos and evaluate the terrain based on everything we've learned so far.

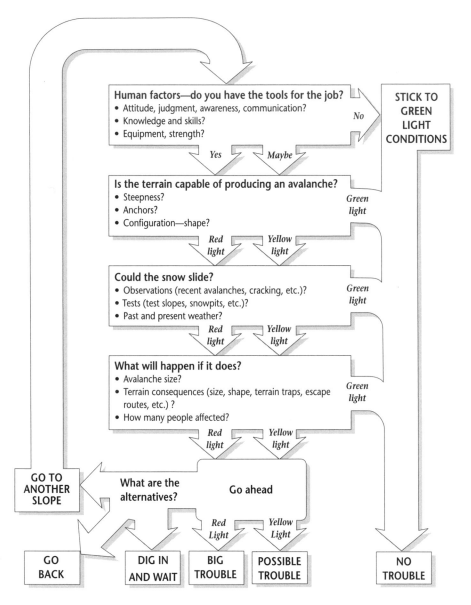

Figure 7-5. Atwater-LaChapelle Risk Evaluation Flowchart. This is my version of how to put Atwater and LaChapelle's ideas into practice.

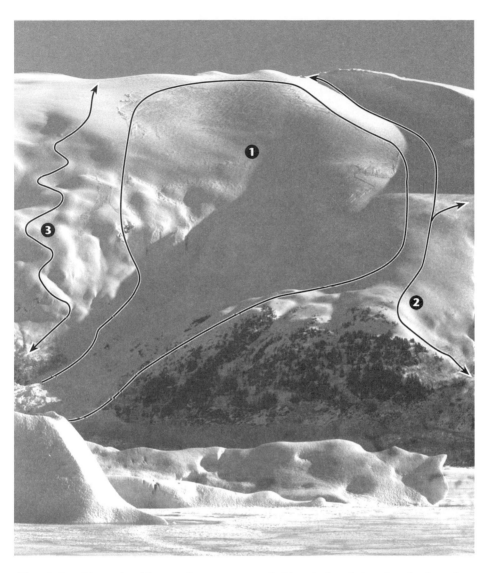

If you look at this terrain with an eye for consequences, the big, ugly, funnel-shaped avalanche path right in the middle (1) jumps right out at you. Even small avalanches can bury you very deeply if triggered anywhere inside of the funnel. Route (2) is safer because it stays on gentler terrain with fewer bad consequences. On Route (3) you have to make like a hound dog and sniff out the gentlest terrain, following subtle spur ridges; but you still would need fairly stable conditions for this route. (Kenai Mountains, Alaska)

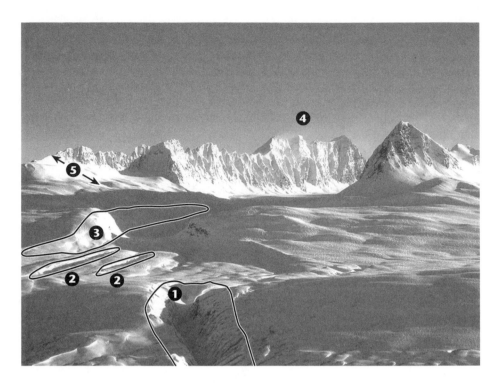

Where's the most dangerous terrain? It's not always the most obvious. I think I would rather take my chances with the steep skyline couloirs than the very ugly terrain trap in the foreground (1). The plumes off the peaks tell you that the wind is blowing (4) and the snow surface patterns tell you that the wind was blowing left to right. Gullies in the foreground have been cross-loaded. The small ones (2) would make good test slopes, but (3) is large enough to kill. The best slope looks like (5), which seems to be more wind-sheltered and generally not steep enough to slide. As for the steep couloirs on the skyline, they're all recently wind-loaded. Some sections of them may be wind-sheltered enough to still be safe, but you'll have to check them out very carefully as you travel. A mistake will send you on a long, possibly unsurvivable ride. (Thompson Pass, Chugach Range, Alaska)

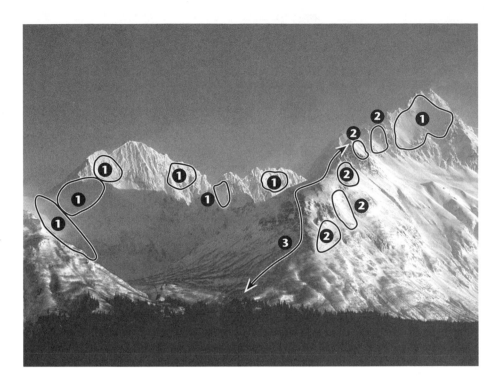

An obviously windy day. All the pockets labeled (1) look like certain death today. All are actively wind-loading, and all have probably unsurvivable consequences. The pockets labeled (2) are also actively wind-loading, but there's at least a possibility of survival. Route (3) looks like the only safe one today as it follows the wind-scoured side of the ridge. Watch out for small wind slabs that could send you for a bone-jarring ride over the scoured rocks. The knife-edge ridge up high looks mighty tricky, though. This looks like a good day to stay home unless you can sniff out a wind-sheltered slope somewhere. Watch out for things coming down from above, because the wind is rapidly loading the slopes. (Thompson Pass, Chugach Range, Alaska)

chapter eight

ROUTEFINDING AND SAFE TRAVEL RITUALS

We write a tale of adventure with our thoughts and actions every day.
And it's a story that we don't get the opportunity to edit and rewrite.
The first draft is the final one. Let's write it well.

—Royal Robbins

Routefinding is a fine art that takes years to master. Making a path on the land—the best path for that particular day in those particular conditions with your own particular party—is the ultimate test of mountain smarts.

TEN COMMANDMENTS OF SAFE TRAVEL

I take a lot of comfort in the fact that only 1.5 percent of the fatalities in the United States in the last 15 years have involved avalanche professionals. This is true mainly because in 90 percent of avalanche accidents, the avalanche is triggered by the victim or someone in the victim's party. Which means that if you know what you're doing, staying alive in avalanche country is predominantly a matter of choice, not chance. Avalanche professionals depend on this fact. But knowledge and experience take us only part of the way. The rest comes from good habits and good techniques.

This section covers a largely unwritten set of safe travel rituals that, through the years, avalanche professionals have developed through trial and, sometimes tragic, error. Make no mistake, these techniques don't guarantee safety, they just help push the safety arrow a couple notches closer to the 100 percent mark. The more techniques we use, and the more often we use them, the higher we push the arrow on the scale. We can never reach 100 percent safety, but we can get very close. How close? As noted in the Introduction, helicopter ski guides have to make the correct avalanche decision better than 99 percent of the time if they expect to have a reasonably long career. Even the cagiest avalanche professional in the world is still a human being and humans make mistakes. We will all make the wrong decision at least once in our life, and more likely, several times.

When the inevitable happens, we had better be practicing our safe travel ritual because this is the only way to push the safety arrow from 99 percent to 99.9 percent. Good rescue skills push the arrow up to 99.99 percent, which is the minimum safety margin for a long career. Safe travel techniques are not something we do only when we think the situation is dangerous. Professionals tend to get caught when they either underestimate the hazard or overestimate their skills and let their guard down. In other words, safe travel is more than a technique, it's a ritual. It works only if you do it *all* the time. It's our habits that save our lives.

Having close friends is important but I draw the line at dying together in the same avalanche. Having a partner works only if you spread out and always leave someone in a safe spot to do the rescue. Going uphill is especially difficult because everyone tends to stack up behind the person breaking trail. Small sluffs like this are normally not too dangerous if you're going one at a time, but they can be deadly when one buries both people at once. (Wasatch Range, Utah)

They are so important that I will call them the Ten Commandments of safe travel because, after all, Moses was right. Humans are a damned mess. We need rules.

When I first started working on the ski patrol at Bridger Bowl Ski Area 30 years ago, I learned several rules I was to never violate when running avalanche control routes. I call them the Richmond Rules because my old friend Doug Richmond taught them to me. Day after day, he would drill the Rules into me, and he would deal out the punishment accordingly when I failed to follow them. He took the Rules seriously, and in later years I could see why. In almost every death of an avalanche professional, if they had been following the Rules, they would probably still be alive. The Richmond Rules have saved my life several times. I have modified and expanded upon Doug's original rules through the years to their present form.

1st Commandment: Thou Shalt Go One at a Time—and Leave Someone in a Safe Spot to Do the Rescue

- Resist the herding instinct. The feeling of safety-in-numbers is hard-wired into the human brain and for good reason. For millions of years, it has been a good defense against lions and tigers and bears, but it has just the opposite effect on avalanche dragons. It's essential to resist the herding instinct because of the following reasons:
  A. If something does go wrong, you *always* need to have someone left in a safe spot so they can dig the other(s) out.
  B. Groups of people weigh more than a single person and are more likely to overload buried weak layers.

Always have an escape route pre-planned. He has built up speed and is headed toward gentler terrain with anchors, which has a lower probability of sliding. (Wasatch Range, Utah)

    C. Several people wandering all over the slope are much more likely to find the trigger point of an avalanche than a single person.
- With small groups, expose only one person to the hazard at a time.
- With larger groups, spread out or split the group in half. Always leave enough people in a safe place so they can carry out a rescue. Sometimes it's better to keep two smaller groups on two different slopes in visual contact than to have two groups on different parts of the same slope.
- Stay in visual, voice, or radio contact.

Corollary 1: Never cross above your partner.

Some ski patrols consider crossing above your partner tantamount to attempted homicide and they deal with the infraction accordingly. If you trigger an avalanche on top of your partner, it's not only a very nasty behavior but there's a good chance that *both* of you will get killed because no one is left to carry out a rescue.

Corollary 2: Get out of the way at the bottom.

I work in the Wasatch Range of northern Utah, where a million and a half people live directly at the base of a large mountain range that rises 7000 vertical feet from the valley floor. It's an extremely crowded place. We have watched with horror as backcountry recreation doubles every five years, with largely avalanche-unaware people who fail to follow the 1st Commandment, causing many shouting matches, not to mention dangerous conditions.

It's hard to follow the rules when everyone around you is violating them, and I sometimes catch myself not practicing what I preach. It's a hard problem, and I'm not sure how to combat the craziness, except to keep preaching and ask all of you to help spread the Gospel.

2nd Commandment: Thou Shalt Have an Escape Route Preplanned

If you trigger an avalanche when you're just standing in the middle of the avalanche path (or you're on a stationary snowmobile), you have almost no chance to escape off the moving slab. That is why for years, ski patrollers and helicopter ski guides have used what they call "ski cuts" as an effective technique to reduce the odds of getting caught. I like to call them slope cuts because snowboarders and snowmobilers can do them as well. The idea is that if you trigger an avalanche, you want to do it when you have your speed built up and are heading for an island of safety so that, in theory, if the slope does fracture, your momentum will carry you off the moving slab. In other words, if the first person down just dives in and starts cranking turns, if an avalanche breaks, their options are very limited. Especially, the first person across the slope should always practice slope cuts.

- Get off the slab! Skiers' and snowboarders' technique: Beginning at the top of a slope, cross the slope rapidly at about a 45-degree angle, aiming at an island of safety, such as trees, rocks, or high ground at the edge of the avalanche path.
- Get off the slab! Snowmobile technique: Unlike skiers and 'boarders, snowmobilers have the ability to do slope cuts from the bottom. Instead of doing your first hill climb up the middle of the slope, either climb off to the side or do a swooping, traversing climb low on the slope where you can get off the slope in a hurry if it does break. If you fracture the slope while going uphill and you can't get off to the side, just grab some throttle and keep heading up in hopes that most of the snow will pass beneath you. If you fracture the slope on the way down and can't get off to the side, your only choice is to try and outrun the avalanche, which might work for small avalanches but probably won't for the big ones.

Slope Cut Caveats

- Although slope cuts work fairly well for soft, shallow slabs, *slope cuts are much less effective for hard or deep slabs.* Nevertheless, you should still practice slope cuts on hard slabs as a good defensive technique, but realize that the third or tenth person across the slope is nearly as likely to trigger the slab as the first one.
- Don't get cocky just because you've successfully cut a few avalanches and escaped. Slope cuts are best used as a defensive technique, not an offensive one. Slope cuts are not a guarantee; they're only one more tool in your bag of tricks to push the safety arrow a little closer to 100 percent.

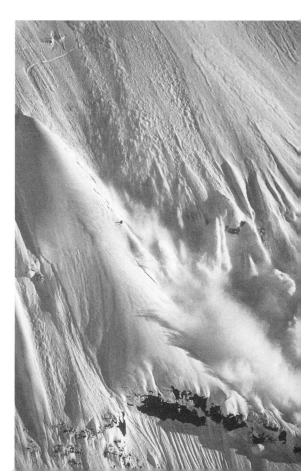

A good example of sluff management. This skier is staying along the crest of the spine and switching to a new spine if things build up too much. Be sure to glance over your shoulder every few turns to see what is chasing you. (Chugach Range, Alaska) © Scott Markewitz

- Keep your speed up. Slope cuts depend on momentum to take you off the slab. Snowmobiles should avoid getting bogged down at the top of a hill climb. When you are on skis or a snowboard, don't poke along like a cow—make like an antelope.

  Corollary: Cross high on the avalanche path. If you trigger an avalanche you want to be as high as possible on the slab for several reasons: First, snow below you can't bury you, but the snow above you can. "Avalanches die from the tail," as the Swiss scientist, Perry Bartlett, puts it. In other words, avalanches lose mass from the tail, or trailing edge, which causes the avalanche to slow and ultimately stop. So the closer you are to the trailing edge, the more likely you will be left behind on the bed surface. Inexperienced people tend to cut too low on the slope and are therefore caught in the leading edge—the most dangerous part—of an avalanche.

Sluff Management Techniques

People who ski, snowboard, snowmobile, or climb in extreme terrain constantly have to deal with sluffs and small slabs. Since the terrain is so steep, even small amounts of sluffing snow can knock you off your feet and send you for a nasty ride. Here are a few pointers from my old friends Doug and Emily Coombs and Jim Conway, ex-extreme skiers who pioneered the Alaska extreme skiing phenomenon. Tragically, Doug recently was killed in France when he slipped and fell off a cliff while coming to the aid of a friend.

First, a sluff is not a sluff. The Alaska helicopter guides generally rate their sluffs in three categories: Class I, Class II, and Class III. Class I sluffs are composed of new, light snow, and you can often ski in them and through them without being knocked off your feet. Class II

A skier descends near a large avalanche that came down the day before. He got away with it because it is slightly less steep with a slightly different aspect. Still, you can bet that I would be the skier waiting on top instead of going first. First tracks are overrated. (Wasatch Range, Utah)

sluffs carry more punch, and they can definitely knock you off your feet. Class III sluffs are composed of dense snow like near surface facets or surface hoar. They can go very fast, and they can easily tumble you down the slope and bury you under 10 feet of debris.

Second, sluffs tend to go slowly at first, but when they reach a certain critical mass, they jump into warp speed and rocket down the mountain, which can take an inexperienced person by surprise.

Third, you should either go slower than the sluff or go faster than the sluff. If you go slower than the sluff, you make a turn or two and wait for it to run out ahead of you. With the new wide skis and snowboards, many of the more elite athletes can stay out ahead of the sluff, but the most important part is to look over your shoulder every turn or every other turn to keep an eye out for when sluffs reach critical mass and suddenly pick up speed.

Fourth, you need to move across the fall line instead of straight up or down. Never turn back into a sluff. Use small sub-ridges (spines and flutes) to your advantage. Stay on or near the crests. When you drop into the gullies, stay up on the sides, never crossing the bottom of the gully when the sluffs you have kicked off will be traveling. When one drainage fills up with sluffing snow, you can often switch into a fresh drainage to your left or right until it fills up with too much snow; then switch again to a fresh slope.

Managing sluffs takes experience and skill. Start practicing in terrain with fewer bad consequences before you jump in big time, which can kill you if you don't know what you're doing.

3rd Commandment: Thou Shalt Never Go First

You should never test the stability of a slope using your most valuable possession—your life. Your parents have invested thousands of dollars in you and only an idiot would risk that kind of investment when there seems to be an endless supply of volunteer stability testers willing to work for free. Snowboarders, skiers, snowshoers, snowmobilers, hikers, Boy Scout troops—they all seem eager for the job. According to Swiss statistics, 90 percent of avalanche accidents are triggered by the first person down. Although there are no good statistics here, I suspect that in intermountain and especially in continental climates of North America this number would be lower because of more persistent weak layers. Still, even in these colder, drier climates, the first person down has a much higher probability of triggering the avalanche than the ones who follow. So, the more tracks in a slope the better. I love going last. All my friends are starting to get wise to me because I have a million excuses. I'll stand at the top and fiddle with my bindings, start chomping on my lunch, call someone on the phone—I'll do anything except go first. Also, when you do go, follow other people's tracks, spooning in your tracks with theirs. Treat an avalanche slope like a minefield. If someone else successfully crossed a particular spot without triggering an avalanche, you probably will too. This is one instance in which the herding instinct works to our advantage.

If you can't find any volunteers, you can use an involuntary stability tester—a cornice, . for example. Just tumble a refrigerator-sized-or-larger chunk of cornice down the slope first (see Chapter 6, Stability, for more details).

4th Commandment: Thou Shalt Never Trust a Cornice

I have personally had three very close calls with cornices and I'm deeply frightened of them. *Never, never, never* walk up to the edge of a drop-off without first checking it out from another angle to see if you'll be standing on nothing but air. If you can't check it out, don't go

to the edge. All too many otherwise sensible people have been needlessly killed this way.

When traveling along a corniced ridge, it's obvious enough that you should travel on the upwind side, but a lot of people travel too close and suddenly get the big elevator ride to hell. Cornices have a nasty habit of breaking farther back than you expect. Most old-time mountaineers have a cornice story or two, and I have seen cornices break farther back than I would have ever imagined. I once saw a cornice break behind a line of trees and behind a large bush that stood between me and the edge. I wore a brace on my knee for a month because of that very close call. Also remember that a person plus a large cornice tumbling down a slope together make a terrific avalanche trigger. Treat cornices with respect, use a belay rope when possible.

Cornices are not all bad. You can use them as a stability test. (See Chapter 6 for the cornice test.)

This cornice was unintentionally triggered by the person who made the tracks shown at the lower right. Never walk up to the edge of a drop-off. (Chugach Range, Alaska) © John Kelly

5th Commandment: Thou Shalt Be Obsessed with Consequences

What will happen if it slides? What's be-

It looks innocent, but this is a nasty terrain trap where even a small avalanche can bury you deeply. This is the site of an avalanche fatality from just such a small avalanche. (Wasatch Range, Utah)

low you? What's above you? What is the slope connected to? If you don't like the consequences, maybe you should find another option.

Always look for the downside of any decision and always challenge your assumptions and beliefs. Continually ask yourself: "Why might this be wrong?"

> Corollary: Remember you can always go back the way you came. The route that got you there will almost always get you back. When all else fails, go underground. Many people have saved themselves during storms by digging a snow cave or creating a snow shelter, which can be surprisingly warm and cozy. Yes, you might be uncomfortable and your loved ones may worry, but at least you will be alive.

6th Commandment: Thou Shalt Start Small and Work Your Way Up

Terrain almost always gives you small gifts—small test slopes—that you can jump on to see how they respond. Never pass up a test slope. It's better to find out the stability of the snowpack on small slopes that won't kill you before you get to the big ones that will. Only a fool jumps into a big slope without first gathering lots of data from other, safer places. This is a standard technique at both ski areas and helicopter skiing operations. They start on gentler, safer slopes and work slowly into more dangerous terrain.

Start gathering information on small, safe terrain before betting with your life on big, dangerous terrain.

7th Commandment: Thou Shalt Communicate

Even here in the Information Age, communication, or lack of it, remains the central problem of our lives. Have you ever noticed that if people would just talk honestly with each other it would eliminate the vast majority of the television and movie plots? It would also prevent most wars.

Professional ski patrols have very strict rules about communication when running an avalanche control route. First, you always need to be in voice or radio contact with your partner. Second, you give clear commands: "You stay on the ridge and I'm going to do a ski cut to the other ridge. After I get there, I'll wave that I'm OK and you come across. Got that?" Or, "I'm going to ski down and around the corner under the cliff; stay here until I call on the radio when I'm safe and you should follow my tracks down and join me."

I love going into the backcountry with other pros because we have all learned the system and operate according to the system. Everything else seems chaotic and dangerous.

"A committee of ordinary people is always smarter than one Einstein."—Roland Emetaz, avalanche expert. Always take advantage of the wisdom of crowds. (Wasatch Range, Utah)

It's not like a military operation in which orders come from the top down. But rather you need to make all your decisions and communicate democratically. (See the "Wisdom of Crowds" in Chapter 10, The Human Factor.)

8th Commandment: Thou Shalt Use a Belay Rope

Most serious avalanche professionals carry and use a belay rope. I usually carry a light-weight piece of 7-mm-by-30-meter rope. You can use a belay rope for digging a snowpit on a suspect slope, rappeling past obstacles, slope cutting, kicking or sawing cornices, waiting for an explosive to go off when standing in an insecure spot, or carrying out a rescue. Ropes are good. Carry one.

9th Commandment: Thou Shalt Use the Right Equipment

Based on many anecdotal examples of victims with releasable bindings ending up on the surface and those without them ending up buried, avalanche professionals doing avalanche control have for many years required releasable bindings and forbidden straps on ski poles. Preliminary analysis of recent Canadian data indicate that, indeed, the likelihood of having a fatal accident is higher with unreleasable bindings. (An update of Canadian avalanche accidents should be published by fall of 2008 from the Canadian Avalanche Centre.)

Also, being tumbled in an avalanche or strained through trees with non-releasable skis, poles, and snowboards attached to your limbs just doesn't seem like a good idea. Finally, every year, many fatalities occur from simply falling head first into a tree well or the bottom of a steep gully, where releasable bindings could help someone escape. Even breakaway pole straps can be dangerous because they may prevent you from getting your hands near your

The importance of consequences and a belay rope: an intentionally triggered avalanche high on Mount Foraker in Alaska. Getting caught here would involve a 10,000-vertical-foot descent that would ruin your day. © Greg Collins

Releasable bindings and no pole straps vs. non-releasable bindings and pole straps. Guess which ones are mine.

face so that you can form an air pocket before the debris comes to a stop. The ski patrol made me cut off my pole straps 30 years ago and I haven't used them since.

Besides the standard rescue equipment of a beacon, shovel, and probe, an avalanche air bag should be the first choice to further increase survivability. They are extremely effective and, statistically, they work much better than beacons. I suspect they will rapidly become lighter and cheaper in the next few years and they will soon be considered standard equipment. I also recommend that everyone wear an Avalung™ and carry a RECCO™ chip somewhere on their body. Both are cheap and lightweight so there is no reason not to use them. (See Chapter 9, Rescue, for details.)

Additional useful equipment: A radio to communicate with your partner(s), an inclinometer to measure slope steepness, a compass or GPS, a first-aid kit, extra warm clothes—a minimum of extra hat, mittens, puff coat and pants—and extra food.

10th Commandment: Terrain, Terrain, Terrain

As Canadian avalanche consultant Chris Stethem says, "Never underestimate the importance or subtlety of terrain. It takes a lifetime to learn terrain—maybe two lifetimes." If you learn nothing else from this book, become a master of terrain management on both large and small scales. Continually choose a route based on steepness, anchors, aspect with respect to the wind and sun, slope shape, and consequences. (See Chapter 3, Terrain Management.)

Canadian helicopter skiers sticking to lower angled terrain during dangerous conditions. The guide approached the edge just to have a look and was almost pulled over the edge. © Mike Welch Photography

STABILITY AND ROUTEFINDING

The old U.S. Forest Service Avalanche Handbook has a diagram of a skier crossing a slope with sparse trees with the caption below telling you to never cross a steep, open slope without trees. I happen to know the guys who wrote that handbook and I can assure you that they spent a lot of their careers skiing steep, open slopes without trees and they had a lot of fun in the process. They just knew enough to do it when the snow was stable. Mountain people live to play on steep, open slopes without trees, in other words, avalanche terrain. The question is, how can we do it safely?

The rules of routefinding are not etched in stone. They depend on the stability of the snowpack, the type of instability, the kind of group, the goals of the group, and the mode of travel. For instance, during green-light conditions, you can go almost anywhere with almost any group and do almost any kind of activity. In yellow-light conditions, your choices become more limited; in red-light conditions the terrain available to you becomes severely limited as well as the makeup of your group and the techniques you use.

Routefinding has just as much to do with what you don't know as what you do. In the avalanche game, you never have as much information as you would like, so you need to adjust your behavior depending on how much you know. For instance, if you have a lot of uncertainty, take a conservative approach and choose a route where you can gather information along the way. Stop by a little test slope, jump on it to see how it responds, and then dig a snowpit on a slope that has the same aspect and elevation as the slope you want to play on for the day.

Routefinding also has a lot to do with your group. How fit are you, what kind of equipment do you have, what is your level of acceptable risk, how fast do you travel, how skilled are you, what are your goals, what kind of communication do you have, and what are your avalanche skills?

The rules of routefinding are a dynamic process that depend on the stability of the snowpack, the weather, and the kind of people you're with. The kind of terrain that is available to you and how you travel on that terrain depends on the conditions. Routefinding also varies depending on what kind of avalanche dragon you're dealing with. (See Chapter 5, Snowpack, for a more detailed discussion.)

For instance, if we consider the stability of the snowpack, we use the Fredston and Fesler stoplight analogy in which we separate the stability of the snowpack into the categories of red light, yellow light, and green light.

Red-Light Conditions
Tests and Observations: Dry Snow
- Localized-to-widespread recent natural avalanches
- Small-to-medium-sized cornice blocks rolling down slopes produce avalanches most of the time
- Collapsing and cracking of the snowpack
- Most snowpit tests show unstable snow
- Recent heavy loading of new and/or wind-blown snow

Tests and Observations: Wet Snow
- Localized-to-widespread recent natural avalanches
- Rain on new snow

Red light conditions—dense, new snow, strong wind, and triggering avalanches from the flat ridges above. (Wasatch Range, Utah)

- Rapid melting of new snow
- Sinking in past your knees while walking in wet snow

Terrain Available
- Avoid slopes steeper than about 30 degrees
- Stay out from underneath any slopes steeper than about 30 degrees
- If you venture into steeper terrain, do so only in dense trees or heavily wind-scoured slope avalanche paths without multiple starting zones that have recently avalanched

People Considerations
- Travel only with strong, well-equipped people with good avalanche skills

Yellow-Light Conditions
Tests and Observations: Dry Snow
- Localized recent natural avalanches
- Large cornice blocks rolling down slopes produce only sporadic or localized avalanches
- Localized areas of collapsing and cracking
- Mixed results on snowpit tests
- More than two days since heavy loading or rapid warming (longer in cold climates or snowpacks with faceted weak layers)

Tests and Observations: Wet Snow
- Localized recent natural avalanches
- Sinking in past your ankles while walking in wet snow
- Rain on old snow
- Rapid warming of old snow

Terrain Available
- Selective slopes steeper than 35 degrees, but you have to really know what you're doing. If you have low avalanche skills, stay on gentle terrain.
- Use full repertoire of safe travel techniques.

People Considerations
- Most avalanche accidents happen during yellow-light conditions. People perceive that conditions are safe, but enough booby traps are still around so that people with low avalanche skills eventually get into trouble. Even someone with good avalanche skills needs to spend a lot of time gathering data to make decisions. Many of the common human factors come into play, such as the herding instinct, impatience, euphoria, positive reinforcement, ego, pride, attitude, etc. Some people with lower avalanche skills can accompany skilled members, but only under supervision.

Green-Light Conditions

Tests and Observations: Dry Snow
- No recent avalanche activity
- No collapsing and cracking
- Large cornice blocks rolling down a slope produce no avalanches
- Snowpit tests show mostly stable snow
- More than several days without heavy loading or rapid warming

Tests and Observations: Wet Snow
- Thick, refrozen snow surface
- Mature, isothermal snowpack (no layers and course-grained with established drainage channels)
- Not sinking in past ankles when walking

Terrain Available
- Most routes are safe.
- This is the time to do those extreme routes you have always dreamed of, but only after carefully checking them out. Avalanches still occur in green-light conditions, they're just very isolated. As always, continue to follow safe travel techniques.

People Considerations
- This is the time to go out with large groups or folks with low avalanche skills. If you get lazy about following the rules of safe travel ritual, this is the time to do it.

ROUTEFINDING BOOT CAMP

Now, no more practice, you have to do it for real—betting with your life, using what we have learned in Chapter 7 about evaluating hazard. Then, on a large scale, use the Avaluator to choose the general area approach for the conditions. As you apporach avalanche terrain, look carefully at the terrain from several angles and draw the various possible routes in your mind's eye from the bottom to the top or from the top to the bottom. List the reasons why you would choose that route from the perspective of steepness, anchors, aspect with respect to both wind and sun, and consequences. Do you see any alternative routes? Where is the crux? Where will you find test slopes? Where will you dig a snowpit? What kind of group do you have? What kind of equipment do you have? Draw each route over and over in your mind looking at pluses and minuses of each one until you eventually zero in on the best one. Know why it's the best one and list the reasons. Then it's time for the final exam.

Take the route and see how it works out. Continually make changes while you travel and gather more information. Afterwards, review your mistakes. Keep doing this every time you go out and by the end of the season you will have much-improved routefinding skills. After several years, you will be well on your way to being a routefinding master.

HOW ROUTEFINDING VARIES WITH DIFFERENT ACTIVITIES

Skiers, snowmobilers, snowboarders, snowshoers, and climbers all must travel differently because of the nature of the equipment and the sport. Also, different kinds of avalanche workers manage the terrain differently. Here is a short list of how routefinding varies with each activity.

Snowmobilers

Advantages
- Modern machines offer a nearly unlimited choice of terrain so snowmobilers can cover nearly as much terrain as a helicopter skiing company. This means they can easily choose alternate terrain if one type of terrain proves too dangerous and they can test many small slopes before getting onto the big ones.
- It's easy to jettison gear and swim if caught in an avalanche.
- A helmet with facemask can provide an air space when buried.
- Warm clothing helps prevent hypothermia when buried, lost, or broken down.
- Power and speed make it easier to escape off a slab.

Disadvantages
- Power and speed allow snowmobilers to cover ten to one hundred times the amount of terrain as a skier in a day. This means if any instability is out there, they will likely find it.
- Snowmobiles are heavy, so they are more efficient as avalanche triggers.
- Helmet, noise, and speed make it difficult to feel or hear obvious signs of instability and also make it difficult to communicate.
- Power and speed easily give a false sense of confidence.
- Traversing on a snowmobile is difficult, so doing slope cuts is harder.
- Snowmobiling is relatively easy to learn compared to skiing, so anyone, regardless of athletic ability or avalanche training, can easily access dangerous avalanche terrain.
- Snowmobiles can break down and leave their riders stranded. (Always ride with a partner.)

Snowmobiler on avalanche debris (Alaska) © Doug Fesler

Routefinding Considerations

- Stop regularly, get off the machine, and examine the snow for unstable conditions.
- Since it's so easy to cover all kinds of terrain, there's no excuse for not testing several small slopes before getting onto the big, dangerous ones.
- Always do a slope cut on the first hill climb of a large slope. Do it lower on the slope as a swooping, traversing cut so that if you do trigger an avalanche, your momentum will take you into safe terrain.
- Do high hill climbing on the side of an avalanche path or turning toward the edge of the avalanche path for a better chance of escape.
- Do *not* come to the aid of a stuck partner in avalanche terrain. (Thirty-three percent of snowmobiler fatalities involve a stuck sled and 34 percent have more than one machine on the slope at the time of the accident.)
- Choose flat or convex terrain to hill climb instead of concave bowls where avalanche debris funnels into a confined area.
- If you must park at the bottom of an avalanche path, at least do it with your sleds parked parallel—not one in front of the other—pointed away from the slope. Have the kill switches up and ready for a quick getaway.
- Many snowmobiles tend to float to the surface of the debris because they are larger objects. Most victims are found within 3 to 10 meters (10 to 40 feet) *uphill* of their sled and in line with their sled.

Matt Turley practicing some transportation between snowpits. (Wasatch Range, Utah)

Skiers

Advantages

- Skis are a practical, time-tested, and efficient vehicle for backcountry travel, and skiers can move fairly quickly over steep mountainous terrain in many different conditions and terrain types.
- Good mobility allows skiers to switch to a more favorable aspect or drainage as conditions change.
- Slow ascent and intimate contact with the snow allows skiers to evaluate snow stability.
- Releasable bindings (except for non-releasable telemark bindings).

Disadvantages

- No power to escape off a slab like a snowmobiler.
- Some free-heel bindings do not release.
- Ascending tends to bunch people together behind the trailbreaker. Spread out.

Routefinding Considerations

- You spend much more time going up than coming down, so the uphill track needs to be in an especially safe place. If you're going to take risks, do it on the descent instead of the ascent, and do it one at a time.
- Don't do jump turns. Ski smoothly and keep your speed up for an easier escape.

Snowboarders

Advantages

- Snowboards have great flotation, making them fast and stable going downhill, so escape off a slab is easier than for skiers.
- Intimate contact with the snow allows for ongoing stability evaluation.
- When traveling uphill on foot, choosing the direct, wind-eroded side of a ridge is easier for boarders on foot than for skiers in slippery plastic boots and snowmobilers.

Disadvantages

- No releasable bindings—dangerous if caught in an avalanche.
- Going uphill is hard, especially on foot. Snowshoes, split-apart boards, or small skis provide better mobility. Boarders on foot tend to walk in ski tracks, which ruins the tracks and can lead to fistfights with skiers.
- Because uphill travel is slow and traversing on foot is difficult, switching to a different aspect or drainage when conditions change is also difficult. If you're traveling on foot, choose the initial terrain carefully.
- Snowboards are very stable in many kinds of conditions that might foil a skier, so boarders tend to get a false sense of security and can end up riding in more dangerous conditions, such as on breakable wind slabs and soggy, wet snow.
- Snowboarding is easy to learn, so inexperienced riders can easily access dangerous avalanche terrain.
- Gullies used as half-pipes or with jumps on the side are dangerous terrain traps where even small avalanches can bury someone deeply.

Utah Avalanche Center forecaster Brett Kobernik on his day off. (Wasatch Range, Utah)
© Howie Garber/ Wanderlust Images

My two best friends on our Muldrow Traverse expedition (Harper Glacier, Mount McKinley, Alaska)

- Cutting cornices for stability tests is harder. (Stomping with skis or using a snow saw on the end of a ski pole works well.)
- Most boarders don't use ski poles, which are handy for probing into the snow to feel for unseen layers below and traversing a slope. With a snow saw attached to the end of a ski pole, cutting cornices and doing rutschblock tests is easy. (More and more boarders carry poles in the backcountry for ascending.)

Routefinding Considerations
- Because of slow speed going uphill and lack of releasable bindings going downhill, you have to be exceptionally conservative with snow stability decisions, both going up and coming down.
- When traveling on foot, choose the initial terrain carefully because switching later is hard.
- When traveling uphill on foot, choose the direct, wind-eroded side of a ridge.

Climbers
Advantages
- Not as much gear to jettison if caught, but attached ice axes can be deadly.
- Intimate contact with the snow allows for ongoing stability evaluation.
- Climbers almost always carry ropes

Disadvantages
- Climbers are often in such dangerous terrain that avalanches are the least of their worries. Sometimes a wise mountaineering decision might be an unwise avalanche decision.

- Climbers often don't carry beacons not only to save weight but because they believe that avalanches in big mountains are often unsurvivable anyway, which is often not the case. Climbers should carry beacons.
- Sometimes lack of good visibility causes climbers to camp under icefalls or beneath obviously dangerous avalanche slopes. Use a map and a GPS or shoot a runout angle in good visibility.
- Escape off a slab is hard because travel is slow going both up and down.
- Even small sluffs on steep terrain can knock climbers off their feet and into terrain with very bad consequences.

Routefinding Considerations
- Objective hazard is often the largest concern. Travel fast in dangerous terrain and choose timing carefully.
- Check out water-ice climbs for looming avalanche hazard above, and choose timing carefully.
- Because you spend so much time in dangerous avalanche terrain, you must be especially diligent about the choice of timing and route.
- Use a map and GPS for choosing camps and routes in poor visibility.

Snowshoers
Advantages
- Intimate contact with snow allows for ongoing stability evaluation.
- Many snowshoers carry ski poles, which work well for probing the unseen layers below. A snow saw attached to the end of a ski pole makes cutting cornices and doing rutschblock tests easier.

Snowshoeing is cheap, easy, and rapidly becoming more popular. (Wasatch Range, Utah)

Disadvantages
- No releasable bindings, so snowshoes are dangerous in an avalanche.
- Traversing steep terrain is difficult.
- Snowshoers lack the power of a snowmobile and the mobility of skiers and 'boarders to escape off moving slabs.
- Snowshoeing is easy to learn, so inexperienced people can easily access dangerous avalanche terrain.

Routefinding Considerations
- Travel is slow both going up and coming down, and traversing steep terrain is difficult, so you must be especially careful about the initial choice of terrain. Switching terrain after the initial decision is hard.
- Because of slow travel and lack of releasable bindings, you can't afford to make mistakes in routefinding and snow stability decisions; choose terrain and conditions very carefully.

Workers (Plow Drivers, Construction Workers)
Advantages
- Workers often have a building or vehicle that can offer some protection from avalanches, but this can also create a false sense of security.
- Workers often have the budget to hire a dedicated avalanche forecaster.

Disadvantages
- Workers often spend large amounts of time at the bottom of avalanche paths, so they must be especially diligent about choosing the proper conditions.
- Workers often operate under intense time or money constraints or intense client pressure and may take risks because of it.

Routefinding and Terrain Management Considerations
- Hire an avalanche specialist to evaluate the terrain, control the avalanches with explosives or defense structures, and forecast avalanche hazard. Or better yet, become an avalanche specialist yourself.
- Workers at the bottom of avalanche paths usually don't trigger the avalanches; instead, avalanches come down from above during times of high or extreme conditions. This is harder to manage than working in the starting zones, because you can't see the conditions that may kill you.

Ski Patrollers (Avalanche Control Workers)
Advantages
- Patrollers operate as a well-rehearsed team in a very controlled environment with route partners, back-up rescuers, and detailed information on path history, snow stability, and weather.
- Patrollers can use explosives to directly and efficiently test snow stability—big advantage.
- Patrollers usually work from the top down. (They seldom have to ascend dangerous avalanche terrain.)
- Patrollers usually have permanent, fixed belay systems in place when necessary.

Ski patroller kicking cornices (Wasatch Range, Utah)

Disadvantages
- Patrollers almost always deal with an "artificial" snowpack, which has been bombed and skied into submission. They can easily develop a false sense of security and then get into trouble when they have to deal with a natural, backcountry snowpack, such as the first few days of the season or when they control areas that have not been open for a few days.
- Patrollers spend large amounts of time in hazardous avalanche terrain and tend to get caught more often because of it.
- Intense time and money pressure from management and customers.

Routefinding and Terrain Management Considerations
- Work from the top down. Never cross beneath uncontrolled terrain.
- Install permanent belay systems where necessary.
- Because you can use slope cuts to keep up on an increasing hazard during a storm, it's easy to misjudge or overuse slope cuts. Sometimes you get into trouble trying to slope cut a hard slab or cut too low on a slope.
- Slope cuts on hard slabs are dangerous. Use explosives.
- Watch out for early season; you are dealing with a backcountry snowpack. Places that usually have moguls can produce dangerous avalanches. Also, in early season you often deal with persistent weak layers, such as depth hoar and surface hoar. The trigger point is often low on the slope, not high in the wind-loaded zones like in midwinter.

Helicopter Ski Guides

Advantages

- Heli guides have a wide choice of terrain and can easily use safe terrain in unstable conditions.
- Heli guides can use explosives to directly and efficiently test for instability.
- Heli guides operate in a more controlled environment than other recreationists. They use "tail gunners" (guides who always go last so they can perform a rescue if necessary), back up rescuers, and detailed information on path history, snow stability, and weather. They usually are highly trained and very experienced.

Disadvantages

- The "magic carpet ride" into the middle of dangerous terrain does not give heli guides nearly as much time to evaluate snow stability as other recreationists. They must rely on scout parties, forecasting, and intimate knowledge of the snowpack and terrain.
- Guides often deal with intense client pressure and money pressure from expensive helicopter time or pressure from film crews. This can push inexperienced guides into unsafe situations.
- With large groups, it's difficult to go one at a time.
- Guides deal with huge areas of uncontrolled, backcountry snowpack and often several days have passed since they last skied a particular slope.
- Digging representative snow profiles on a daily basis can be difficult.
- Because of euphoria, managing a client's routefinding decisions is difficult.

Routefinding and Terrain Management Considerations

- Keep a close eye on clients—close communication—close supervision. They tend to stray off the safest line and can endanger themselves and others.
- Start on gentle terrain and work your way onto steeper terrain as you gather more snow stability information for that area. Or start on a safe aspect and work your way onto a suspect aspect as you gather more information. Never dive in without gathering information.
- If possible, send an advance "scout party" to check out new terrain the day before you plan to fly there.
- Maintain close communication with other avalanche workers in the area (ski patrols, avalanche forecast centers, other helicopter companies, etc.).
- Guides should regularly practice slope cuts at the top of each slope and at each breakover.
- When possible, use a tail gunner or use an experienced client as a tail gunner.

chapter nine

RESCUE

Remember the avalanche does not know you are an expert.
—Andre Roch, retired Swiss avalanche scientist

The good news is that humans make mistakes because that's how we learn. The bad news is that mistakes in avalanche terrain can lead to very expensive lessons. This is the nub of the dilemma; by our very nature, we will make mistakes yet in avalanche terrain we can't afford to make mistakes, at least very many of them. So what do we do? We minimize the damage.

As we saw in Chapter 8, one way to minimize the damage of mistakes is to ritualistically practice safe travel techniques and when those don't work, depend on rescue. This is the place we all hope that we will never have to visit because it means that everything else has failed. Even when we do everything right, sometimes we have to rescue another party in need of help. Eventually, if you spend much time in avalanche terrain, there's a good chance you'll be glad that you've been regularly practicing your rescue techniques.

Here's another sobering fact: Avalanche rescue doesn't work very well. As we will see, rescues—even by professionals—are usually a mess. With the inherent problems of wild emotions, impossible time constraints, lack of resources, nightmarish communication

Not using beacons is not only dangerous, but it usually means drudgery for searchers. If rescuers cannot locate the victims using dogs or probe lines, they have no choice but to leave their bodies to melt out in spring. Here family and friends continue efforts for several days after rescuers have given up on this snowmobiler. (Wasatch Range, Utah)

problems, and foul weather, it's a wonder that any rescues succeed at all. Yet something about rescue captures our imagination. There's action and drama and the potential for heroism, life and death, and a race against time. Television programs love the subject of rescue and in nearly every avalanche talk I've ever given, that's all people want to know: What do you do when you get caught? How do you save someone's life? Now I don't fight it anymore. I talk about rescue in the first part of the talk—get it out of the way—because after that everyone realizes that, sorry, most of the time there's not a whole lot you can do after you get caught and rescue doesn't work very well anyway. Then everyone is ready to listen to the important part—that the best avalanche rescue is to never need one.

TABLE 9-1. TIMETABLE FOR A TYPICAL AVALANCHE*	
Time	What to Expect If Caught
Fracture	You may hear a muffled whoomph sound; sometimes a loud CRACK. You notice cracks around you.
1 to 2 seconds	The slab starts to move. It feels like someone pulled the rug out from under you. Most people almost invariably fall down. The slab shatters into blocks. The slab quickly picks up speed and after 2 seconds is moving about 15 km/hr (10 mph). In other words, in order to escape off the slab, you need to take action *now*. After this, it will be too late. If you haven't preplanned your escape route, you probably won't be able to pull it off.
2 to 5 seconds	After 5 seconds, the avalanche is moving 15 to 40 km/hr (10 to 30 mph). The blocks are now tumbling furiously. Skiing, snowboarding, and snowmobiling become impossible. Ski bindings release. It's now too late to grab a tree because you're definitely moving fast enough to cause injury or death. After this, you are, as Doug Richmond says, "a fly in the toilet bowl."
5 to 10 seconds	The avalanche is traveling 70 to 130 km/hr (40 to 80 mph). You are being tumbled hard and do not know which way is up. With every breath, you suck in a snow-air mixture that forms a plug of ice in your throat. Breathing is difficult. Hats, mittens, goggles are gone. Impacts with trees or rocks cause injury or death.
10 to 15 seconds	The avalanche slows down and the debris solidifies into a cohesive block even well before it comes to a complete stop. Make sure you bury your mouth in the crook of your elbow to make an air pocket.
Avalanche stops	Debris instantly sets up like concrete often while it is still moving. You are frozen in place and cannot move. Completely buried victims cannot dig themselves out or form an air pocket.
4 minutes	As you rebreathe the carbon dioxide that builds up in the snow around your mouth, you begin to lose consciousness.
15 minutes	Most of those buried will still be alive but unconscious, and some may have brain damage.
25 minutes	Half of completely buried victims not already killed by trauma will be dead.
35 minutes	73 percent of completely buried victims not already killed by trauma will be dead. Anyone who survives after this time must have an air pocket, which slows the build up of carbon dioxide.
90 minutes	81 percent of victims are dead.
130 minutes	97 percent of victims are dead.
* Also see Figure I-1 in the Introduction.	

Yes, sweet air at last. Unless this happens in the first 15 minutes, most rescues don't have a happy ending (Wasatch Range, Utah)

STRATEGY FOR VICTIMS

Most people don't make it off a moving slab. Everything happens *very* fast and unless you are practicing a slope cut or already have an escape route pre-planned and have been rehearsing everything in your mind, you most likely won't be able to do it. Most people don't even know what's going on until it's too late. If you are caught, some of these techniques may work.

A. While the Avalanche Is Moving

1. *Yell.*

   Let your partners know that you are caught. **Note:** Some folks are what we call "hooters"—they like to hoot and holler on the way down to let everyone know how much fun they are having. Save the yelling for when you need it. Besides, we all go to the backcountry for peace and quiet. It's just bad form to make a racket in a quiet place.

2. *Try to escape off the slab.*

   Remember that the snow below you can't bury you, but the snow above you can. So do whatever it takes to let as much snow pass below you as possible. If you are still able, use your momentum (or the power of a snowmobile) to move toward the edge of the avalanche where you can ride onto non-moving or slower-moving snow. If you are near the upper fracture line of the slab, sometimes you can climb uphill and dig into the bed surface. Try to grab a tree if you can. Even if you still get taken for the full ride, at least some of these techniques give you a chance to be on the slower, dying part of the avalanche where you stand a much better chance of ending up on the surface.

3. *If you can't get off the slab, get rid of your equipment.*

Release your ski bindings. Skis with releasable bindings will be torn off quickly, but snowboards and snowshoes don't have releasable bindings, which is a big problem. Some 'boarders rig their bindings with a ripcord to get out of them in an avalanche. For instance, plate bindings for hard boots can be fitted with a cord on the latches and Clicker bindings can be fitted with a cord on the release.

4. *If you have one:*

- Get Avalung™ mouthpiece in your mouth. (See the "Avalung™" section below.)
- Deploy avalanche air bag. (See the "Avalanche Air Bags" section below.)
- If you do not have an Avalung™, you should use the technique suggested by Halstead Morris, an avalanche educator with the Colorado Avalanche Information Center: Reach across your face and grab the pack strap by your opposite shoulder and bury your mouth in the crook of your arm. This will help to strain the snow out the air you will breathe, protect your face from trauma, and create an air pocket when the debris solidifies.

5. *Leave your pack on.*

You should leave your pack on for the following reasons:

- A pack provides valuable padding to your back and kidneys when bouncing off trees and rocks.
- Should you survive, your pack contains everything you'll need: shovel, probe, extra hat, mittens and warm clothes, food, water, first-aid kit, etc.
- Larger objects tend to end up on the surface, similar to shaking a bag of tortilla chips to get the largest pieces. Your pack helps make you a larger object, which will help keep you near the surface.

6. *Discussion—To Swim or Not to Swim*

Every avalanche instructor since the beginning of time has instructed their students to swim hard to stay on the surface. Since riding in avalanche debris feels very similar to floating through a rapid in a river, almost everyone will automatically swim anyway, since swimming in water is hard-wired into every living creature on Earth. Although avalanches move in both laminar and turbulent flow, like water, much of the avalanche moves in "granular flow" where larger objects rise to the surface through "inverse segregation." And lucky for us because the human body is three times denser than snow and it would instantly sink to the bottom if avalanches flowed like water. Instead, most buried avalanche victims are within the top meter of the snow surface and deeper burials usually only occur in terrain traps such as gullies.

Although some articles have been written lately that question the wisdom of swimming in avalanche debris, avalanche scientists agree that there is no data to support the idea that you should not swim. In fact, something that supports swimming is that European professional guides tend to end up on the surface of avalanches more often than do their clients. Presumably guides struggle harder because that is what every guide has been trained to do; but also, guides tend to carry larger packs than their clients, making them larger objects, which tend to rise. The only thing we do know for sure about inverse segregation is that avalanche air bags have been phenomenally successful, leading to as much as a ten-fold decrease in mortality (see discussion on air bags below). Until more research settles the question, I will continue to advocate swimming in avalanche debris as long as you protect your airway when the avalanche begins to slow, which brings us to our next point.

B. As the Avalanche Slows Down

7. *With one arm, make an air space around your mouth.*

As avalanche debris slows down, friction tends to cause the leading debris to pile up in front and we often see large areas of debris solidify into a solid mass even before it comes to a complete stop. For this reason, victims often report that they were frozen in place much sooner than they expected. Far too often, we uncover victims with their arms frozen in swimming motions. Instead, it's important to make an air pocket in front of your mouth.

If you don't have an Avalung™ (see below), make sure to bury your mouth in the crook of your arm by reaching across your face and grabbing the pack strap by your opposite shoulder, even as you continue to struggle with your other limbs. The larger the cavity around your mouth, the longer you will live under the snow. If you can get rid of your carbon dioxide along your arm you will last longer than if your mouth is in direct contact with the snow. Plus, it helps prevent the formation of an impermeable ice mask, which exacerbates CO_2 buildup.

Snowmobilers: A helmet with a full facemask seems to help prevent the formation of an ice mask, at least in smaller avalanches. In larger avalanches, the helmet is often filled with snow or the mask flips up. Even with a face mask it's probably best to practice the same technique mentioned above.

8. *Extend a hand toward the surface.*

You might not even know which way is up, but still try to push a hand to the surface. It's much easier to find a victim using a visible body part than it is using a beacon or probe. But make sure your other arm is covering your mouth. Remember you must do this *well before* the avalanche comes to a complete stop. Once it stops, it will set up firmly and you will not be able to move even your little finger unless you are very near the surface or the debris is unusually soft, for example in a very small avalanche.

C. When the Avalanche Comes to a Stop

9. *Relax*

Relax. Right! Even Zen masters will have a hard time relaxing after all that. But remember that the clock is ticking until the carbon dioxide builds up and puts you to sleep, so do your best to go into hibernation mode. You won't be able to move anyway so there's not much choice. If you're lucky enough to have a hand above or very near the surface, you may even be able to move snow, which could help to create a channel to disburse carbon dioxide. But the vast majority of completely buried victims quickly lose consciousness.

D. Equipment considerations:

- Snowmobilers should always wear a helmet with a face shield and a good seal around the neck. It helps protect you from trauma and, at least in smaller avalanches, the helmet may not fill up with snow. I'm hopeful that helmet makers will soon offer a model with an Avalung built into it.
- Snowmobilers should wear a shovel on their back in a small pack instead of on the snowmobile. If you survive and your snowmobile is buried, you will need a shovel to dig out your friends.

- Skiers should always wear releasable bindings and not use pole straps. There is good anecdotal evidence and some data that indicates that victims with releasable bindings tend to end up on the surface significantly more often than victims with skis, a board, or snowshoes attached.
- Snowboarders should rig their bindings with a ripcord to get out of their snowboard in a hurry.
- Avalung™s and especially avalanche air bags work very well. Everyone should use an Avalung™ since they are light and cheap. Those that can afford the extra expense and weight of an avalanche air bag should use one. As these get lighter and cheaper, they will soon be considered standard equipment, like wearing a PFD on a white-water river.
- Most trauma deaths among avalanche victims involve head and neck injuries. Everyone should wear a helmet.

STRATEGY FOR SURVIVORS

This is your basic nightmare. You have just watched your partner, friend, or loved one trigger an avalanche, get swept away, and vanish in the debris. Now their survival depends only on you! In stressful situations like this, the brain's frontal lobe (logic and judgment) usually shuts down and you operate on a deeper, reptilian level. In fact, I know one beacon manufacturer who tests the usability of their products using people with mental handicaps because it mimics how most of us operate under stress. Like everyone else in these situations, you will make stupid mistakes. Even rescues by professionals are often a mess. When the guacamole hits the fan, everyone operates on autopilot, and the more you have practiced beforehand, the more likely your autopilot will make the right choices. Practice, practice, practice. It's the only way to do a rescue quickly.

So here are the steps you should practice beforehand:

Last-Seen Area

First, if you can see the victims, watch them closely. Memorize exactly where you saw them last and watch them travel down the mountain to see where they end up. If they are swallowed up by snow, watch the parcel of snow to see where it ends up. Often the victims travel straight down the flow line from their last-seen area and clues such as gloves and hats also line up with the victim. Knowing approximately where to start searching will make things go much faster.

Do Not Send Someone for Help

That's right. Do not send someone for help. This is why:

1. You don't even know yet if the victim needs help. They may be just fine. Don't endanger the lives of organized rescuers unless you know you will need the extra resources.
2. An avalanche victim is essentially a drowning victim. Time is of the essence. A rescue crew won't show up for at least another hour or two, even in the best of circumstances. By that time, the rescue operation will likely have turned into a body recovery. You need all your resources to stay and help get your friend out of the snow and breathing as soon as possible.
3. If you have trouble locating a completely buried victim or you have a victim with trauma injuries, then you can probably take an extra minute to call on a mobile phone

for help. But don't send someone for help because you will need *all* your resources for the search. Remember, even if you have contact with a cell phone you should still not call for help until you know you will need it.

Witnesses and Survivors

If you didn't see the accident but others did, keep close track of the witnesses. Witnesses have a wealth of valuable information that you need to speed up the rescue, plus witnesses and survivors are often in a difficult emotional state and they need someone to keep track of them. Witnesses, especially frantic witnesses, have a habit of bolting off to call for a rescue party, wandering away from the scene—perhaps into the next avalanche path—or interfering with the rescue efforts. Sit them down. Calm them down. Find out what you can. How many people? Were they wearing beacons? Exactly where did they last see the victim? These are all critical questions that only the witnesses or survivors can answer. Countless rescues have been delayed because the witnesses got away or the rescuers failed to interview them adequately.

Off to the Rescue!

Every fiber in your body urges you to hurl yourself after your friend who has just been swept away, find them, dig them out— *It's off to the rescue!* Right? Wrong.

One of the chief reasons we have been so successful as a species is because compassion is hard-wired into the human brain. Yet there are times—difficult times—when our individual survival depends on being able to suppress our instincts. Take a step back, calm down, and *stop, think, plan.* No one said this would be easy.

In an avalanche rescue, your priorities are as follows, listed in order of importance:

1. Yourself
2. The other survivors
3. The victim

First of all, the victim may be just fine and not even need help—or the victim may be mortally injured or already dead. In either case, it makes no sense to risk your life for someone who doesn't need it. Remember that the number-one rule of rescue is to look out for number one. Stop, think, plan.

Is it safe? This is a classic example of a path with multiple starting zones that all terminate in the same narrow gully. If one section has run out but the others have not, you have a tough decision to make. (Wasatch Range, Utah)

Is It Safe?

Stop and take a minute to add up the facts. If you can't get to the debris safely, don't go. If a loved one is buried under the snow, this will likely be the most difficult decision of your life.

The good news is that most of the time, conditions will be safe, for the same reason that a stick of dynamite is safe after it has already gone off. Most of the time, you can safely descend into the avalanche path or, better yet, come up from the bottom. Whatever you do, don't be tempted to cross an adjacent avalanche path that has not yet slid. Remember the best sign of avalanches is avalanches. If one slope has just avalanched, the identical one next to it will likely do the same if you give it a thump. Choose your route carefully.

When to Consider Saying No

1. If you're standing above the avalanche and there is too much "hangfire" (unslid snow above the crown face) to cross over to get to the crown face. I am not aware of any case where hangfire has come down on its own if it is left undisturbed. Usually you can cross short sections of hangfire safely, say 10 meters (33 feet). However, if the avalanche broke mid-slope and a disconcerting amount of snow hangs above the fracture, you should try to find a better way onto the debris. This is a tough call.

Figure 9-1. Is it safe to do the rescue? When the accident site sits at the bottom of multiple avalanche paths, you have a tough decision to make.

2. If you're standing below the avalanche, it's almost always safe to travel uphill onto the debris, unless you are faced with the following combination of circumstances:
    - Multiple avalanche paths drain onto the rescue area (Figure 9-1) and
    - The victim was buried by a spontaneous avalanche that descended from above and
    - The weather that caused the avalanche will likely cause more avalanches in the immediate future (heavy loading of new or wind-blown snow, rain, or rapid melting).

Obviously, this situation is another very tough call. Numerous times organized rescue groups have decided to abandon a search because of dangerous or deteriorating conditions—often amid heated debate. But first things first. Look out for number one. Personally, in this situation, I might risk doing a quick scuff search or a beacon search, but I would not risk bringing in a larger group of searchers, especially an organized probe line that could take considerable time.

Stop, Think, Plan

If it is safe to go in, then we go to the next step. As Dough Fesler says, sometimes the best way to go faster is to go slower. Strong emotions, poor communication, equipment problems, logistical problems—they all conspire to make rescues a mess—nearly every one of them, even among professionals. So to reduce the mess factor, stop, think, plan.
- Any witnesses? Don't let them get away. Ask them for information.
- Figure out which group member has the most avalanche rescue experience and appoint that person as the leader.
- Take a quick inventory of your equipment—beacons, probes, shovels, first-aid kit.
- Turn your beacons to receive and check everyone's beacon to make sure, because one inadvertently transmitting beacon can short-circuit the entire rescue. (This mistake occurs in many rescues.)
- Find out who's good at what. Put your best beacon people on the job.
- Remind everyone to communicate with the leader.
- Remind everyone to keep their equipment with them. Don't litter up the debris. Otherwise, you won't know which equipment belongs to the victim and which belongs to the rescuers.

RESCUE WITH BEACONS
Turn Beacons to Receive

In nearly every avalanche rescue practice I have done with beginning students, someone fails to turn their beacon to receive. As a result, the searchers spend the first 10 minutes hopelessly confused by a "mysterious" signal that seems to come and go until they finally trace it to one of their own (we have met the enemy and he is us). Instead, if you hear a signal that doesn't make sense, stop and listen. If the signal changes, that means it's coming from a moving source. In avalanche classes, I don't fight it anymore; I just let the inevitable happen and it always turns out to be a great learning experience. But if it happens when your friend is buried for real, then you're in deep trouble. (Practice, practice, practice.)

Another common mistake is that people won't even remember how to turn their beacon to receive. A final common mistake: some beacons automatically return to transmit after a few minutes, which is very confusing if, like most people, you read the directions for the first and last time on Christmas day.

Unless you practice regularly with your beacon, you probably won't be able to find your partners in time to save their lives. (Wasatch Range, Utah)

When everyone is safely on the avalanche debris, the leader should check to make sure that *all beacons are set to receive* and that everyone knows how their beacon works. (See the Rescue Technology section below for a detailed discussion on how beacons work.)

How to do a Beacon Search

Beacons are "directional," meaning that the receiving beacon gets a stronger signal in one orientation than another, but they are not directional in the way you may think. They don't point directly at the transmitting beacon. Instead, they point along the lines of the magnetic field (Figure 9-2). (As my friend—and engineering PhD—Ian McCammon tells me, it doesn't become an "electromagnetic field" until you get farther away than about 400 meters.) This magnetic field is an extremely important concept to grasp and I'll take some time here to explain.

Take yourself back to the science experiments you did in grade school in which you put iron filings on a piece of paper and then put a magnet under the paper. The iron filings lined up along the lines of the magnetic field. This is a way to visualize the lines of force in two dimensions (the plane of the paper). It's important to realize that the lines of force exist in three dimensions and look kind of like the shape of an apple. You need to be solid with this concept, so be sure to practice mapping out the curving field with two beacons until you are comfortable with how they work.

Next, let's learn both of the common methods for finding buried beacons: the induction method and the grid method. You will use the induction method at a distance and the grid method when you get close.

Induction Method

The induction method is also called the "flux line method" or the "tangent method." Simply follow the lines of the magnetic field (Figure 9-3) as they lead you on a curving path to the beacon (or in a straight line if you are directly in line with the axis of the buried beacon). Most modern beacons have digital lights or an arrow to show you which way to turn the beacon. With the old analog units, you must continually reorient the beacon and listen for the strongest signal. Realize that the beacon will point you in one of two, opposite directions; so if the signal gets weaker (the distance numbers go up) you're heading the long way around the semicircle. Turn around (180 degrees) and march in the other direction. Just follow the lights or the arrow, which will lead you on a curving path to the transmitting

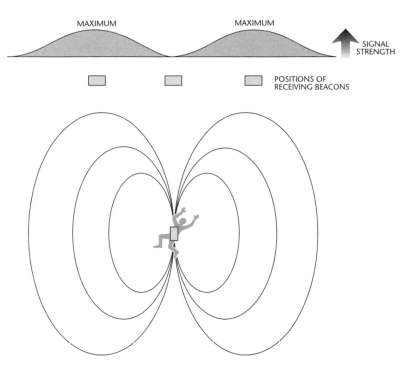

MAXIMUM   MAXIMUM   SIGNAL STRENGTH

POSITIONS OF RECEIVING BEACONS

Figure 9-2. Especially with older, single-antenna beacons, the receiving beacons get stronger signals when their antennas are aligned parallel to lines of magnetic force, which creates a "double maximum" in this example. This is the reason most modern beacons use 3 antennas, which help to eliminate this confusing phenomenon.

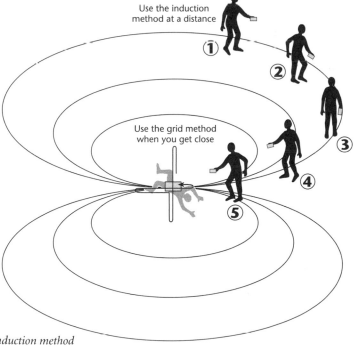

Use the induction method at a distance

Use the grid method when you get close

① ② ③ ④ ⑤

Figure 9-3. The induction method

255

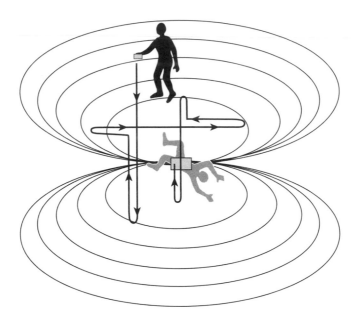

Figure 9-4. The grid method

beacon. If you have an analog beacon with a volume control, *turn it down as you get closer.* Otherwise, you will never be able to locate the beacon.

Simple. Or at least it's simple in a parking lot. It gets a lot more complicated on a slope, since a curving path sometimes makes you walk uphill (more huffing and puffing just when you need it the least). It can also be complicated on small avalanche paths, when the curving line takes you outside of the avalanche path (possibly dangerous territory) or into a cliff (impenetrable territory). With practice, though, you can figure out ways to get around these problems.

This induction method works well at a distance but when you get close to the buried beacon, you will need to switch to the grid method (described below).

Grid Method

The second method is the grid method, which you will need to use when you get close to the buried victim (Figure 9-4). For older, analog beacons, many prefer to use the grid method to do the entire search since following a magnetic field with an analog beacon is harder. Hold your beacon vertically. Start moving in a grid of perpendicular lines, first moving across the slope then up and down the fall line. Where you think the signal is strongest (or, better yet, midway between fade points), you simply make a perpendicular turn (90 degrees to the old direction) and follow this new line. You have two choices of direction. If the signal fades (distance numbers increase), you're going the wrong way, so turn around (180 degrees) and march in the other direction until you hear the strongest signal. Turn 90 degrees again and repeat the process over and over until you zero in on the buried beacon. When you get within a couple of meters, it's best to bend over and run the beacon over the snow surface. Don't bounce up and down doing the "mating flamingo dance" as Doug Fesler likes to call it. Keep the beacon near the snow all the time. Remember that if you use an analog beacon, you will need to continually turn down the volume to where you can barely hear it. If it's too loud you can't hear the changes and subtleties of the signal. Think string quartet, not heavy metal.

When coming from the top, I like to use the funnel method—a variant on the grid. This method is very fast and works well on skis or a snowboard that can traverse easily, and even on foot. Simply zigzag down the avalanche path. When you first pick up the signal, figure out where the signal is strongest and concentrate your downward zigzags in that area, making them smaller and smaller as you "funnel" in on the transmitting beacon. It's simple, easy, and quick. Zigzagging down the slope is the easiest way to descend on skis or a board anyway, since avalanche debris is difficult to negotiate and zigzagging is a good way to efficiently cover the terrain in a pattern tight enough to avoid missing a beacon signal.

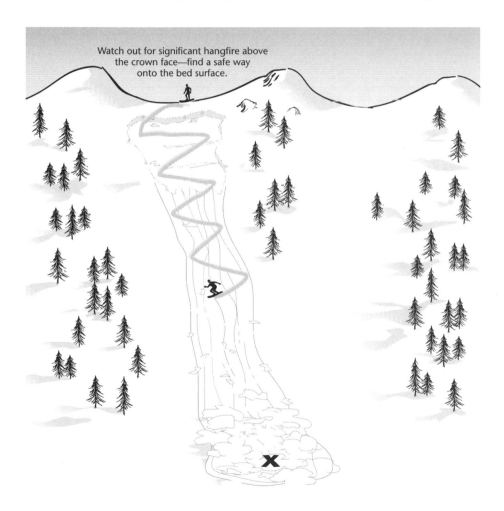

Figure 9-5. Zigzag down or up the avalanche path.

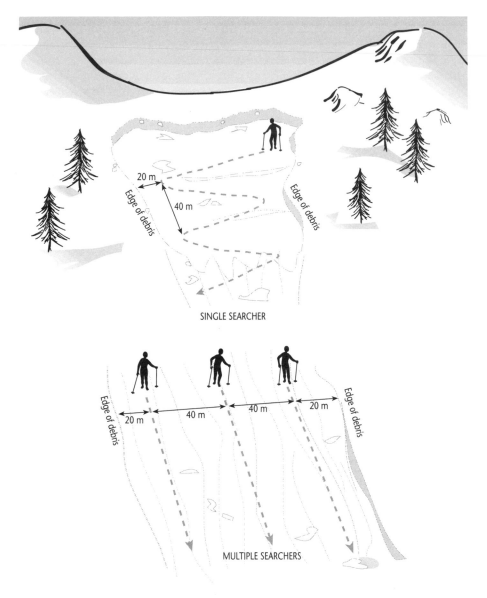

Figure 9-6. Make sure your switchbacks are spaced close enough not to miss a beacon signal (about 40 meters for most beacons but 20 meters for some brands with shorter range).

Start Doing Zigzags and Watch Your Spacing

The best way to search a large area with a beacon is to do zigzags (Figure 9-5). This is especially effective if you are descending from the top on skis or a snowboard. Pick a width for your zigzags so that you won't miss a signal. The spacing will depend on the minimum range of your particular brand of beacon. For most beacons, the zigzags should be around 40 meters. (Figure 9-6.) Remember that some beacons have half the range of other beacons so your spacing should be around 20 meters. **Note:** Especially in maritime climates the bed surface can be very hard and icy, and descending a 35 to 45 degree icy slope can be dangerous. Sometimes people are tempted to descend the snow to the sides of the slide, but this is where you can easily trigger the snow that hasn't yet slid. Hopefully, you have been regularly practicing with your beacon and you have some intuitive sense for its receive range. Remember that the buried person may have weak batteries or a cold beacon or an old, out-of-date beacon, in which case, their transmit range will be less than ideal, which is why we use a distance of 40 meters between zigzags instead of the maximum range of the beacon. You should continually rotate your beacon on all three axes to find the most favorable orientation. (The searching beacon receives the strongest signal when its longest antenna is parallel to the lines of the magnetic field. Since you don't know the orientation of the buried beacon, you need to continually reorient your beacon until you get the first signal.)

When You Receive the First Signal

Don't spend a lot of time with the details here. This is the time to move fast and get a *general* idea of where the signal is coming from. If you're using the induction method, don't worry about getting the exact direction. If the signal is getting stronger you're going in the right direction. Keep pointing your beacon in the direction of the arrows on the beacon or the strongest signal (if you are using an old analog beacon), and keep moving. As the Swiss avalanche rescue specialist Manual Genswein puts it, "It's like an airplane coming in for a landing: go fast when you are far away and go progressively slower the closer you get." At a distance, you should be running or traveling at a fast walk or cruising fast on your skis, snowboard, or snowshoes.

When You Get Close

With an analog beacon you are now on the lowest or next to lowest volume setting, or if you have a digital-display beacon without a volume control, the distance is under about 4 meters (12 feet). Now, you need to slow way down. Don't even think about digging yet. Take some time—perhaps 30 seconds to a good minute—and get it down to the *exact* location, or as close as you can. If you're good with a beacon, you should be able to guess the approximate depth and be able to take out your probe and hit the victim on the first try (Figure 9-7).

Failing to get an exact location is probably the second most common mistake among novices (after failing to set the beacon to receive). It's only natural to get excited and shout out, "Here! It's right here!" and several people whip out their shovels and start flinging snow. After 5 minutes of furious digging, they still haven't hit anything. Wisely someone grabs their beacon and

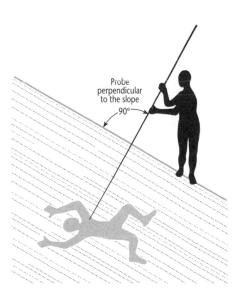

Figure 9-7. *Probe perpendicular to the snow surface. Don't worry about injuring the victim with the probe or shovel, which is the least of their worries when they can't breathe.*

Searchers narrowing in on the victim of an avalanche. (Wasatch Range, Utah)

takes time to get a more exact location and find that they have been digging 1 meter (3 feet) away from the victim. I can't tell you how many times I have seen overly excited students start digging in the wrong place, sometimes 10 meters (30 feet) away from the victim. Slow down. Get as close as you can.

After you have zeroed in on the beacon, don't start digging. First, take out your collapsible probe and get an *exact* location. Start where you think the signal is strongest and probe in an expanding spiral until you hit the victim (Figure 9-8). When you get a strike, leave the probe in place. It takes about 10 seconds to probe an area 2 meters by 2 meters and it takes about 10 minutes to dig a hole that large. A probe can locate a victim many times faster than by shoveling. Shoveling takes a *huge* amount of time,

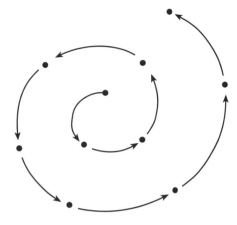

Figure 9-8. When you locate the strongest signal, probe in an expanding spiral until you get a strike. Leave the probe in place and start digging downhill from the probe.

especially in dense avalanche debris that is often as hard as concrete.

If you find that the victim is buried deeply and you also have multiple burials, you have a tough decision to make. See the "Triage" section below.

Digging

Digging usually takes more time than searching so it's essential to practice digging techniques. That's right. Practice digging. I'm not winning many friends here but it's important to talk about the very loathsome topic of digging techniques.

Digging the wrong way:

Most people dig completely wrong. They stand on top of the victim, dig straight down, and make the hole far too small: all wrong. First, a buried victim has a hard time breathing because the snow presses on their rib cage and diaphragm making it hard to expand their lungs. Rescuers standing on top of the victim while they dig further exacerbate the problem. For this reason, you dig downhill from the victim and dig into them horizontally. Also, it is always much easier to move snow horizontally out of a hole than lifting it vertically. Third, you need a much larger hole than you might imagine because you will need room to work on the victim. Often you must completely extricate them and turn them over to begin CPR.

Digging the right way:

Leave the probe in place. Dig *downhill* of the victim and dig horizontally to them. With several diggers, make like a flock of geese and dig in a V shape so each person can chip away at the side walls and pass the snow out in the middle (Figure 9-9). The V should be about twice as long as it is deep. The person digging at the point of the V will do the most work, so it's important to rotate the diggers every two minutes, the same way bicycle racers take their turn in the lead, then rotate to the back of the pack to recover. Pass the debris down the middle of the V. Don't lift the snow, but instead, slide it sideways, which takes much less effort.

Figure 9-9. Shoveling technique is even more important than beacon technique because it takes more time. Recent research from Europe indicates that shovelers should make like a flock of geese and form a V on the downhill side of the probe (victim). Move the debris out of the middle of the V. Move snow horizontally instead of trying to lift it out of the hole. Rotate positions every couple of minutes. (From Manuel Genswein, www.genswein.com/manuel_lawine_english.html.)

Multiple Victims

Even though your chance of actually having to perform a multiple beacon search is small, we still need to practice multiple search techniques for the small percentage of the time when we may need it. Unless you have been regularly practicing with multiple beacon problems, pulling off such a rescue in a realistic situation will likely be an insurmountable problem. Again, practice, practice, practice.

When using beacons with analog sound, you will easily hear if there is more than one beacon transmitting. It will sound like a staggered beep-beep…beep-beep. Since beacons usually transmit at different rates, you can hear the interaction of the cadence overlap change through time as well. With practice you will be able to tell how many beacons are transmitting and also concentrate on the strongest signal while tuning out the others the same way you can follow one person's conversation at a crowded dinner table.

Many brands of digital beacons produce a sound that is digitally filtered so that it locks onto the strongest signal and suppresses the sound from other beacons. For a single burial this might be an advantage, but it can be a disadvantage in multiple burials because you have to be more careful not to miss other beacons. Personally, I like hearing the analog sound, or at least having the option to hear it if I want. That way I can instantly tell if one of the searchers inadvertently returned to transmit or if a searcher forgot to turn their beacon to receive. Most digital beacons have a lockout feature, which "flags" or locks out the signal from the beacon that you just found so that you can hear the signal from the next closest beacon. The lockout feature works fairly well but perhaps 10-20 percent of the time, it fails to work (because the cadence of the two signals happen to be right on top of each other), in which case, you will have to use one of the following methods. The multiple search strategies are slightly different for each brand of beacon so be sure to follow the directions from the manufacturer and, again, practice a lot.

Micro search strip:

Traverse back and forth in much smaller search strips of about 2 to 5 meters (Figure 9-10). This is a very thorough method, and one that is unlikely to miss a buried victim. Recent research seems to support that this is the most effective method because it is more thorough and it involves less walking back uphill.

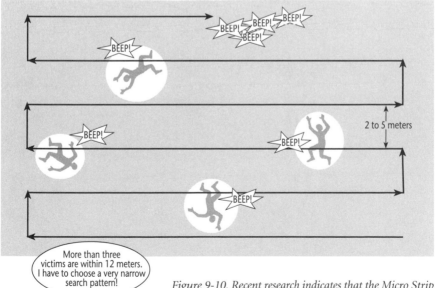

Figure 9-10. Recent research indicates that the Micro Strip Search works best for multiple burials. Even with beacons that have a "lockout" feature, you should practice this technique because the lockout will not work some of the time because of signal overlap. (From Manuel Genswein, www.genswein.com/manual_lawine_english.html.)

Triage

Unfortunately, with multiple burials you sometimes have to make some hard choices. In the backcountry, most of the time you will have limited resources and you will need to evaluate which victims are most likely to live and go for them first.

Go for the shallow burials first. After you get all the shallow burials breathing, then go back for the deep ones. Deep burials, say 1.5 meters (5 feet) or more deep, have a very small chance of survival. How fast can you dig a 5-foot hole in dense avalanche debris? The numbers usually don't add up to a happy ending. A scenario like this takes a lot of discipline and hard choices are required. Wasting valuable time digging out a deep burial doesn't make sense when you may be able to get a shallow burial out of the snow much more quickly.

Also, ignore the person on the surface who is screaming in pain or fear. We're worried about the ones who can't scream because they can't even breathe. Deal with the screamers later. The only exception to this is if the person on the surface is losing blood rapidly or has some other condition that requires immediate attention. Plug the holes quickly and return to the task of getting everyone breathing.

Note: As of this writing, the Barryvox Pulse beacon has sensitive motion detectors that can tell whether a buried victim is breathing or not. The beacon transmits this information via a separate frequency to other Barryvox beacons and it allows rescuers to not waste time digging for a victim that shows no breathing motions. This seems like a cruel feature that flies in the face of our most basic human instincts but, statistically, it can help save more lives.

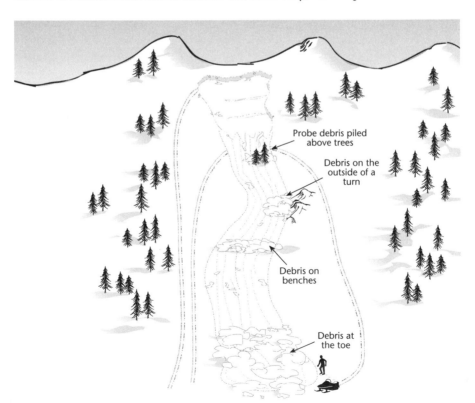

Probe debris piled above trees

Debris on the outside of a turn

Debris on benches

Debris at the toe

Figure 9-11. Concentrate your initial search on places where avalanche debris has piled up.

First Aid

ABCDEs. Airway, breathing, circulation, disability, environment. Are all the rescued people breathing? Now go back and stop the bleeding, stabilize the spine if they show a mechanism of injury, get them out of the snow, keep them warm, and do the splinting. When keeping them warm, don't forget that what's under them is just as important as what's over them. (See Bibliography for good first-aid books.) Remember that trauma sustained on the way down the mountain kills about a quarter of people who die in avalanches in the U.S.; once you've dug them up there likely won't be much you can do about them except stop the bleeding, treat for shock, and keep them warm. Among all avalanche victims only about 2 percent will live long enough to die from hypothermia. The rest die from asphyxia—breathing their own carbon dioxide.

In recent years, most people carry a cell phone and probably as a result, it seems that fewer people carry an adequate first-aid kit and extra warm clothes. Don't fall for this trap. Helicopters can't fly in poor weather or after nightfall and even when they can fly, often they can't land or long-line someone in from complex, steep terrain. As a minimum, you should always carry a basic first-aid kit, extra hat and mittens, a down or synthetic-fill jacket, and puff pants. A lightweight bivy bag is also a good idea, especially in more remote areas.

Go for Help

Yes, now—finally—is the time to go for help. Aren't you glad that you didn't send someone for help earlier? First things first. You needed all your resources at the scene to get everyone breathing as soon as possible. Now you can take the time to plan how someone is going to go for help without getting killed. Now you have the time to write down all the details so that you can communicate to the rescuers exactly what kind of injuries the victims have and the exact location of the accident. (Many people who frantically call for help early in a rescue don't know either of these details, which are essential information for a rescue team—especially the exact location—and countless hours have been wasted because of this, not to mention putting rescuers' lives at risk.)

RESCUE WITHOUT BEACONS

The only thing worse than doing an avalanche rescue is doing one without beacons. It's not only a needle-in-a-haystack situation but it's looking for a needle with a needle. Not surprisingly, very few complete burials without beacons will survive. Beacons are very inexpensive when compared to a human life, especially your own. Even if they fail to save a life, beacons also save your friends from having to spend all night probing for you. Life without beacons is not good and it's everyone's responsibility to use a beacon even if you are traveling alone.

Rescue without a beacon means using a probe. Everyone in your group should have either collapsible probe poles or avalanche probe ski poles; if not, then you will need to go all the way back to the Stone Age and use tree branches or whatever else you can find.

Initial Search

Some people also refer to this as a "hasty search," but I don't like that term because it implies that speed is more important than thoroughness. In what is more commonly called an "initial search" or "scuff search," move quickly down or up the avalanche path and concentrate on places where the avalanche debris has piled up such as:

- Debris piled on the uphill side of trees
- Debris collected on the outside of turns
- Debris at the bottom

Also concentrate on areas around clues, such as a ski, a glove, or a snowmobile (Figure 9-11).

In each one of these areas, do the following:

- Look carefully for something sticking out of the snow—a hand, a glove, or a ski—and follow it to see if the victim is attached. Probe around these areas. Too many tragic deaths have occurred because the victim's partners noticed a ski or a snowmobile on the surface but did not check the evidence out further. **Note:** Because they are larger, snowmobiles usually end up on the surface and their riders end up buried less than 1 meter (2 to 3 feet) deep and 3 to 10 meters (10 to 40 feet) uphill of and in line with the snowmobile.
- Spot-probe these likely areas by random probing. Don't spend a lot of time probing at this stage. Try to cover the entire avalanche path in about 10 to 15 minutes.
- Occasionally shout and listen for the victim's response. Some people have been found this way. Also, although the snow absorbs most of the sound coming out of the snow, the victim can usually hear sound filtering into the snow from outside.

Organized Probing

If the initial search turns up nothing, then your victim(s) are most likely completely buried. Don't send someone away from the scene to get help, at least not yet. You need all your resources to search. If you have no luck after about an hour, then send someone to get help.

Without beacons, it's like finding a needle in a haystack with a needle. Probing is very time-consuming and exhausting work. (La Sal Mountains, Utah) Photo courtesy of the U.S. Forest Service

If you have a cell phone or radio coverage, then go ahead and call for help, because you will likely need more resources.

If you have only a couple of searchers, it's probably best to continue to do spot probing of likely areas. If you have, say, four or more people, then you should organize them into probe lines, but only after doing a complete initial search of the debris.

Start in the most likely area, for instance, in line with a clue (ski, snowmobile, glove, etc.) or downhill from the last-seen area. Start at the *bottom* of the avalanche debris and work your way uphill. Especially for small groups of searchers, the three-hole probe has the highest probability of finding someone. Line up fingertip to fingertip and then probe three times, once to the left, once in the center, and once to the right, keeping the holes about 60 cm (2 feet) apart. (Figure 9-12). Keep track of the probe holes to keep the probes evenly spaced and watch to make sure everyone stays in a straight line. Probing is much easier if one person can take the lead and call out the signals, "Probe right. Probe center. Probe left. Step forward."

This kind of "course probing" has about an 80 percent chance of finding a victim on the first pass. Statistically, this is the most efficient use of resources with the combination of speed and thoroughness. Probe all the likely areas. If you have reason to think that you may have missed a victim on one pass, make another pass.

If you have not had any success after about an hour, then it's time to send someone for help. An organized rescue team will come in with search dogs and, if the dogs can't locate the victim, then they will form larger teams of probers to cover the entire area. If they have no success with probes and dogs—which is common with very deep burials—they will

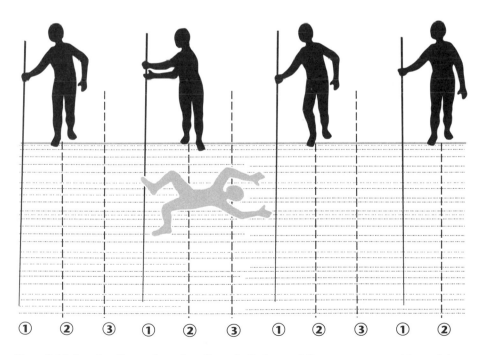

Figure 9-12. Searchers line up fingertip to fingertip. Probe once left, once center, once right, and then move forward one step.

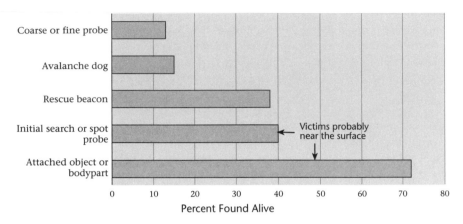

Figure 9-13. The success of these various rescue methods is a function of how fast the victim was rescued and how deeply they were buried. Most victims found by attached body part or hasty search were probably at or near the surface and found quickly by partners. Avalanche dog and coarse probing are usually done by organized rescue teams, which often take several hours to get to the accident site.

have no choice but to leave the victim to melt out in spring. And yes, the price of a beacon is always better than putting loved ones through that. (Figure 9-13).

DEALING WITH THE AFTERMATH

The death of a friend or loved one is one of the most difficult chapters most of us have to face in our lives and I have, unfortunately, faced it several times. Luckily we don't have to do it alone. Don't try to be a tough guy and shove it back in some hidden place or dissipate the pain through work, alcohol, drugs, or fooling around. I've seen post-traumatic stress syndrome significantly disrupt the lives of several of my colleagues as well as myself. So take it from me. Get some professional help. That's what it's for.

Even if there is no death, perhaps you just took a very scary ride in an avalanche and suddenly came face to face with your own mortality. This is often a life-changing event. You have to expect it to take some time before the echoes quit reverberating off the canyon walls of your psyche. It takes time and work. Don't cheat yourself.

RESCUE TECHNOLOGY

It's our birthright as Americans that we always look for the perfect technology so that we don't have to think anymore. Rescue technology has made great strides, especially in the past 10 years and many people have been saved because of it. So it's important to know how the technology works. But as history has repeatedly shown, technology often doesn't save lives. Why? Because we humans tend to practice "risk homeostasis," i.e., if conditions (or technology) make things safer, we tend to raise our level of risk back to what is often our irrationally high comfort level. Our gizmos just give us a false sense of security, which makes us do even crazier things, and the death rate remains about the same. (See Chapter 10, The Human Factor, for more details.) Remember that these new, revolutionary devices work only if we resist ratcheting up our levels of risk. Very few people are able to resist that

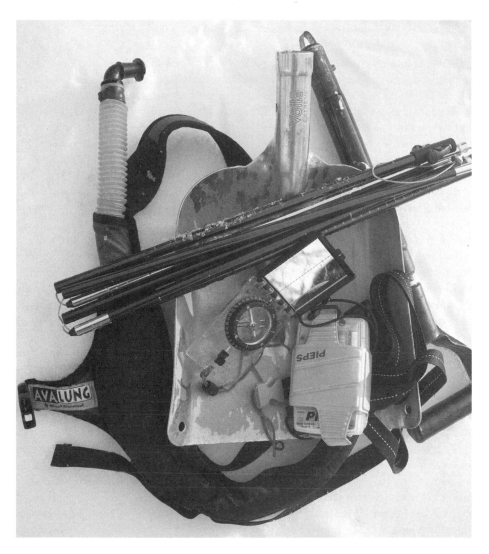

This is the minimum equipment I always carry: beacon, shovel, probe, compass, and Avalung™.
Note: *Our staff usually cycles through different brands of beacons so we become familiar with all of them. This is the one I happened to have with me. Many makes and models work well and the best beacon is the one you practice with.*

siren song. Rescue technology has not, nor probably ever will, replace avalanche avoidance. The best rescue technology is never needing a rescue in the first place.

Avalanche Beacons
Beacons—Do They Help or Hurt?
I hate to admit that I am old enough to remember when beacons arrived on the scene back in the 1970s. We all assumed that beacons would dramatically reduce avalanche deaths, yet the opposite occurred. What happened?

First, better equipment combined with large population booms in the western states has led to more and more people recreating in avalanche terrain. And second, because of the aforementioned, risk homeostasis, beacons tend to give us a false sense of security, which not only causes us to jump onto slopes we would normally avoid, but encourages even more people to recreate in avalanche terrain, making it a self-perpetuating system.

Beacons give us a false sense of security because the sad truth is that beacons work well, but the people who use them don't always work so well. Many recent studies have shown that at least among recreational users who do not practice enough, the use of beacons reduces mortality only about 10 percent (some studies have shown zero percent). More recent studies with the new generation of digital beacons have pushed that number up to 15 percent, which is still not very high. I remember my first year on the Bridger Bowl Ski Patrol back in 1977, we discovered that although beacons seem like a simple device, even professional patrollers flailed when doing beacon searches in realistic situations, so we instituted weekly practice sessions. Because of regular practice, pros today enjoy around a 60 percent reduction in mortality due to beacon use. Also, in Switzerland, a country with a highly avalanche-educated population, the reduction in mortality even among general users is 75 to 80 percent. Yet the vast majority of recreational users rarely practice and when they do, it is rarely in realistic scenarios. As a result, beacons give a false sense of security and some have argued that they have actually led to more avalanche fatalities than they have saved people from dying in avalanches.

The take-home point here is that beacons work only if 1) you practice often in realistic situations and 2) you behave as if you were not wearing a beacon. I now recommend, too, that beacons always be combined with an Avalung™ and especially an avalanche air bag (see sections later this chapter).

Beacon Technology

Beacons are simply small, electronic devices costing $150–$500 that both transmit and receive an electronic signal. Everyone in the party wears one and each member turns it on when they leave the house or leave the car to head into the backcountry. (Wear it *under* your jacket to keep the batteries warm and to keep it from being torn from your body during the ride.) When turned on, the beacon automatically starts transmitting, about one electronic "beep" per second. If someone is buried, everyone else in the party turns their beacons to receive, so that they can hear the beeping of the buried victim's beacon; the signal gets stronger the closer you get. The range of most beacons is 60 to 80 meters (yards and meters are about the same), or about half that range for some makes and models.

This book would be twice as thick if I discussed the technology behind the various brands of beacons and the pros and cons of each. And even if I did, the technology changes so fast that by the time you read this, it would be out-of-date. So you should monitor the various websites and discussion forums if you are in the market for one—www.beaconreviews.com is a good place to start. As to which is the best brand, they all work well and there are pros and cons to each. When I take informal polls among professional avalanche forecasters, about which beacons they use, the results are scattered all over the map and when they have competitions on how fast people can find beacons, no one brand stands out. The best beacon is the one you practice with.

Here is a short synopsis of the current technology: The older generation of analog beacons uses a single antenna and in the past 10 years there has been an explosion of digital beacons with multiple antennas designed to speed search, reduce confusion, and offer more sophisticated features for multiple burial situations. At the simple, inexpensive end of the spectrum is the Ortovox F1, which quickly became a classic after it was introduced around 15 years ago and still remains popular. It is an analog beacon with a single antenna and a volume control dial. At the far end of the spectrum, the Ortovox S1 looks like a *Star Trek* tricorder and plots the beacons on an LCD screen in their approximate locations. The Barryvox Pulse includes a sensitive motion detector that can even tell if a buried victim is breathing or not, which helps the searcher to do triage during a rescue. When you buy a new beacon it's important to match the beacon not only to your budget but to your technological aptitude and your willingness to practice regularly. For instance, most of the sophisticated, expensive units are designed for professionals who practice enough with all the features to use them intuitively. A novice who practices once per year should stick with the simpler models.

The statistics indicate that the new generation of beacons has improved search times. Yet I know many avalanche professionals who prefer the older, analog beacons and they can solve even complex, multiple burial scenarios just as fast. It is far more important to practice regularly with the beacon you already own than to run out and buy the latest model. Unfortunately, in our time-constrained world, far too many people find it easier to whip out their credit card than to regularly conduct practice sessions.

Note on multiple burial features: In 1999, Manual Genswein and Stephan Harvey from the Swiss Federal Institute for Snow and Avalanche Research published a study of 30 years of Swiss statistics and they found that 35 percent of all accidents involved multiple burials and 61 percent of completely buried victims were multiple burials. This prompted most manufacturers to produce beacons with features for solving multiple burial scenarios, which digitally analyzed the signals and allowed the user to "flag" or lock out the signal from each beacon as it was located, so you could move on to the next signal without the distraction from the found beacon. The occurrence of multiple burials in Europe was so high because 1) many were guided parties, which tend to travel as a group, 2) the Alps are very crowded, and 3) since the statistics included 30 years, many of the victims from older incidents did not have very good avalanche education and trips then commonly exposed too many people at once.

More recent statistics from both Austria and the U.S. indicate that far fewer multiple burials are occurring, probably because of better avalanche education. Although statistics on recent incidents of multiple burials are inconclusive or lacking, the take home point is that we all still need to practice our multiple burial rescue skills.

Always do a Beacon Check at the Beginning of the Tour and Always Practice with Beacons

The good news on beacons: Despite a huge amount of research and money thrown at other ways of finding an avalanche victim, locating a victim through the use of electronic avalanche rescue beacons remains the most widely used way to find someone completely buried in avalanche debris. With regular practice in realistic situations, you should be able to find a buried beacon in under 10 minutes. Among people who practice regularly, beacons work and they work well.

Another reason to practice: I can't count the number of times I have forced one of my friends to practice with their beacon and put up with their whining only to learn that their beacon didn't even work. Either it had a compromised transmit or receive range or it wasn't

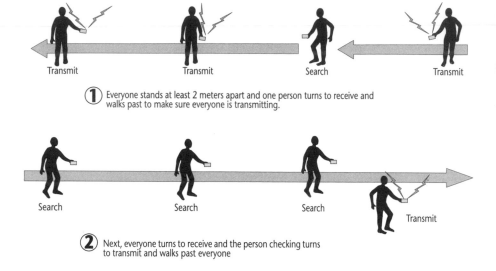

Figure 9-14. I always do a beacon check at the beginning of every tour. Otherwise, you have no way of knowing when someone's beacon is not working or defective. Also, it reminds everyone how to use the basic features of their beacon. (From Manuel Genswein, http://www.genswein.com/manuel_lawine_english.html.)

transmitting or receiving at all. (I always carry a spare in my car because it happens so often.) Also, I can't count the number of times that my supposedly competent friends have forgotten how to turn their beacons to receive or forgotten that they have it programmed to return to transmit after 5 minutes. How are you going to know there's a problem with your beacon unless you practice? Practice may be a pain, but it sure beats finding out that your beacon doesn't work during a real rescue or that you were just not practiced enough to save your friend or spouse.

Always do a beacon check at the beginning of every tour (Figure 9-14). The person doing the check should stand well away from the others, turn their beacon to receive and listen for each person's signal as they pass. This way you can check the transmit range of each beacon. (Weak batteries or an aging beacon can dramatically reduce transmit range.) Finally, someone else in the group should check the checker.

How to Practice

At home: Do a shell game. If there's no snow in your backyard, take a bunch of grocery bags out of the recycle bin and head outside. Turn a beacon on, hide it in one of the grocery bags, and scatter the other empty grocery bags on the lawn. Put a rock in each one if the wind is blowing. (Windy! First clue. Beacon practice might be a good idea today.) Then tell your partner to find the beacon. Now switch roles. If you have more than two beacons, "bury" two of them to do a multiple beacon practice, which is much harder.

Also, if you don't have enough time, hide a beacon in the house. (Remember, though, that the electric currents in the house or around your yard can confuse digital-display beacons and make analog beacons hard to hear.)

In the field: While you're waiting for someone to run a car shuttle or unload snowmobiles or perhaps during lunch, put a transmitting beacon into your spare mitten (to protect it from cold and snow). *Make sure it's transmitting.* Stuff the beacon into the snow, the deeper the better. Make some tracks around the area so your partners can't use visual clues, then have them search for the beacon.

As you gain more skill, make your practice sessions harder with more realistic situations.

HOT TIP!

With a ski pole, it's easy to bury a beacon for rescue practice. Ram the basket end of the pole into the snow and pump it up and down to drill a deep hole, then put the beacon in the hole and shove it down with the ski pole. Cover up the hole. If you don't have a ski pole, push the beacon in with your arm but don't shove it straight down, shove it sideways or at a 45-degree angle so that the beacon will be under undisturbed snow. (This is to make sure that people are not just looking where the tracks are. Force them to believe what the beacon is telling them.)

Now that you can find beacons in the parking lot, move onto steeper slopes, and after you master that, move up to multiple burials and then graduate to finding multiple burials in realistic situations, namely on slopes and in jumbled avalanche debris. Add several rescuers looking at once so you have the usual cluster of communication and logistics

Doing a beacon search at lunch. It doesn't take long—just hide it in one mitten or bury it in the snow.

problems. Then, finally, add a frantic or uncooperative witness or two, and do it during a blizzard. You will quickly discover that your beacon skills are not nearly as good as you thought. For multiple burials, you will need to use the micro strip search method mentioned previously. Remember, you need to practice with multiple burials or your beacon training is not complete.

Avalanche Probes

I carry a collapsible avalanche probe in my pack all the time. Even when I carry my probe ski poles, I still carry the collapsible probe pole in my pack. Why? Because out of the hundreds of students I have taught through the years, I have almost never seen anyone who could assemble their ski pole probes in under 10 minutes. It takes a while to remember how they work, then it takes a long time to get the baskets off. By that time the folks with the collapsible probes have already been probing for several minutes.

Collapsible probes assemble quickly, they're longer, and they slide through the snow much more easily than ski pole probes. Finally, they are very lightweight and I don't even notice one in my pack. Many pros strap a collapsible probe to their shovel handle along with flagging for marking the perimeter of avalanche debris, clues, and the route to the avalanche accident.

Shovels

Probably the only item more important than a beacon is a shovel, because digging someone out of avalanche debris without one is nearly impossible. I like the lightweight, heat-tempered, aluminum shovels that break apart in two pieces for easy storage in any pack. Get the ones with the D-shaped grip and the extendable handle. You can buy them in most outdoor shops. The somewhat lighter weight Lexan ones seem to break more often and they don't seem to chop through ice chunks and tree branches as well, and yes, many avalanche debris piles are mixed with tree branches.

Snowmobilers, be sure to wear your shovel and probe in a small pack on your back instead of carrying it on the machine. If your snowmobile gets buried with your shovel on it, you won't be able to dig anyone else out who might also be buried.

Avalanche Air Bags

Judging from the statistical success of avalanche air bags over the past few years, it appears that avalanche air bags are the most promising technology to come along in the past 60 years—perhaps since explosives were introduced to control avalanches. As I mentioned earlier, avalanche beacons do not work well among recreational users because users almost never practice enough; beacons decrease mortality only about 10 percent among recreational users, while they decrease mortality 70 percent among pros. The avalanche air bag, however, has been used primarily in Europe for the past few years and as of 2007, 168 persons with avalanche air bags have been caught and only two have died—both because they initially ended up on the surface but were subsequently buried by a secondary avalanche. Of the 168 people with air bags caught, 151 people had successfully inflated their air bags, ten did not pull the ripcord, one did not carry the handle, two had empty cartridges and four experienced technical failures (most of these technical failures occurred with the early versions).

Among people caught, normally about 10 percent die, even with beacons. With avalanche air bags, only 1.5 percent have died. This is nearly a tenfold reduction in mortality

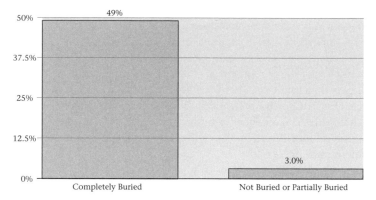

Figure 9-15. Avalanche air bags work so well because, as statistics indicate, half of completely buried victims (including ones with beacons) will die in avalanches, whereas only 3 percent of unburied or partially buried victims will die. In other words, avoiding a burial works far better than trying to survive a burial.

(Figure 9-15). Since beacons only slightly decrease mortality among recreational users, it's fair to say that avalanche air bags are the best technology to come along in the history of people's interaction with avalanches. In fact, they arguably work better than avalanche forecasts, education, or research, which is a humbling admission for someone like me who has spent a lifetime providing exactly that. Yes, the avalanche air bag is clearly here to stay, but no, it will not solve all of our problems.

Nearly all of these statistics come from Europe, where, unlike recreation in the U.S. and Canada, most recreation occurs on smooth, cultivated land above tree line. In Europe, only 6 percent of avalanche victims die from trauma. In the U.S., 25 percent of victims die from trauma and in Canada it is around 50 percent because more people recreate in and above trees. Air bags will not prevent most of these trauma deaths, but among those not killed by trauma, an incredible 98 percent of the victims will likely live.

How do they work? For many years, people have noticed that larger objects tended to rise to the surface in avalanche debris. For instance, larger trees seem to end up on the surface; even snowmobiles often end up on the surface of avalanche debris while the victims are often buried just uphill of them. This is because avalanches do not flow like water; they flow through a process called "granular flow" like millions of bouncing ping-pong balls. In granular flow, objects don't float to the surface because of buoyancy but because of "inverse segregation" the same way we have all learned to shake a bag of tortilla chips or a can of mixed nuts to make the larger ones rise to the surface. Avalanche air bags work and work well. It is likely that in a few more years none of us will consider going out without one.

The current generation of avalanche air bags are attached to a pack. When you find yourself on the wrong side of the fracture line just pull the ripcord and—whoosh!—a 150-liter air bag deploys, making you a much larger object. Victims tend to rise to the surface very quickly. Thus, avalanche rescues can dispense with two of the most time-consuming parts of the rescue, searching and digging. Also, there is some evidence that victims with air bags suffer less trauma because victims ride higher in the debris, farther away from rocks and stumps near the ground.

The only down side is that they add 3 pounds (1 to 1.5 kg) to your pack and subtract $500-$1000 from your wallet. Currently, two models are available in North America. One model deploys two bags, one from each side of a pack; the other features air bags that pop out of the pack straps and the top of the pack, encircling the victim's head to help prevent trauma. (See Bibliography for sources.) Air bags have become common in Europe among off-piste skiers and ski patrollers. They are offered as optional equipment at many helicopter skiing operations in North America and required equipment among some hut guiding operations in Canada. As more manufacturers enter the market, they will undoubtedly become lighter and cheaper. This technology will evolve rapidly, so be sure to monitor websites for the latest information.

Note: Since avalanche air bags work so well, it seems reasonable that wearing a larger pack would also help to keep you on the surface. Partially for that reason, I usually wear a larger pack than I need and I always carry a lightweight down jacket and puff pants to help fill the volume, which should be part of everyone's emergency gear anyway. The larger pack has the added benefit of making me look like a real he-man while only adding about a pound to the pack. The downside is that it only adds perhaps 20-40 liters to your volume, a bit less than the 150 liters in an avalanche air bag. I am anxiously awaiting the new generation of lightweight, inexpensive air bags.

Avalung™

After nearly every avalanche talk I have ever given, someone, usually an engineer or doctor, comes up afterward and says, "Hey, has anyone ever thought about…" and they keep me pinned for about 10 minutes while, wild-eyed, they tell me about their brilliant contraption for saving the avalanche world. Unfortunately, I have to explain that most of them have already been tried or they're too expensive or too heavy or too something. The Avalung™ is the only one that I said, "Hmmm, that's a great idea."

Tom Crowley took his idea and developed it into the Avalung™. It's simply a lightweight tube worn over the outside of your jacket or attached to a pack. If you get caught in an avalanche, you push the plastic mouthpiece toward your mouth—kept properly positioned in case of such an occurrence—and start breathing through it. The tube allows you to breathe in through the intake near your chest (thus filtering out the snow that normally plugs up your throat). When you breathe out, a flapper valve directs your air out through the end of the tube, which is near your side or back, keeping the carbon dioxide well away from the intake. In tests, buried volunteers have been able to breathe under the snow for over an hour with no ill effects. Since it was introduced only recently, there are not enough statistics to show its effectiveness. But as of this writing, there have been ten incidents in which the buried victim used an Avalung™ and in several of these incidents, out of multiple people buried, the one using the Avalung™ survived while their companions without Avalung™s died.

The obvious question with the Avalung™ is whether you will be able to chomp down on the mouthpiece in time. Unless you get it in your mouth in the first few seconds, you won't be able to do it while you're getting thrashed around during the ride. The prognosis seems good. It's stiff enough that you can position it near your mouth when you need it. Also, it's apparently tough enough to withstand the forces inside most avalanches. It appears that the victims to date did not have trouble getting it in their mouth and keeping it there on the descent.

The bottom line is that the Avalung™ is light and cheap and there's no excuse not to wear one. I use a pack that has an Avalung™ manufactured into the pack strap, so I always have it with me, and now would not think to go out without it. Since most recreational users just don't practice their beacon, probing, and digging skills often enough, few can locate and extricate their partner in time to save them. Want to keep breathing while your friends are trying to remember how to turn on their beacons? That's why I always use an Avalung™.

RECCO™

RECCO™ is a rescue system in which people wear small, inexpensive chips manufactured into many popular brands of helmets, clothing, and boots. The chips don't emit a signal or use batteries, they are simply an antenna attached to a diode that doubles the frequency of the broadcast microwave signal from a searching unit, allowing the operator to quickly locate a buried victim. The downside is that the receiving units are still too expensive and heavy for everyone to carry in the backcountry; they also take some training and experience for a searcher to operate. Thus, mainly ski areas and rescue squads purchase them and they are used mostly for locating ski area customers who don't normally wear beacons. Almost all avalanche-prone ski areas throughout the world have a RECCO™ locator in the top of their ski areas ready to be quickly dispatched to an on-piste or off-piste accident site. Because almost no avalanche fatalities occur at ski areas, and since the receiving units have to be transported via helicopter to backcountry accidents, as of this writing, no live recoveries have occurred in the backcountry of North America using RECCO™, though there have been a number of body recoveries. However, there have been several live recoveries in Europe and as rescue times become faster and faster in North America, we will likely see more live recoveries using RECCO™. In some cases, RECCO™ receivers can detect weak signals from other electronics such as cell phones or a snowmobile but their record on this to date has been spotty.

Although an avalanche air bag or a beacon and a skilled partner still provide the best chance for a live recovery, it's cheap insurance to buy clothing or gear with RECCO™ chips. It is possible to purchase a "loose" RECCO™ chip—one not manufactured or sewn into gear—but the practice is discouraged because people have a habit of losing them when they fall out of a pocket or a pack compartment, which can disrupt searches in that area for years in the future. If you ever do lose one, contact someone with a locator to find it before it can disrupt a future search. They cost under $20 and they weigh under 4 oz. and you can find them sold by some websites.

The Perfectly Equipped Avalanche Geek

By now your head is probably swimming—beacon, probe, shovel, Avalung™, avalanche air bag, RECCO™—how much of this stuff do you really need and what does it cost and weigh? Where to draw the line? The bare minimum for everyone should be a beacon, shovel, probe, and Avalung™. Except for the beacon, these are all cheap and light. I have an avalanche air bag pack that I demo in my avalanche classes, and though I have to admit that it's just too heavy and lacks enough cargo space for me to use every day, I do use it on the sketchy days. I would love to use it every day and as they get lighter and cheaper we will doubtless see avalanche air bags become standard equipment and I look forward to that day.

Good News—Bad News

The good news is that these gizmos can help to save lives. The bad news is that they probably won't save nearly as many as we hope. It's basic human nature to adjust our level of acceptable risk upward with each "revolutionary" safety device that we use. Seatbelts, airbags, and safer highways have not decreased automobile deaths, because we all just drive that much faster and crazier. (More on this in Chapter 10, The Human Factor.) Yes, some people will be saved who would have otherwise died, but probably more will die overall because the technology gives them the confidence to venture into progressively more extreme activities. It's no wonder that as many people wearing beacons are recovered dead as those who are found alive. And as avalanche air bags gain widespread use, we will undoubtedly see people bring spare cartridges so that they can go back up and take another ride in an avalanche. Laugh if you will, but if the past is any indicator—mark my word—it will come to pass.

chapter ten

THE HUMAN FACTOR

We are imperfect beings. No matter what you know or how you operate 95 percent of your life, you're not a perfect person. Sometimes those imperfections have big consequences.
>—Mary Yates, widow of a professional avalanche forecaster who, along with three others, was killed in an avalanche they triggered in the La Sal Mountains of southern Utah

Trading is a brutal profession because you have to control your emotions. As humans, we generally stink at that. Therefore, most people make lousy traders.
>—Gary Smith, successful stock trader

In the mid 1980s I was lucky enough to work for avalanche professionals Jill Fredston and Doug Fesler at the Alaska Avalanche Center and they were the first ones to clue me into what has come to be known as the "human factor." There are two kinds of avalanche accidents. First, an estimated two-thirds of fatalities are caused by simple ignorance, and through education, ignorance is relatively easy to cure. The second kind of accident is the subject of this chapter—when the victim(s) knew about the hazard but proceeded anyway. They either simply didn't notice the problem, or more commonly, they overestimated their ability to deal with it. According to Jill and Doug's impeccable incident database, in almost all accidents there are not one, but many, obvious clues present. Likewise, in 2001 a study by Dale Atkins of the Colorado Avalanche Information Center confirms the importance of the human factor: of victims who had at least some level of avalanche education, human factors accounted for 82 percent of accidents and human factors accounted for three times more accidents than lack of judgment. These numbers parallel those found in many other industries, for example the airline industry (Figure 10-1). Smart people regularly do stupid things.

These kinds of accidents are especially problematic because 1) they are hard to prevent, 2) they speak poorly of human nature, and perhaps most disturbingly, 3) if smart, avalanche-educated people are getting caught in avalanches where obvious clues exist, it means that any of us can too.

At first, I didn't entirely believe Jill and Doug because I was a trained scientist, after all, and I prided myself on regularly practicing evidence-based decision making and critically analyzing all the facts, and I believed others could too. If everyone just had enough

It seems that this backcountry access gate at a Utah ski area would leave little doubt about the dangers of entering uncontrolled avalanche terrain, yet hundreds of people without beacons regularly parade through the gate every day. A snowboarder was killed in a massive avalanche he triggered in the second photo, just past the ski area boundary; my cohorts are examining the fracture for scale. It's hard to believe something is dangerous when everyone else is doing it, and it's hard to switch your thinking from the Disneyland safety of a ski area to the stone age savagery of the backcountry when merely crossing a thin, little rope line. Each year several people die exactly this way.

information, I thought, they would automatically make the right decision. But after investigating accident after accident, it became increasingly clear that Jill and Doug were right, as usual. More disconcertingly, I began to notice how often I did stupid things even when I knew better, not just in avalanche terrain, but when driving my car, when mountaineering and rock climbing, in relationships, and even while shopping at the grocery store.

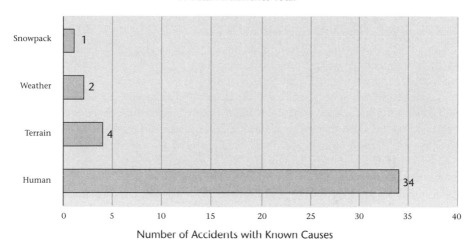

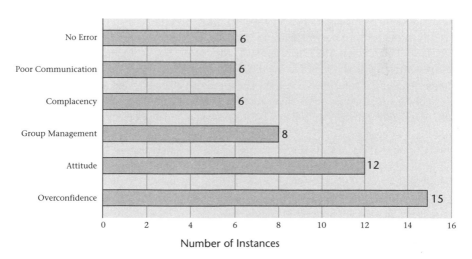

Figure 10-1. Primary factors in fatal avalanches involving people with at least some avalanche training (From Dale Atkins, Human Factors in Fatal Accidents, *1990–2000,* International Snow Science Workshop, *2000, pp. 46–51)*

Finally, in 1992, Mark Yates, a friend and fellow avalanche forecaster I trained, was killed along with three others when they were ascending what, in 20/20 hindsight, was an obviously unstable slope in the La Sal Mountains near Moab, Utah. As the story slowly came out, two people in the group had taken an avalanche class from me the previous month and they had both held a running argument for much of the day with my friend Mark, the only professional avalanche forecaster in the group. They believed the conditions were dangerous and Mark believed otherwise. Yet somehow one of the two who was adamant about the danger was in the lead, breaking trail, up the middle of a large, high-elevation cirque when they collapsed the slope and avalanches descended upon them from three different directions, burying everyone in the party and killing four.

I spent many agonizing, sleepless nights not only grieving for my lost friend, but wondering how something like this could have happened. I didn't have to look too far for the answer. All I had to do was to rewind the tape of my own life and recall all the similarly arrogant, boneheaded decisions I'd made, and the close calls I'd experienced. I'd always chalked my success up to skill, training, and talent. But the more I reeled through the instant replays, the more I had to admit that it was all just a grand delusion. Often the only difference between me and all the dead and injured was that I got lucky and they didn't. Was I next to go, I wondered? It all scared the hell out of me. Plus, it meant that my strategy in teaching avalanche classes—simply giving people information—just didn't work. Thus began my long quest to find out why smart people make dumb decisions and to uncover how I could not only become a more effective avalanche educator but save my own life in the process.

We are astoundingly social and emotional creatures and, as a vast body of research clearly shows, we make most of our decisions based on emotion, feeling, and beliefs that, more often than not, have no basis in fact. Just look at Congress or the stock market or the plots for made-for-television movies and you can see this is true. Don't forget that we share 99.3 percent of our genetic code with pygmy chimpanzees, our closest relative. Logic clearly does not come naturally to our species.

Anyone who knows me will tell you than I'm all too human. I make mistakes all the time. As a fourth generation Montanan on both sides of the family, I come by pride and stubbornness honestly enough, not to mention overconfidence and many other things I would rather not admit. I'm terrified because I know that if I ever get killed in an avalanche it will probably be because I was not practicing proper humbleness and have allowed my human foibles to control my perceptions and decisions. Like most people, I need to be forced to make good decisions by relying on a set of established procedures and checklists. After a 30-year career of documenting a very long, sad list of smart people doing stupid things in avalanche terrain, I've come to the inescapable conclusion that Moses was right. Human beings are a damned mess. We need rules. Facts alone don't do the trick; it's analysis of the facts. We need a system to stay alive in avalanche terrain.

It seems that we are both blessed and cursed by our humanness. The same species that has probed the depths of astrophysics and quantum mechanics also regularly practices acts of unspeakable stupidity and even cruelty. We seem cursed to forever walk the tightrope balanced somewhere in between, and it certainly makes life as a human being an interesting way to pass the time. One lesson I continually have to relearn—the lesson that avalanches teach so well—is that in order to survive in the mountains, we must learn to leave some of our individual and collective human foibles behind. Around humans, be human. In the mountains, think like a mountain. As Canadian helicopter skiing guide Roger Atkins always reminds me, "Staying alive in avalanche terrain probably has more to do with mastering yourself than mastering any knowledge of avalanches."

WHAT ARE THE HUMAN FACTORS?

In investigating avalanche accidents, we invariably find that the victim either didn't notice the danger or they overestimated their ability to deal with it: the human factor.

The human factors that repeatedly get people into trouble in avalanche terrain include familiarity, peer pressure, the herding instinct, competition, money considerations, poor communication, and as Fredston and Fesler call it, the "sheep syndrome" (blindly following whoever is leading), the "horse syndrome" (a rush to get back to the barn), and the "lion syndrome" (a rush for first tracks or summit fever).

Not surprisingly, avalanche people are not the only ones to recognize this problem. Anders Ericsson writes in the introduction to *Cambridge Handbook of Expertise and Expert Performance* (2006), "The number of years experience in a domain is a poor predictor of attained performance." As I noted in the Introduction, people with a lot of education and experience tend to perform at the same level as novices when: 1) they don't get regular, accurate feedback, 2) their judgment is clouded by human factors, or 3) when they encounter unusual conditions.

On this last point, I have, known a number of avalanche professionals who unfortunately are no longer with us, all of whom were killed during unusual conditions. Among close friends was Doug Coombs who during an interview for the recent movie *Steep*, noted the dangers of complacency. He said something to the effect that if anything was going to get him in the mountains, it was complacency. Shortly after that interview, while skiing in France, he slipped and fell to his death when he approached the edge of a cliff to come to the aid of a friend who had slipped and fallen just before him.

Among other close friends, both Alex Lowe and Seth Shaw used to work for me at the Utah Avalanche Center. Alex was killed on Sishapangma in Tibet while traveling along a low-elevation glacier in relatively flat terrain. A massive, natural avalanche broke out 5000 vertical feet above his party and descended into the valley. Similarly, Seth Shaw was mountaineering in Alaska, and after being stuck in their tent for several days during a storm, starved for exercise, he and his partner visited a small piece of exposed ice on the glacier where they found a small ice cave. While taking photos and standing just outside the entrance to the cave, it collapsed, killing Seth and breaking the leg of his partner. Both Alex and Seth just happened to be in the wrong place at the wrong time.

Among other friends, Mugs Stump was mountaineering in Alaska when he approached a crevasse to scout a route around it; the crevasse collapsed farther back than expected, and he was buried under tons of ice. Most recently, Mike O'Leary, the local avalanche forecaster in Cordova, Alaska, was skiing his favorite backcountry slope with friends adjacent to the ski area he helped manage, when he triggered a massive avalanche. The avalanche was 10 to 15 feet deep, took out a couple of bowls, and buried him 18 feet deep.

Yes, years of experience make us perform better, but experience can also lead to overconfidence. The journal *Accident Analysis and Prevention* found that licensed racecar drivers had more accidents than did a control group when the racecar drivers drove on regular roads. I have known a number of cagey, old avalanche professionals, me included, who midway through their careers made the conscious decision to significantly notch back on their exposure. They realized that they felt so comfortable operating in dangerous terrain that it was just a matter of time before something unusual or a simple mistake could kill them.

Pick up a book on stock trading and you often find chapters—sometimes half the book—dedicated to psychological traps that get in the way of making logical decisions under pressure. The airline industry has spent many millions of dollars researching human factors in aviation accidents because, like avalanche accidents, most aviation accidents are caused by pilot error. Look through the popular books on business and you find similar discussions. We all are, after all, humans and there's just no escape from being what we are.

After every avalanche accident we invariably hear the well-worn refrain: what were they thinking? We have often heard that we only use 10 percent of our brain, or something to that effect, which really means that most of our decisions occur on an unconscious level, even the ones that we think we are making consciously. Scientists notice that even something as simple as making a "conscious" effort to move your finger actually is initiated in the unconscious part of the brain; in fact, most of what we attribute to self will, is really just an illusion (read *The Illusion of Conscious Will* by Daniel Wegner, 2002). Engineering consultant and avalanche educator Ian McCammon has spent a good portion of the past couple of years—including a semester at Harvard University—studying human factors and our decision-making process. He writes, "The vast majority of our cognition, learning and routine risk management takes place below the conscious level. When rational processes fail to provide quick and easy risk management, unconscious processes are ready to take over."

I have presented Ian's work, and that of others, here, which has had a profound effect on the avalanche community. Until just a few years ago, avalanche educators and avalanche forecasters assumed that if we just gave people information about how avalanches work, or the conditions they will likely encounter that day, they will make the right decisions based on the facts. But it's clear that strategy just doesn't work. Similar results have occurred in many other fields such as the campaigns against illegal drug use, risky sexual behavior, traffic safety, etc., and in the industries of aviation, automotive, industrial, addiction, investing, real estate, engineering, combat, medicine, etc. So to answer the question: what were they thinking? They were *not* thinking. The vast majority of the time none of us think. Mostly, we just operate on autopilot, and for all these years we have been using the wrong tool for the job. Instead of appealing to reason, we need to find ways to reprogram the autopilot. Following an established system will do that.

In this book, I've presented some approaches that have been found to work better:
- Simple recognition shortcuts such as hazard evaluation worksheets and rule-based decision-making cards (Chapter 7).
- Graphics-based avalanche bulletins and danger level scales (Chapter 7).
- Rituals such as safe travel ritual and operational procedures (Chapter 8).
- Simple mitigation measures such as rescue equipment (Chapter 9).
- Stories and anecdotes including photo galleries, blogs, and avalanche incident reports on avalanche center websites (Bibliography).

Also important is getting regular, accurate feedback through effective communication and networking, for instance, making use of the "wisdom of crowds." And now we come to our final chapter, The Human Factor, which, in terms of importance, could easily have gone first. Along with the systematic methods discussed earlier in the book, it's important to learn to recognize the human factor pitfalls that affect all of us, so that when we see them occurring to us or to others, we can intervene or use some of the approaches above to mitigate their influence.

MENTAL SHORTCUTS

> *All there is to thinking is seeing something noticeable, which makes*
> *you see something that you weren't noticing, which makes you see*
> *something that isn't even visible.*
> —Norman Maclean, *A River Runs Through It,* 1976

The good news is that we critically depend on mental shortcuts, what behavior scientists call "heuristics," to get us through the day-to-day of our complex world. The bad news is that our mental shortcuts can lead us astray. It's well proven that we tend to take more risks when we utilize some of the common mental shortcuts in the following table. After all, a multi-billion dollar advertising industry is built around skillfully exploiting mental shortcuts in an attempt to separate us from our potential retirement income. In *Evidence of Heuristic Traps in Recreational Avalanche Accidents* (2002), Ian McCammon analyzed nearly 600 avalanche accidents in the U.S. and found that people took more risks in the face of obvious hazard when they were also operating under one or more of the following six important mental shortcuts. Advanced users were just as susceptible to these shortcuts as individuals or groups with less experience and training. Let's explore them one by one:

Common Mental Shortcuts (we tend to take more risks in these situations)	How the Advertising Industry Uses (and abuses) Mental Shortcuts
Familiarity (we feel more comfortable with what is familiar)	"Serving our community since 1938"
Acceptance (seeking acceptance by others)	"Get that Cover Girl look"
Commitment (committed to a goal or an identity)	"If you CARE about your family, you'll use this disinfectant"
Expert Halo (following an "expert" who really isn't one)	"Doctor recommended"
Scarcity (competition for resources or among others)	"Big Sale—One Day Only!"
Social Proof (the herding instinct)	"Come on down and join your friends at the gala grand opening"

Familiarity

We all feel more comfortable in familiar terrain and we take more risks because of it.

This probably doesn't surprise most of us. It's only natural that we take more risks on our home turf because we know it so well. But how well do we really know it? Since the snow is stable about 95 percent of the time, we get a disproportionate amount of positive feedback. Like I mentioned in the introduction, the avalanche game is like playing a slot machine in which 19 out of 20 times, we pull the handle and quarters jingle into our cup. Then on the 20th pull, it suddenly takes back all the money we won, it charges our credit card $10,000 and a gang of goons throws a blanket over our head, pummels us with baseball bats and throws us into the street. After we recover, we think it *must* have been a fluke. I mean we were winning every time. So we go back at it, and once again we win and win until wham,

the blanket, the goons, the credit card all over again. In a system like this it takes a lot of pulls at the handle to learn the downside of the game. In other words, if we ski a particular slope once per week all season, it will feel very familiar to us but we probably haven't seen it when the avalanche dragons were cranky. If we wisely stay away when the avalanche center tells you to, it might take years to see conditions hazardous enough for an accident. So it's no wonder that people take more risks in familiar terrain and avalanche accidents occur because of it.

I have witnessed perhaps a dozen examples, some involving myself, in which professional ski patrollers have close calls or get caught in the early season before their ski area opens. When they do avalanche control on a steep, low-elevation slope usually covered with moguls, the habituated part of their brain tells them that this slope never slides even though their eyes see the epitome of dangerous avalanche conditions. Ironically, the same patroller would instinctually tremble in fear if they encountered an identical-looking slope in unfamiliar backcountry terrain.

The bottom line is you need to remember that the snowpack, weather, and terrain are exactly the same in familiar and unfamiliar terrain, yet we all behave much differently. Watch out for familiar terrain.

Acceptance

We all want acceptance from our peers. Consequently, it's always easier to go along with the crowd than to speak up when we think there's a problem. We often hear people say after an accident that they did not feel comfortable about what the group was doing but they just didn't speak up. Practicing good communication can help alleviate this (more on this later).

Mixed groups of men and women can be an especially dangerous combination, especially when the men are trying to impress a woman in the group, in which case, we not only have competition for powder and admiration of the other males but we also have the age-old displays of preening, strutting, and chest-thumping that have made the world go around since the beginning of life on Earth. Wildlife biologists have wondered for many years about behaviors such as "stotting" among animals like deer or gazelles in which they bounce along in front of a pursuing predator instead of just running. There is good evidence that they are showing off to potential mates that they are so fast and fit that they can afford to show off in the face of danger. Sound familiar?

In Utah where I live, even though women comprise over a third of the backcountry recreationists, since 1980, only four fatalities out of 66 (6 percent) involved a female and all were relative novices accompanying males at the time. Nationally, 7 percent of fatalities are female. I don't think that it's a coincidence that these are exactly the same proportions of men to women in U.S. prisons. Almost all avalanche victims in North America are male and between 16 and 40 years old. Males, especially young males, always have, and most likely always will have, the inexorable need to go out into the world and slay dragons. When we go out to slay the avalanche dragon, there will always be a certain percentage who don't come back alive.

Opposite: It's a case of familiarity and acceptance. In this obvious avalanche path near Anchorage, Alaska, I couldn't figure out why everyone always marched right across the steepest part of it...until I discovered that the summer trail crosses here. (Chugach Range, Alaska)

Testosterone makes the voice deep, the chest hairy, the muscles strong, the ego huge! But the avalanche doesn't care about these things. Avalanches hew down the strong and weak alike, but avalanches do not hew down the aware and the unaware alike.

Because so few women get killed in avalanches, I like to go into the mountains with women as long as it's someone I'm not trying to impress, which as a middle-aged bald guy is an increasingly moot point anyway. It seems like women are not afraid to be afraid and are quick to balk at unnecessary risk. When I'm out with my male friends, I know that I have to keep a sharp eye out for competition, pride, and all the other traits that tend to go along with groups of men, because at least in my younger days, I was often the worst of the bunch.

Acceptance also takes the form of what we used to call "Kodak Courage" back in the pre-digital days. I'm also a photographer and I've always been amazed at what kind of craziness people are willing to perform if they think they might get on the cover of a magazine.

To make matters worse, the outdoor equipment manufacturers and filmmakers constitute a multi-billion dollar industry, and they unabashedly capitalize on the extreme end of their sports. It seems like you can't buy any outdoor clothing without the word *extreme* written on it, or buy a snowmobile not named after a predatory animal. In paging through a few of the popular outdoor magazines on my desk, I see that the advertisements tell me "Just do it," "Why ask why?" "Break your limits," "The ultimate adrenaline rush," "Snatched from the jaws of death," and so on. These advertisements are sandwiched between articles about shark attacks, alligator wrestling, dangerous bears, first ski descents, first river descents, first mountaineering ascents, and other cool people doing cool things.

As my old friend, the late extreme skier Doug Coombs, told me, "The 'E' word [extreme] has definitely gotten out of hand. . . . I think the ski movies have put this fallacy that you can just rage, just go for it. . . . They don't talk about all the people who get hurt making the movies. I don't think people realize the danger they're getting themselves into because of the Kodak Courage. You don't see a whole lot of ski movies with people with shovels and probe poles. . . . I think the ski movies should have that incorporated into them, because it's an education, it's just common sense that you have to have these certain tools with you."

Bottom line: be wary in situations where you are either trying to get famous, or to earn acceptance or admiration from a group of peers or the opposite sex.

Commitment

Commitment means more than just commitment to a goal, like summit fever, but commitment to an identity. For instance, someone might consider themselves to be a hot snowboarder and much of their identity and self-worth is wrapped up in it. So their unconscious mind (which makes the majority of decisions) says, "Hot snowboarders go down steep powder slopes including this one here in front of me. What are you going to do, hot snowboarder?" And they jump on in despite the obvious signs of instability they noticed on the way up. Hot snowboarders, after all, don't turn around and walk back down the way they came up.

Commitment also means stick with the plan or "sick with the plan" as Canadian helicopter guide Roger Atkins likes to put it. I usually avoid making detailed plans in the outdoors, and I'm especially suspicious of set destinations or plans that stick to a pre-defined time schedule. My friends are always calling me up to say, "Let's climb the Pfeifferhorn next Saturday." And I always respond, "OK, let's get out and do something on Saturday and let's decide Saturday morning where we should go." And even if we do end up going to the

Pfeifferhorn, we stop several times on the way to reevaluate conditions and quite often we end up going someplace else. The only concrete goal you can usually pin me down to in the backcountry is to get out and enjoy the mountains and good company. Most of the time, I really don't care where I go. The bottom line is to be suspicious of goals and identities. Go where it seems safe, and be who you are—not someone you saw in a video. Take the Zen approach: the journey is the destination.

Expert Halo

Obviously, I think listening to experts is a good thing, especially buying their books. The trouble comes when the expert is not really an expert. For instance, let's say your friend Joe brings you to his favorite spot. Everyone is following Joe and when Joe says, "Let's rip it up," everybody does. Joe might be an expert on how to get to his favorite slope but he might not be an expert at avalanches, yet we follow him anyway. Sometimes the expert is the best rider in the group, or the oldest person, the most vocal, the best looking, or the most charismatic. Often people bubble to the top of the pecking order for reasons other than their avalanche expertise.

I once had a close call with an avalanche because we were all following the Ski Patrol director to a recent accident site. Even though his route had to traverse slopes identical to the one that just killed someone the day before, I didn't speak up because after all, he was the local expert and he should know. But the "expert's" halo slipped off as soon as one of our party triggered an avalanche and had to grab a tree to keep from being swept down the slope.

Mr. Gizmohead does not seem to be impressing Ms. PhD. A shovel, snow saw and avalanche smarts beat gizmo madness every time. (Wasatch Range, Utah)

The bottom line is to be careful about who you trust to be the leader. It's up to you to make your own decisions when theirs just don't seem right.

Scarcity (Competition)

Scarcity means scarcity of resources (powder in our case) with two or more groups trying to get to it first. It also means competition among group members. I live in a very urban environment in which a million and a half people in greater Salt Lake City live directly at the base of a large mountain range, where scarcity and competition are always at work. On a sunny powder weekend, nearly every backcountry slope in the entire range is tracked out. This seems to create a nerve-wracking, feeding frenzy for powder and for the attention and admiration of others. I regularly see people doing all kinds of insanity that they would never do if they were alone in the backcountry. Yet, it's exactly the same snowpack, weather, and terrain, just different human factor conditions. Something to consider: if another group wants first tracks, let them have it (the first people down tend to trigger more avalanches). Competition and danger go hand in hand.

Social Proof (The Herding Instinct)

Social proof means that we look to others for clues to appropriate behavior, like at a fancy dinner when you're not sure which fork to use for the lobster—you watch to see what others are doing. I also like to call this the herding instinct.

I think the herding instinct is one of the major causes of avalanche accidents. Humans are clearly one of the most social creatures on Earth. Safety in numbers is hard-wired into our brains as it is for most other species. For humans, it has certainly served us well through the eons when lions, tigers, and bears were our greatest fear. But our herding instinct has just the opposite effect in avalanche terrain because it not only means more triggers but also more people to be buried if something goes wrong.

But I think the most important effect of herding instinct is on perception. Most people will admit that they are bolder in a group than when alone, a phenomenon called "risky shift" by behavioral scientists. It was first noticed in the business community in which people in larger committees tend to make riskier decisions than in smaller committees. In avalanche terrain, it doesn't matter if you're alone or in a large group—the instability remains the same. Since risk doesn't exist until we add people to the equation, the more people we add the greater the risk, not only because of the increased numbers but because of the shift in perceived safety. In other words as group size (and risk) increases, our perception of hazard decreases. Bad combination.

I'm always suspicious of large groups. Two to four is the perfect number. There are others to help if something goes wrong, but there aren't too many people to start biasing decisions toward risk. I have noticed on the many outdoor trips and expeditions I've done through the years that communication and logistical problems start skyrocketing in groups larger than four. Once you jump above the magic number four, there's always someone who doesn't hear the discussion and doesn't know the plan. It's harder to form a consensus and travel slows by an hour per day with each additional person you add to the group. That's why I almost always keep my groups at four or less unless it's just a social outing in safe terrain. Big groups usually mean big frustration and big danger.

Bottom line: avoid groups larger than four and be especially suspicious of several groups together because acceptance and competition also add to the fire.

① Everyone has a level of risk that they not only tolerate but seek.

② Often we take mitigative measures (engineering, enforcement, and education) to make our risky behaviors safer.

③ Unfortunately, we then tend to choose even riskier behavior, keeping our level of risk the same. This is called risk homeostasis. The end result is no decrease in accidents.

Figure 10-2. Risk homeostasis (adapted from J.S. Wilde, Target Risk, 1994)

ADDITIONAL HUMAN FACTORS
Raising The Stupid Line (Risk Homeostasis)

> *The two biggest problems are the new guys who don't know anything and the old guys like me who think they know everything but don't.*
> —Onno Wieringa, longtime snow safety director
> at Alta Ski Area (now general manager)

Many risk researchers talk about crossing what has been called the "stupid line"—the invisible line that separates acceptable risk from unacceptable risk (Figure 10-2). Each one of us draws the stupid line in a different place, depending on 1) our penchant for risk, 2) our knowledge of the hazards, and 3) our perceptions of the hazards. People not only have a certain tolerance for risk but also most have a preference for it. Risk, after all, makes life more interesting.

This penchant for risk as affected by other factors has been described as "risk homeostasis." For instance, traffic studies have shown that when we added seatbelts and airbags to cars and made highways safer, the automobile accident rate did not drop. People just drove faster and crazier. In Alaska when bush pilots had too many accidents, they added many more fixed navigational devices; yet it did not decrease accidents, pilots just flew in worse conditions. And it turns out that adding crosswalks can actually increase pedestrian accidents because people are less likely to look before crossing the street. We tend to adjust our risk thermostat in all aspects of our lives, in sports, business, money, our love life, and we have different risk comfort levels for each activity. If we drop below a certain level, we feel bored; above that level, we feel fear.

Be sure to avoid the trap of what I call "gizmo madness." All too often, the mirror on the compass indicates exactly who is lost, the GPS indicates exactly where you are lost, the microscope indicates exactly the kind of weak layer that is about to kill you, the inclinometer indicates the steepness of the slope that's about to kill you, the radio is used to call your

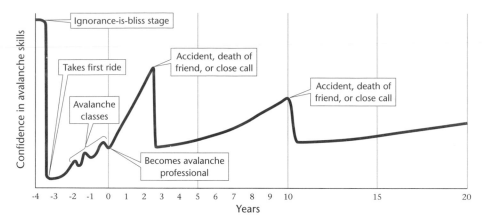

Figure 10-3. A conceptual illustration of how avalanche professionals' confidence in their own avalanche skills follows a cyclical pattern throughout their lives. (Adapted from Clair Isrelson)

friend at the top of the slope that's about to kill you to say, "Come on down, everything's fine," and the beacon will tell the rescuers exactly where to find your body.

Where we place the stupid line often changes dramatically throughout our lifetime. When I was 16, I would jump off tall cornices and jump into steep couloirs with hardly a thought. Now you can't get me to even approach the edge of a cornice unless I'm wearing a rope. Certainly, I've become more cautious with age and responsibility, but it's also because as Barry LePatner says, "Good judgment comes from experience, and experience comes from bad judgment."

Several longtime avalanche professionals have noticed that our placement of the stupid line also follows a cyclical pattern throughout our lives. For instance, Clair Isrealson, a prominent Canadian avalanche specialist, notices that if we graphed our confidence in avalanche skills on the vertical axis and time on the horizontal axis, that confidence among avalanche workers slowly climbs and reaches a peak at about three years, whereupon they usually have a close call or a friend dies and their confidence suddenly drops. Then it slowly starts to rise again, reaching a second peak around 10 years and another close call or a death of another friend and another sudden drop and so on (Figure 10-3).

From my experience, we can modify Clair's graph to begin several years before someone becomes a professional, in which case, confidence starts out at a lifetime high—the ignorance-is-bliss stage. Then we learn a few things and get scared, or we have a close call, and confidence plummets to a lifetime low. Then we take a few avalanche classes and confidence slowly rises to join Clair's graph when we become professionals. Past 10 years, I'm still not sure whether confidence slowly rises through time or sinks, but I have optimistically drawn it slowly rising. At least for me, that's the case, but then again, it may be rising up to yet another downfall.

Belief

> *Don't confuse me with the facts.*
> —Late Senator Roman Hruska, during the Watergate hearings

It isn't what we know that gets us into trouble, it's what we know that ain't so.

—Will Rogers

When the facts change, it's time to change your mind.

—John Maynard Keynes

We often hear people say, "I'll believe that when I see it." But really, it's the other way around.

When we believe the snowpack is stable, all we see are signs of stability, because we can't see something until we first believe it. For instance, survivors of avalanche accidents often say, "The avalanche bulletin said that the hazard was 'moderate,' so we didn't expect to get caught," (expert halo) or "There were tracks on the slope, so we assumed that it was safe" (herding instinct) or "I snowmobile here all the time, and I've never had any trouble" (familiarity).

We don't have to look very far through history books, or even current events, to see how powerful belief can be even in the face of contrary evidence. Belief is such a powerful force that in the geology summer field camp I attended in undergraduate studies, the professors required that we keep our field notebooks separated into two sections. On the left-facing pages, we wrote only facts and on the right-facing pages we wrote only opinions, speculation, or anything else that was not a concrete fact.

It's like the old story of three blind men trying to describe an elephant. The person feeling the leg says, "An elephant is like the trunk of a tree." The person feeling the tail says, "No, you're wrong, an elephant is like a rope." The person feeling the ear says, "No, you're both wrong, an elephant is thin and wide and moves like a fan." The good news is that each one is simultaneously right, but the bad news is that each one is also simultaneously wrong.

The human brain has a strong tendency toward what scientists call "confirmation bias," which means belief comes quickly and naturally while skepticism is slow and unnatural. Recent research has demonstrated that each is processed in different parts of the brain: belief in the part of the brain associated with learning by rewards, and skepticism in the part of the brain associated with pain and disgust (as in "not passing the smell test").

In other words belief is faster and feels better so we have to force ourselves to be skeptics. For this reason, scientists operate by trying to disprove hypotheses instead of proving them, which runs counter to our natural tendency but works much better. The bottom line: Nurture your inner skeptic and you will live longer in a dangerous environment.

It's a hard truth, but most of what we believe is wrong. Try this experiment: if you take the time to look deeply into any subject, we invariably discover that our pre-existing beliefs were either partly wrong or completely wrong. It's the Dilbert Principle: we're all idiots. Each of us only has time in their life to be experts at a very tiny piece of the world and for everything else, we're idiots. We have no choice but to use one of the many mental shortcuts to make our decisions. If we take the time to really look into the matter, we invariably change our belief. Yet the facts (and the danger) remain the same in either case.

Be very careful of unexamined beliefs. If you believe the world is flat and the ground is solid, that's exactly what you will see. For this reason scientists are trained to watch out for "confirmation bias." (Wasatch Range, Utah)

We have noticed for years that most people getting caught in avalanches are very skilled at their sport. Newspaper accounts often report that they were very "experienced." But experienced at what? True, they may have years of experience as a snowmobiler or climber but almost invariably their sport skills outpace their avalanche skills by a significant margin. How many years have you spent learning how to be a good skier, snowmobiler, climber, snowboarder (pick your sport)? How many years have you spent studying avalanches? See what I mean? We have also found that people highly skilled in their sport tend to consistently overestimate their avalanche skills, often they vastly overestimate them.

This situation is true in almost all endeavors. A 1981 study found that most drivers rate themselves in the top 50 percent of safe drivers. Stock traders consistently mistake favorable market conditions for personal stock-picking skill. (Only a tiny minority of stock pickers have been able to consistently beat the market year after year.)

All scientists are systematically schooled, from early years, to identify their assumptions and check them out. Scientists are a notoriously cynical and suspicious lot, and successful avalanche forecasters, because their lives intimately depend on it, are doubly so. For years I thought that something was wrong with me because in the outdoors I was always looking for what could go wrong. But I have read that successful stock traders are similarly skeptical—always looking for the downside. The ones who see only sunny days will quickly get washed away in the next storm. Incorrect assumptions, erroneous beliefs, mistaking opinions for facts, and mistaking one perspective for the whole truth have caused uncountable death, injury, and heartache in avalanche terrain. Be very careful of belief and always be prepared to abandon it at the first contrary evidence.

Belief Inertia

Not knowing is true knowledge. Presuming to know is a disease.
                                                              —Lao-tsu

On one hand, investors exaggerate their stock-picking abilities. On the other, they form initial impressions that persist and are hard to change, even if they are based on random or irrelevant information. As a result, investors are slow to change.
          —Louise Witt, *Overconfidence and the Illusion of Validity*

A time delay always exists between when we learn the facts and when the facts sink in and we finally get it, which I call "belief inertia." This is a common problem even among professional avalanche forecasters—either a rapidly building avalanche hazard catches someone or the slope or the road remains closed too long after conditions stabilize. A good avalanche forecaster who is paying attention will have a close match between the actual and the perceived hazard (Figure 10-4). Someone with poor avalanche skills usually doesn't believe there's danger until someone triggers an avalanche. Then they spend the next several days, or sometimes weeks, tiptoeing around long after the instability has abated. The truly clueless not only have a large time delay but their belief curve hardly even budges in the face of obvious facts.

Successful avalanche forecasters (among others) operate using what scientists call a Bayesian approach, in which your mind cycles through countless iterations of gathering new evidence and updating your belief until you eventually funnel into the correct belief.

In Lawrence Gonzales' book *Deep Survival, Who Lives and Who Dies*, he notes that people who tend to survive in outdoor accidents are the ones who can quickly and efficiently update their beliefs based on new evidence. In other words, survival favors those who make evidence-based decisions and disfavors those who cling to beliefs.

If you make decisions based on experience alone, the final exam sometimes comes before the lesson.
          —Dave McClung, prominent avalanche researcher
                    and co-author of *The Avalanche Handbook*

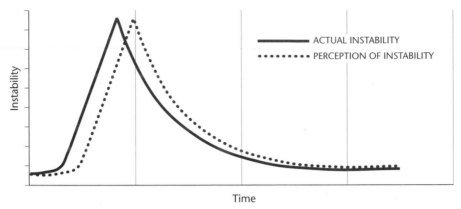

A good avalanche forecaster will have a close match.

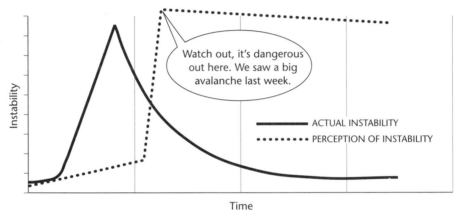

Belief inertia of someone with poor avalanche skills who is reactionary as well. This is often how the media responds.

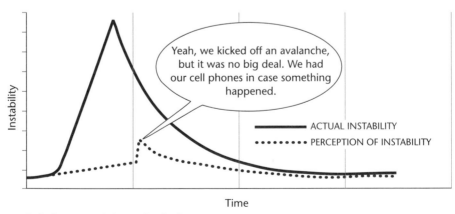

Belief inertia of the truly clueless.

Figure 10-4. There is always some time mismatch between actual and perceived instability. The closer the match, the better the avalanche forecaster. People who survive in the mountains tend to be those who are quick to modify their beliefs in the face of contrary evidence.

When people are free to do as they please, they usually imitate each other.

—Eric Holffer

Know the male yet keep to the female.

—Lao-tsu

Weather and Perception

We know that most avalanches occur during or immediately after storms, but avalanche *accidents* tend to occur during blue-sky days following storms. It is true that more people are out during sunny days, but I think that sunny days have a more important effect, namely, sunny days make us feel good, but the snowpack doesn't necessarily share our opinion. Most of our non-avalanche-related experience teaches us that the danger is over when the storm is over. Avalanche hazard notoriously lingers after storms, especially with persistent weak layers such as faceted snow and surface hoar. Once again, our perception of the hazard is out of sync with the actual hazard. Always be suspicious of the first sunny day after a storm and be especially suspicious of sunny Saturdays after a storm.

On the other side of the coin, travel during foul weather can also be just as dangerous but for the opposite reason. Being cold and wet gives us what Fredston and Fesler call the "horse syndrome," the rush to get back to the barn. We tend to cut corners and rush decisions. Just when we need to pay attention the most, the weather pushes us to do the opposite.

Any astronomer can predict where a star will be at half past eleven. He can make no such prediction about his daughter.

—James Thurlow Adams

Unfortunately, the sort of individual who is programmed to ignore personal distress and keep pushing for the top is frequently programmed to disregard signs of grave and imminent danger as well. This forms the nub of a dilemma that every Everest climber eventually comes up against: in order to succeed you must be exceedingly driven, but if you're too driven you're likely to die. Above 26,000 feet, moreover, the line between appropriate zeal and reckless summit fever becomes grievously thin. Thus the slopes of Everest are littered with corpses.

—Jon Krakauer, *Into Thin Air*, 1997

Communication

Here in the "information age" communication is, more than ever, the central problem of the human race. Have you ever noticed that if people would just *talk* to each other, most of the conflict that drives the plots of television and movie dramas would be eliminated? It would put thousands of entertainment workers out of a job. In a world where communication is a commodity, profits as well as marital bliss depend on it; without communication, there is chaos. Poor communication is a common denominator in almost all

avalanche accidents. As Fredston and Fesler have noted, poor communication typically takes several forms:

- One or more people fail to speak up for fear of being the "nerd."
- Incomplete communication leads to incorrect assumptions or limited sharing of important information.
- Misunderstanding of the group's plan or the group's opinion of the potential hazard.
- No communication at all.

Once again, avalanche professionals are certainly not immune. Some of the most dangerous group dynamics situations in which I have participated involved larger groups of helicopter guides, avalanche forecasters, or ski patrollers in their early season training. In such a high-level group, no one wants to speak up and risk offending their peers. Yet we will all willingly dive into a dangerous situation that afterward we all agree was foolhardy.

When we look at avalanche accidents, it's clear that democratic decision-making works best. The central premise of James Surowiecki's bestselling book, *The Wisdom of Crowds*, is that groups of people almost always make better decisions than individuals. This notion often flies in the face of con-

Most avalanches happen during storms but most avalanche accidents occur on the sunny days following storms. Sunny weather makes us feel great, but the snowpack does not necessarily share our opinion. (Wasatch Range, Utah)

ventional wisdom because we often hear derogatory phrases like, "it's like it was designed by a committee." It's also basic human nature that we look for the one, great leader or lone, great genius who will show us the best way, but the evidence simply does not support that this happens very often. Even highly paid CEO's don't make better business decisions alone than they do by using a more collaborative approach. I, likewise, have learned the hard way that all too many of my ideas and decisions have turned out to be embarrassingly lame-brained. So through my past 35 years of being a boss and supervisor, my management style has evolved into a democratic process in which ideas come from the bottom up and we make all our important decisions as a group. In fact, I first heard these ideas many years ago from the venerable avalanche specialist Roland Emetaz who liked to say, "A brainstorming group of ordinary people is almost always smarter than one Einstein."

An effective way to demonstrate this principle in an avalanche class is to have everyone in the class guess your weight. Have each student write their guess down on a scrap of paper, collect the papers, have one student calculate an average and the result will almost invariably be very close to correct. Notice that the average is closer to the right answer than most of the individual guesses. Averaging eliminates the individual human errors. As

James Suroweiecki puts it, "Every data point has two components, information and error. Eliminate the error and you are left with the information." I've actually spent a lot of time watching ants, and I have always been amazed at how individually, they seem like bumbling idiots, but collectively they represent a great intelligence. In fact, this same strategy is employed by most species on Earth, including humans.

However, democratic decision making only works in groups when the following conditions are met.

ESSENTIAL CONDITIONS FOR THE "WISDOM OF CROWDS"

- At least some expertise or knowledge among individuals
- Diversity of opinions
- Free competition of ideas
- Mechanism to narrow the choices (secret ballots or nonjudgmental voting)

In the backcountry, we would obviously have a hard time voting by secret ballot, but we can at least make sure that members are encouraged to vote without judgment or pressure. The "wisdom of crowds" does not work when these conditions don't exist. Here are some ways that group decisions can go haywire:

As we know, in any group, a natural leader almost always rises to the occasion—usually because of a strong personality, organizational skills, familiarity with the terrain or route, or a number of other reasons. Usually, group leaders don't rise to the top just because of their avalanche skills (the "expert halo" strikes again), though that's what is most needed. So it often takes courage for a shy person with good avalanche skills to speak up and attempt to sway the momentum of their peers. And it also takes uncommon good judgment for a group leader to ferret out opinions from soft-spoken members who might know something but don't want to say.

Communication is always a problem, and the larger the group, the larger the problem. (Wasatch Range, Utah)

If we always go out with the same group of like-minded people we automatically eliminate a diversity of opinions. Many successful businesses make it a policy to include dissenting views on every committee and even invite representatives from competing companies to participate on committees.

Finally, we don't have to look far in human history, or even in current events, to see the folly of eliminating dissent. A healthy democracy depends on dissent and dictators, who thrive in dissent's absence, seldom last long. Thus, a leader's main job is not to make decisions, but to ferret out other opinions from the group and listen carefully. Any mountaineering party can accomplish only what its weakest member can accomplish. Often the weakest member doesn't speak up or the decision-makers fail to adequately consult everyone in the group. Different members of the party may also have different levels of acceptable risk, expectation, travel skills, and avalanche skills and there's invariably too little communication about it.

Yes, using the wisdom of crowds certainly takes more time, but we almost always make better decisions because of it.

The best way to combat inevitable human factors that lead us astray is to use a time-tested system. Without a system, the world is too complicated and we simply rely on mental shortcuts. The first photo shows someone else's office (believe it or not, this really is his working office). The second (opposite) is my home office where everything is in its place. My mind may resemble the first office but I try to make up for it with good organization and habits.

When people think that they know the answers, people are difficult to guide. When they know that they don't know, people can find their own way.

—Lao-tsu

HOW TO AVOID THE DREADED HUMAN FACTOR

Through the years I have tried a number of ways to keep human factors from making me do stupid things even when I know better. Early on, I believed that just studying them and being vigilant for them would help me avoid falling in their traps. After a few years I realized that this helped but only a little. Next, I needed to get a better handle on my own mind. I read a lot about psychology and once again, yes, it helped, but only a little.

So I just dove in deeper. So for five years I attended a world-class Zen center, which just happened to be a couple of blocks from my house. Every morning at 6:00 AM I marched over for an hour-long meditation; I attended classes and lectures in the evenings, went to week-long retreats, and received regular, personal coaching from several of the top Zen masters in the world. At least for me, Zen practice has been a fundamental, life-changing, ego-smashing, delusion-obliterating experience, which I would recommend to everyone.

Although Zen practice has improved my ability to stay alive in avalanche terrain by reducing the human factors or mistakes created by ego or close-mindedness, I also realize that Zen practice is damned hard. The vast majority of those who travel or recreate in avalanche country would have neither time, desire, nor the motivation required. Zen practice may be the answer to a lot of other things but it is not the answer to the avalanche problem.

Finally, I decided I should just see what worked in other fields (you would think I would have tried that first). Thus, we return to the theme of this book. What saves our lives is application of a thorough system of procedures, checklists, rules, coaching, and good avalanche habits. Because avalanche professionals operate within a time tested high-success system of analysis they enjoy a very low fatality rate. Because backcountry recreationists for the most part operate completely outside such a system they account for the vast majority of avalanche accidents and fatalities (98.5 percent in the U.S.).

Part of the system is to maintain a strong "situational awareness," which is a fancy term for paying close attention or maintaining key awareness (back to Zen again). Here is one simple habit of conversation between partners that has been used in many other industries to force people to pay attention.

- Here's what I think we face.
- Here's what I think we should do.
- Here's why.
- Here's what we should be alert to.
- What do you think?

Probably the most effective way to combat the ravages of belief is to always challenge it. Continually ask yourself, "How might I be wrong?"

RAP ON RESPONSIBILITY

Our culture rejoices in the concept of individuality, that we have the right to do as we please, even to the point that if we kill ourselves through risky endeavors, well, then it's nobody's business but our own. I have, unfortunately, participated in several dozen missions of either rescue, body recovery, or accident investigation and have attended the funerals of a half

dozen friends and coworkers who have died in the mountains. With every one of them there were the tears of spouses, children, parents, siblings, and friends whose lives will never be the same. There were also the invisible strings attached to the rescuers who risked their lives, the innocent people below on the trail or road who were nearly buried by the avalanche they triggered, and the lawmakers who passed restrictive rules for others in the wake of an accident or lawsuit. Catastrophe and sorrow, it seems, always make ripples that travel to the edges of every pond. So where is the individual? I don't think I have ever seen one.

Everything we do affects others. When we break a trail through the snow, others will follow. When we decide not to cross a slope, others will listen. When we check everyone's beacon at the beginning of an outing, everyone will think about avalanches. When we see young people doing stupid things in the mountains and we teach them a better way with patience and compassion, everyone will be safer. There are no unconnected dots.

Opposite: Avalanche control with explosives and heavy ski compaction are very effective at preventing large, slab avalanches at ski resorts. However, especially with depth hoar near the ground, when the entire snowpack becomes saturated for the first time, it's possible for large, wet slabs to fracture, taking out the entire season's snowpack, complete with moguls. This was an explosive-triggered avalanche at a resort around noon on a very hot, spring day. (Wasatch Range, Utah)

APPENDIX

UNITED STATES AVALANCHE DANGER DESCRIPTORS

Danger Level (and Color)	Avalanche Probability and Avalanche Trigger	Degree and Distribution of Avalanche Danger	Recommended Action in the Backcountry
What	*Why*	*Where*	*What to Do*
Low (green)	Natural avalanches very unlikely. Human-triggered avalanches unlikely.	Generally stable snow. Isolated areas of instability.	Travel is generally safe. Normal caution is advised.
Moderate (yellow)	Natural avalanches unlikely. Human-triggered avalanches possible.	Unstable slabs possible on steep terrain.	Use caution in steeper terrain on certain aspects (defined in accompanying statement).
Considerable (orange)	Natural avalanches possible. Human-triggered avalanches probable.	Unstable slabs probable on steep terrain.	Be increasingly cautious in steeper terrain.
High (red)	Natural and human-triggered avalanches likely.	Unstable slabs likely on a variety of aspects and slope angles.	Travel in avalanche terrain is not recommended. Safest travel on windward ridges of lower-angle slopes without steeper terrain above.
Extreme (black)	Widespread natural or human-triggered avalanches certain.	Extremely unstable slabs certain on most aspects and slope angles. Large, destructive avalanches possible.	Travel in avalanche terrain should be avoided and travel confined to low-angle terrain well away from avalanche path runouts.

Avalanche Safety Basics

Avalanches don't happen by accident, and most human involvement is a matter of choice, not chance. Most avalanche accidents are caused by slab avalanches, which are triggered by the victim or a member of the victim's party. However, any avalanche may cause injury or death and even small slides may be dangerous. Hence, always practice safe routefinding skills, be aware of changing conditions, and carry avalanche rescue gear. Learn and apply avalanche terrain analysis and snow stability evaluation techniques to help minimize your risk. Remember that avalanche danger rating levels are only general guidelines. Distinctions between geographic areas, elevations, slope aspects, and slope angles are approximate and transition zones between dangers exist. No matter what the current avalanche danger, there are avalanche-safe areas in the mountains.

NORTH AMERICAN PUBLIC AVALANCHE DANGER SCALE (2008 DRAFT)

Danger Rating (and Color)	Advice for Public Recreation
Low (green)	Generally safe conditions. Watch for unstable snow on isolated terrain features.
Moderate (yellow)	Locally unsafe conditions. Evaluate the snow and terrain carefully. Use good travel habits to minimize risk.
Considerable (orange)	Variable conditions and uncertainty require conservative decision making. Careful route selection and good travel habits are required.
High (red)	Widespread dangerous conditions. Exposure to avalanche terrain is not recommended. Extensive experience assessing snow and terrain is required for safe travel.
Extreme (black)	Avoid all avalanche terrain. Travel only on gentle slopes well away from avalanche paths and runout areas.
The avalanche danger rating is only a starting point. **YOU CONTROL YOUR OWN RISK** *by choosing where and when you travel.*	

Note: These descriptors are currently being rewritten by a joint U.S.–Canada committee. Check www.avalanche.org and www.avalanche.ca for current updates.

GLOSSARY

anchors Trees, rocks, or bushes that help to hold the snowpack in place.

aspect The direction a slope faces with respect to sun and wind. For instance, a slope may be north-facing, or it may be a leeward slope.

avalanche air bag Victims caught in an avalanche pull a rip cord to deploy this air bag mounted on their packs to help the victims rise to the surface of avalanche debris.

Avalung™ A device that delays the dangerous buildup of carbon dioxide for a buried avalanche victim. Buried victims breathe through a tube that exhausts carbon dioxide on the back side of their bodies and allows them to breathe in air from the front side.

beacon An electronic device used to locate buried avalanche victims. Also called transceivers or locators.

bed surface The snow surface on which an avalanche slides.

bridging The ability of a relatively stiff slab to spread a person's weight over a wider area, making that person less likely to trigger an avalanche. However, if an avalanche is triggered, it is often larger and more dangerous than an avalanche with a softer slab.

cirque A large bowl-shaped concavity formed by glaciers in mountainous terrain.

climax slab avalanche An avalanche that involves the entire season's snowpack and slides either on a weak layer near the ground (usually depth hoar), or on firn, or on a glacier.

clustered snow *See* melt-freeze snow.

collapsing Also called "whoomphing." A snowpack collapsing onto a buried weak layer, which is an obvious sign of instability. It often produces an audible whoomphing sound. (Sometimes incorrectly called "settling.")

concave slope A slope shaped like the interior of a circle or sphere. When descending it becomes less steep. A double concave slope is shaped like the inside of a bowl.

continental climate The snow climate found in mountains far from the influence of the ocean's weather. Characterized by thin snowpacks, cold temperatures, and more persistently unstable snowpack.

convex slope A slope shaped like the exterior of a circle or sphere. When descending it becomes steeper. A double convex slope is shaped like the outside of a basketball.

corn snow *See* melt-freeze snow.

cornice An overhanging mass of snow created by the wind, usually near a sharp terrain break such as a ridge.

couloir A steep gully in alpine terrain. In winter, a couloir is usually filled with snow bound by rocks on either side.

cross-loaded Snow blown by the wind across a slope, depositing drifts on the sides of gullies or other terrain features.

crown The snow that remains on the slope above the crown face of an avalanche.

crown face The top fracture surface of a slab avalanche. Usually smooth, clean-cut, and angled 90 degrees to the bed surface. *See* fracture line.

deep slab avalanches Avalanches that break deeply into old weak layers of snow that formed some time ago. Often persistent weak layers such as facets or surface hoar are the culprit weak layer.

delayed action avalanches Avalanches that occur a day or more after a storm, usually with persistent weak layers such as faceted snow or surface hoar as the culprit.

depth hoar Large-grained, faceted, cup-shaped crystals near the ground. Depth hoar is caused by large temperature gradients within the snowpack, usually in the early winter, by large temperature differences between the warm ground and the cold snow surface.

direct action avalanches Avalanches caused directly by storms, usually from loading of new, wind-blown snow or rain.

diurnal recrystallization Faceted snow created by large temperature gradients near the surface of the snow from strong heating and cooling of the snow surface between day and night.

dry avalanche An avalanche that occurs in snow of below-freezing temperature.

equilibrium A situation that occurs when the snowpack has a low temperature gradient, which metamorphoses rounded crystals instead of faceted crystals. Usually, less than 1°C per 10 cm. is considered to be equilibrium conditions.

faceted snow Angular, larger-grained snow with poor bonding created by large temperature gradients within the snowpack. Different kinds of faceted crystals include depth hoar, diurnal recrystallization, melt layer recrystallization, and radiation recrystallization.

firn Snow that did not melt in the previous summer. After one or more seasons, firn can become glacial ice.

flagged trees Trees with the branches ripped off on the uphill side, indicating that they have been hit by an avalanche in the past.

flux line search *See* induction search.

fracture The separation of a solid body into two parts under the action of stress. Fracture usually requires both initiation and propagation of the fracture. Fracturing must occur for a snow avalanche to release.

fracture line The visible crack in the snow after a slab avalanche has released. The fracture line is composed of the crown face, flanks, and staunchwall of the avalanche.

glide The entire snowpack slowly moving as a unit on the ground, similar to a glacier. This is usually caused by melt water lubricating the snow-ground interface. Slabs of snow can release catastrophically at random intervals. Not to be confused with climax slab avalanche.

grain The smallest distinguishable ice particle in a snowpack. Synonymous with crystal in avalanche applications.

graupel New snow that looks like little Styrofoam balls. Mechanically, it behaves like ball bearings but it can also form slabs.

grid search A rescue technique with beacons in which the rescuer uses a series of perpendicular grids to find the transmitting beacon.

hang fire Snow that remains above a crown face after an avalanche. Hang fire seldom avalanches naturally but if disturbed it can sometimes release, which is a danger to rescuers below or to avalanche geeks doing a fracture line profile.

hard slab A snow slab having the density of 300 kg/m³ prior to avalanching. Hard slabs usually include layers of older, harder snow but they can be formed within new snow by strong winds. Hard slabs are considered difficult to manage because they tend to break above you instead of at your feet as soft slabs often do.

humidity The amount of water contained in air. *See also* relative humidity.

icefall The glacial equivalent of a waterfall. A glacier slowly moves over a drop-off, such as a cliff or bulge, creating jumbled ice that can calve off ice blocks.

icefall avalanche An avalanche of ice falling from an icefall.

induction line search A rescue technique with beacons in which the rescuer follows the curving magnetic lines of force that emanate from a transmitting beacon. Also called tangent line search or flux line search.

intermountain climate The snow climate commonly found in intermountain areas midway between maritime and continental climates. Characterized by intermediate snow depths and intermediate temperatures.

isothermal The state of equal temperature, that is, temperature does not change with depth. This usually occurs in spring after the entire snowpack warms up to 0°C.

leeward The downwind side of an obstacle such as a ridge. Wind can deposit snow onto leeward terrain, creating wind slabs or wind pillows, which are often dangerous.

loading The addition of weight on top of a snowpack, usually from wind, new snow, transport, or rain.

loose snow avalanche An avalanche of loose snow—not a slab avalanche. Small loose snow avalanches are called sluffs. They often start from a point and fan out. Also called point releases.

maritime climate The snow climate near the oceans, characterized by deep snow and warm temperatures. Also called coastal climate.

melt-freeze snow Large-grained, rounded, and clustered crystals formed by the repeated melting and freezing of the snow. It typically forms in spring conditions near the snow surface. Also called clustered snow or corn snow.

melt layer recrystallization Faceted snow created by large temperature gradients between a wet, warm snow layer and the overlying colder new snow. This typically occurs when a cold storm deposits snow on top of a wet, warm rain crust. Also called melt layer recrystallation.

persistent weak layers Weak layers within the snowpack that continue to produce avalanches several days after they were subjected to a rapid change such as loading of new or wind-blown snow or a rapid temperature rise. Persistent weak layers include faceted snow and surface hoar. These layers account for about 80 percent of avalanche fatalities in North America and Europe.

point release *See* sluff.

probe A rod used to probe avalanche debris for buried victims.

propagation The spreading of a fracture or crack within the snowpack. During very unstable conditions, fractures can propagate for long distances.

radiation recrystallization A thin layer of faceted snow created in the top centimeter or two of the snow surface by strong heating by the sun combined with strong surface cooling from outgoing radiation. This is usually a high-elevation phenomenon at lower latitudes.

rain crust A clear layer of ice formed from rain on the snow surface, which later freezes. Not to be confused with sun crust or melt-freeze crust.

relative humidity The amount of water air holds compared with the amount of water it can hold at a certain temperature.

remote trigger When a person triggers an avalanche some distance away. Sometimes incorrectly called sympathetic trigger (sympathetic trigger is when one avalanche triggers another avalanche some distance away). Remote triggers are usually seen as a sign of very unstable conditions.

rime A Styrofoam-textured snow that forms on solid surfaces during storms. Rime forms when supercooled water droplets in the clouds freeze upon contact with a surface. Rime can form on the snow surface, trees, and other snowflakes as they fall.

runout The zone where an avalanche loses speed and deposits debris.

runout angle The angle, measured from horizontal, between the toe of the avalanche and the crown. Also called the "alpha" angle.

sastrugi Wind-eroded snow, which often looks rough as if it were sandblasted.

settling, settlement The slow deformation and densification of snow under the influence of gravity. Sometimes settlement is incorrectly used to describe collapsing or whoomphing snow.

ski cut *See* slope cut.

slab A relatively more cohesive layer of snow overlying a relatively less cohesive layer of snow. You can also think of a slab as strong snow sitting on top of weak snow. A slab avalanche is similar to a magazine sliding off an inclined table.

slope cut Moving rapidly across an avalanche starting zone, aiming at safe terrain on the side, so that if an avalanche breaks, your momentum will hopefully carry you off the moving slab onto safe terrain. Skiers call them ski cuts.

sluff A small, loose snow avalanche—not a slab. Sometimes called "point releases."

slush flow avalanche An avalanche composed of slush—very saturated snow. They usually occur in arctic climates on permafrost soil when dry cold snow becomes rapidly saturated with water in spring. Slush avalanches can run long distances on very gentle slopes.

snowpit A hole dug in the snow to examine snowpack properties. This is a very powerful tool used by avalanche forecasters and recreationists. Also called snow profile.

snow profile *See* snowpit.

soft slab A snow slab with a density less than 300 Kg/m^3. Soft slabs are usually composed of new snow without strong winds. Soft slabs tend to be more manageable than hard slabs because they tend to break at your feet instead of above you.

stepping down A slab avalanche sliding a short distance and breaking down into deeper weak layers, forming a stair-step pattern on the bed surface.

sun crust A thin, clear layer of ice formed by radiation from the sun. Not to be confused with melt-freeze crust or rain crust.

surface hoar Frost that forms on the snow surface during calm, clear, humid conditions. When buried, surface hoar forms a thin, persistent weak layer within the snowpack—a very dangerous weak layer. Also called frost, hoar frost, or feathers.

sympathetic trigger One avalanche triggering another avalanche some distance away. Sometimes incorrectly called remote trigger (remote trigger is when a person triggers another avalanche some distance away).

tangent line search *See* induction line search.

temperature gradient The change of temperature over a certain distance within the snowpack. Large temperature gradients (generally more than 1°C per 10 cm.) metamorphose crystals into weak, angular, faceted snow. Small temperature gradients (generally less than 1°C per 10 cm.) are called equilibrium conditions, which metamorphose the snow into more well-bonded, rounded crystals.

terrain trap Terrain in which the consequences of an avalanche are especially hazardous. Common terrain traps include gullies, an abrupt transition, or an avalanche path that terminates in trees, a crevasse field, or a cliff.

trigger A disturbance that initiates fractures within the weak layer, allowing the slab to slide off a slope. In 93 percent of avalanche accidents, the victim or someone in the victim's party triggers the avalanche. Natural triggers include new snow, cornice falls, wind, rapid warming, or percolated water. Contrary to popular myth, avalanches are not triggered by noise.

trigger point A place where a person can trigger an avalanche, usually in an area where the slab is thinner or is poorly bonded to the underlying snow. Sometimes called "sweet spots" or "deficit areas" or "super weak zones."

upside-down snow New snow with relatively stronger snow on top of relatively weaker snow.

weak interface A poor bond between two layers of snow without a distinct weak layer.

weak layer A relatively less cohesive layer of snow underlying a relatively more cohesive layer of snow. In a slab avalanche, the weak layer fractures, allowing the overlying slab to slide off the slope.

wet avalanche An avalanche caused by snow losing its strength after becoming damp, moist, or saturated with water.

whoomph Snowpack collapsing on a buried weak layer—an obvious sign of instability.

wind loading Loading of weight on top of a snowpack when wind drifts snow onto lee terrain. Wind can deposit snow much more rapidly than snow falling from clouds. Wind loading is a common denominator in most avalanche accidents.

wind slab A slab of snow formed when wind deposits snow onto lee (or downwind) terrain. Wind slabs are often smooth and rounded and sometimes sound hollow.

windward The upwind side of an obstacle such as a ridge. Usually snow is eroded from windward slopes making them relatively safer.

BIBLIOGRAPHY

AVALANCHE BOOKS AND PUBLICATIONS

American Avalanche Association. *Snow, Weather and Avalanches: Observational Guidelines for Avalanche Programs in the United States.* American Avalanche Association, 2004. See www.avalanche.org for an online version.

Avalanche.ca–The Journal. Monthly publication of the Canadian Avalanche Association, See www.avalanche.ca for ordering information. This is a must-have monthly magazine for avalanche professionals in both the U.S. and Canada

The Avalanche Review. Monthly publication of the American Avalanche Association, See www.AmericanAvalancheAssociation.org for ordering information. This is a must-have monthly magazine for avalanche professionals.

Canadian Avalanche Association. *Observation Guidelines and Recording Standards.* Canadian Avalanche Association, 2002. See www.avalanche.ca for ordering information.

Colbeck, S., E. Akitaya, R. Armstrong, H. Gubler, J. Lafeuille, K. Lied, D. McClung, and E. Morris. "International Classification for Seasonal Snow on the Ground." Boulder, CO: International Commission of Snow and Ice, World Data Center-A for Glaciology, 1990. An updated version will be published soon.

Daffern, Tony. *Avalanche Safety for Skiers and Climbers.* Seattle: The Mountaineers Books, 2000.

Fredston, Jill, and Doug Fesler. *Snow Sense: A Guide to Evaluating Snow Avalanche Hazard.* Anchorage, AK: Alaska Mountain Safety Center, Inc., 1999. This is the most popular avalanche book ever written and is highly recommended, especially for beginning avalanche students.

"International Snow Science Workshop Proceedings." American Avalanche Association. This international conference occurs on even-numbered years and is the leading vehicle for publication of scientific avalanche literature. Its motto, "Merging of Theory and Practice," says it all. My copies of each "Proceeding" are heavily dog-eared, underlined, and gritted with desert sand from bedtime reading during summer vacations. See www.avalanche.org and click on ISSW for ordering information.

Jamieson, Bruce. *Backcountry Avalanche Awareness.* Revelstoke, British Columbia, Canada: Canadian Avalanche Association, 2000. A new version will be published soon.

Jamieson, Bruce, and Torsten Geldsetter. *Avalanche Accidents in Canada*, Volume 4, 1984–1996. Revelstoke, British Columbia, Canada: Canadian Avalanche Association, 1996.

Jamieson, Bruce, and Jennie McDonald. *Free Riding in Avalanche Terrain: A Snowboarder's Handbook.* Revelstoke, British Columbia, Canada: Canadian Avalanche Association, 1999.

Jamieson, Bruce, and Darcy Svederus. *Sledding in Avalanche Terrain: Reducing the Risk.* Revelstoke, British Columbia, Canada: Canadian Avalanche Association, 1998.

LaChapelle, Ed. *Field Guide to Snow Crystals*. International Glaciological Society, 2001.
———— *Secrets of the Snow: Visual Clues to Avalanches and Ski Conditions*. Seattle: University of Washington Press, 2001.
Logan, Nick, and Dale Atkins. *The Snowy Torrents: Avalanche Accidents in the United States 1980–86*. Colorado Geological Survey, Special Publication 39, 1996.
McCammon, Ian. *Evidence of Heuristic Traps in Recreational Avalanche Accidents*, 2002. Available from Snowpit Technologies, www.snowpit.com.
————. *Snow and Avalanche Field Notebook*. Available from Snowpit Technologies, www. snowpit.com.
McClung, David, and Peter Schaerer. *The Avalanche Handbook*, 3rd editon. Seattle: The Mountaineers Books, 2006.
Munter, Werner. *3x3 Lawinen* (in German). Agentur, Poht and Shellhammer, 1997.

FIRST-AID BOOKS

Auerbach, Paul S. *Medicine for the Outdoors: The Essential Guide to Emergency Medical Procedures and First Aid*. New York: The Lyons Press, 1999.
Isaac, Jeffery. *The Outward Bound Wilderness First-Aid Handbook*. New York: The Lyons Press, 1998.
Schimelpfenig, Todd, and Linda Lindsey. *NOLS Wilderness First Aid*. Mechanicsburg, Pa.: Stackpole Books, 2000.
Weiss, Eric. *Wilderness 911*. Seattle: The Mountaineers Books, 1998.
Wilkerson, James A. *Medicine for Mountaineering and Other Wilderness Activities*, 5th edition. Seattle: The Mountaineers Books, 2001.

WEATHER BOOKS AND DVDS

Whiteman, C. David. *Mountain Meteorology: Fundamentals and Applications*. New York: Oxford University Press, 2000.
Williams, Jack, and *USA Today*. *The Weather Book*, 2nd edition. New York, Vintage Books, 1997.
Woodmencey, Jim. *Reading Weather: Where Will You Be When the Storm Hits?* Helena, MT.: Falcon Publishing, 1998.

AVALANCHE VIDEOS AND DVDs

"Avalanche!" *Nova*, #2148, November 25, 1997. Produced and directed by Beth Hoppe. 60 min. WGBH Boston, 1997. Call (800) 949-8670 ext. 498 to order. More information about this episode is available at www.pbs.org/wgbh/nova/avalanche.
Avalanche Rescue Beacons: A Race Against Time. Written by Dale Atkins. 38 min. People Productions, Boulder, CO, 1995. Call (303) 866-2611 or visit www.caic.state.co.us to order.
Beating the Odds. Revelstoke, British Columbia, Canada: Canadian Avalanche Association. Call (250) 837-2435 or visit www.avalanche.ca to order.
The Discovery Channel. *Raging Planet: Avalanche.* 1997. Call (800) 889-9950 or visit http://shopping.discovery.com to order.
The Discovery Channel. A variety of avalanche documentaries and avalanche stories. Visit http://dsc.discovery.com/ and search for "avalanche."

National Geographic. A variety of avalanche videos, documentaries and articles on avalanches. Visit http://dsc.discovery.com/ and search for "avalanche."
Riding Safely in Avalanche Country. 30 min. Forest Service National Avalanche Center
  and Idaho Department of Parks and Recreation, 1998. This video is specifically for
  snowmobilers. To order, call the Friends of Sun Valley Avalanche Center, c/o the
  Environmental Resource Center, (208) 726-4333.
Rules of the Snow. Written and directed by Valerie Schramm. 50 min. SavaFilm, 1997. A
  safety video for snowmobilers. Call (307) 739-2256 or visit www.savafilm.com to order.
Think Like an Avalanche. Forest Service National Avalanche Center. Available through
  Black Diamond, (www.bdel.com).
Time is Life: Medical Training in Avalanche Rescue. 78 min., 10 languages. Protocols for av-
  alanche rescue. Recommended for avalanche and medical professionals and advanced
  users. Available through the Canadian Avalanche Centre (www.avalanche.ca).
Violent Planet. 25 min. National Geographic Explorer Series, 1995. Call (800) 647-5463 to
  order.
White Risk. A slick, interactive CD produced by the Swiss Institute of Snow and Avalanche
  Research. Available in English (www.slf.ch/welcome-en.html).

Websites

www.avalanche.ca
Website of the Canadian Avalanche Association. Complete avalanche information for
Canada.

www.avalanche.org
Official website of the American Avalanche Association. Supported and run by avalanche
professionals, it offers one-stop shopping for a wealth of avalanche information and links
to a multitude of other avalanche sites. It also maintains a current list of classes taught in
each area of the United States.

www.nsp.org
National Ski Patrol

www.slf.ch/laworg/map.html
European avalanche centers

www.slf.ch/welcome-en.html
Swiss Institute for Snow and Avalanche Research

www.snowmobilers.org/saferider/homepage/page°00.html
The International Association of Snowmobile Administrators' website includes avalanche
information for snowmobilers.

INDEX

ABOUT THE AUTHOR

BRUCE TREMPER grew up skiing in the mountains of western Montana, where his father taught him the basics of avalanches at the age of ten. He was a member of the Junior National Ski Team and the U.S. Ski Team Talent Squad; in 1973, he was NCAA Division Downhill Champion. Tremper went on to earn a master's degree in geology from Montana State University, studying under the well-known avalanche researchers Dr. John Montagne and Dr. Bob Brown. His professional avalanche experience began in 1977 when he did avalanche control for Bridger Bowl Ski area. Tremper was the director of avalanche control at Big Sky Ski Area and then a backcountry avalanche forecaster for the Alaska Avalanche Center. He has been the director of the Forest Service Utah Avalanche Center since 1986 and, in that capacity, coordinated backcountry avalanche safety preparations for the 2002 Olympic Winter Games in Salt Lake City. He has been featured on many news programs and national and international television avalanche documentaries, including those produced by National Geographic, PBS, and Discovery Channel.

THE MOUNTAINEERS, founded in 1906, is a nonprofit outdoor activity and conservation club, whose mission is "to explore, study, preserve, and enjoy the natural beauty of the outdoors...." Based in Seattle, Washington, the club is now the third-largest such organization in the United States, with seven branches throughout Washington State.

The Mountaineers sponsors both classes and year-round outdoor activities in the Pacific Northwest, which include hiking, mountain climbing, ski-touring, snowshoeing, bicycling, camping, kayaking and canoeing, nature study, sailing, and adventure travel. The club's conservation division supports environmental causes through educational activities, sponsoring legislation, and presenting informational programs. All club activities are led by skilled, experienced volunteers, who are dedicated to promoting safe and responsible enjoyment and preservation of the outdoors.

If you would like to participate in these organized outdoor activities or the club's programs, consider a membership in The Mountaineers. For information and an application, write or call The Mountaineers, Club Headquarters, 300 Third Avenue West, Seattle, Washington 98119; 206-284-6310.

The Mountaineers Books, an active, nonprofit publishing program of the club, produces guidebooks, instructional texts, historical works, natural history guides, and works on environmental conservation. All books produced by The Mountaineers fulfill the club's mission.

Send or call for our catalog of more than 500 outdoor titles:

The Mountaineers Books
1001 SW Klickitat Way, Suite 201
Seattle, WA 98134
800-553-4453
mbooks@mountaineersbooks.org
www.mountaineersbooks.org

The Mountaineers Books is proud to be a corporate sponsor of Leave No Trace, whose mission is to promote and inspire responsible outdoor recreation through education, research, and partnerships. The Leave No Trace program is focused specifically on human-powered (non-motorized) recreation.

Leave No Trace strives to educate visitors about the nature of their recreational impacts, as well as offer techniques to prevent and minimize such impacts. Leave No Trace is best understood as an educational and ethical program, not as a set of rules and regulations.

For more information, visit www.lnt.org, or call 800-332-4100.